In Our Clients' Shoes

Theory and Techniques
of Therapeutic Assessment

COUNSELING AND PSYCHOTHERAPY
INVESTIGATING PRACTICE FROM SCIENTIFIC, HISTORICAL,
AND CULTURAL PERSPECTIVES

A Lawrence Erlbaum Associates, Inc. Series
Editor, Bruce E. Wampold, University of Wisconsin

This innovative new series is devoted to grasping the vast complexities of the practice of counseling and psychotherapy. As a set of healing practices delivered in a context shaped by health delivery systems and the attitudes and values of consumers, practitioners, and researchers, counseling and psychotherapy must be examined critically. By understanding the historical and cultural context of counseling and psychotherapy and by examining the extant research, these critical inquiries seek a deeper, richer understanding of what is a remarkably effective endeavor.

Published

Counseling and Therapy with Clients Who Abuse Alcohol or Other Drugs
Cynthia E. Glidden-Tracy

The Great Psychotherapy Debate
Bruce Wampold

The Psychology of Working: Implications for Career Development, Counseling, and Public Policy
David Blustein

Neuropsychotherapy: How the Neurosciences Inform Effective Psychotherapy
Klaus Grawe

Forthcoming

The Pharmacology and Treatment of Substance Abuse: Evidence and Outcomes Based Perspective
Lee Cohen, Frank Collins, Alice Young, Dennis McChargue

Making Treatment Count: Using Outcomes to Inform and Manage Therapy
Michael Lambert, Jeb Brown, Scott Miller, Bruce Wampold

The Handbook of Therapeutic Assessment
Stephen E. Finn

IDM Supervision: An Integrated Developmental Model for Supervising Counselors and Therapists, Third Edition
Cal Stoltenberg and Brian McNeill

The Great Psychotherapy Debate, Revised Edition
Bruce Wampold

Casebook for Multicultural Counseling
Miguel E. Gallardo and Brian W. McNeill

Culture and the Therapeutic Process: A Guide for Mental Health Professionals
Mark M. Leach and Jamie Aten

In Our Clients' Shoes

Theory and Techniques
of Therapeutic Assessment

Stephen E. Finn

Psychology Press
Taylor & Francis Group

New York London

Psychology Press   Psychology Press
Taylor & Francis Group   Taylor & Francis Group
711 Third Avenue   27 Church Road
New York, NY 10017   Hove, East Sussex BN3 2FA

© 2007 by Taylor & Francis Group, LLC
Psychology Press is an imprint of Taylor & Francis Group, an Informa business
Originally published by Lawrence Erlbaum Associates

Printed and bound in the United States of America by Edwards Brothers Malloy
10 9 8 7 6 5

International Standard Book Number-13: 978-0-8058-5764-1 (Hardbound)
International Standard Book Number-13: 978-0-8058-5764-8 (Softbound)

Cover Design by Kathryn Houghtaling-Lacey

Library of Congress Cataloging-in-Publication Data

Catalog record is available from the Library of Congress

Visit the Taylor & Francis Web site at
http://www.taylorandfrancis.com

and the Psychology Press Web site at
http://www.psypress.com

Contents

~

Part III
Theoretical Developments

Descriptive Contents

Part I
The History and Development
of Therapeutic Assessment

Part III
Theoretical Developments

Foreword

Some 15 years ago, as I read and reread the inch-thick handout that Steve Finn had given me from his Society for Personality Assessment workshop, tears eased their way down my face. They were the tears that accompany being in touch with shared core but vulnerable values. This man whom I had just met had explicitly incorporated aspects of my *Individualizing Psychological Assessment* into his independently developed practices. I found throughout the handout that after Steve had reflected thoroughly on test patterns, theory, research, and what he already knew of the person's situation, he posed his impressions to the client in that person's terms. He collaborated respectfully, so as to truly individualize his descriptions, all the while helping the person to realize greater possibilities. I was moved by the openness and depth of his care for and faith in his clients, and by their profound experiences while working with Steve. I had always thought that collaborative/individualized assessment was necessarily growthful for clients as well as immediately helpful to readers of assessment reports. But Steve often went further, planning for clients to experience therapeutic insights—lived as well as understood. That workshop handout presaged what Steve soon named "Therapeutic Assessment."

I've often been asked whether Therapeutic Assessment is appropriate for when clients have been referred by professionals who are unfamiliar with it. I reply that even when clients are referred more traditionally, therapeutic insights are not only helpful to the clients but provide the referring party with understandings of the clients' openness to new experience. Many persons self-refer and many professionals do refer their clients for this service.

The title of this book, "In Our Clients' Shoes," evokes for me the collaborative assessor's practice of exploring the client's world by traveling with that person, through tests and talk, catching glimpses of his or her goals, horizons, hopes, and perceived dangers and obstacles. The therapeutic assessor accompanies and guides clients into test-related experiences through which they come to personal discoveries that are comprehended both affectively and conceptually. Clients grasp connections with the questions that were presented for the assessment, and also apprehend personally viable means of altering course to their goals. The assessor has not unilaterally presented clients with "feedback" nor told them what to do. Indeed, Steve's quiet, receptive presence to clients, evident in the case excerpts in this book, often has reminded me of Buber's "encounter" with the other—a profound respect for the other's being and for the intangible "between."

I am appreciative of and grateful for Steve's brave, creative, enthusiastic, unstinting, and effective outreach—giving national and international workshops, making his Therapeutic Assessment approach accessible through filmed excerpts, invitational writings, symposia, and extensive supportive consultation with students and colleagues. He has developed charts showing concrete steps for conducting Therapeutic Assessment, published articles that integrate diverse theories into collaborative practices, provided a broad range of clinical examples, and published and encouraged research on the outcomes of collaborating with assessment clients. Steve regularly seeks consultation with colleagues on theory and on clinical cases, always evolving his own understandings and practices. Due primarily to Steve's dedicated efforts, collaborative and Therapeutic Assessment practices are being adopted, adapted, and advanced by practitioners across the country and in many international settings.

In Our Clients' Shoes illustrates Steve's steady development of Therapeutic Assessment's approach and practices. Every chapter is readily understood and helps the reader to imagine undertaking Therapeutic Assessment practices in his or her own way.

Constance T. Fischer
Duquesne University

Preface

I coined the term *Therapeutic Assessment* in the late 1980s to describe an approach to psychological assessment that I was developing with the help of my colleagues in Austin, Texas. As the clinical methods and theory of Therapeutic Assessment evolved, and as my colleagues and I gained experience working with diverse groups of clients, I became convinced that we had found a powerful way to impact clients' lives and help them with their persistent problems in living. I also witnessed (and knew from my own experience) that practicing psychological assessment in this way enhanced the wisdom, compassion, and personal and professional development of most clinicians. I felt a strong urge to share with others what I had learned.

Thus, I began to travel and speak about Therapeutic Assessment to different groups of psychologists around the world. I often showed videotape excerpts from my assessment sessions with various clients, who altruistically waived their rights to confidentiality so that other psychologists could learn a new approach that had proved helpful to them. Other clients generously consented to be assessed "live" before a group of psychologists, so that those clinicians could observe and collaborate in the assessments. The response to these various workshops has been tremendous, and at this point I estimate that over 3,000 clinicians have attended one or more of my training sessions in Therapeutic Assessment. I know that many others have learned about Therapeutic Assessment in their graduate training, or have read something that explicated or referred to its principles and techniques. Now, every week I receive inquiries about Therapeutic Assessment, with requests for readings, training workshops, consultation, or help with research proposals.

I am excited and somewhat humbled by this growing interest; excited because of the number of clients who may be having positive experiences with psychological assessment, and humbled because my own writing and formal research on Therapeutic Assessment has not kept pace with my thinking, clinical work, or training workshops. I conceived of this book as a way to partially remedy that situation, by assembling—in one place—a number of my papers on Therapeutic Assessment that jointly explicate some of its history, theory, techniques, and impact on clients and assessors. Most of the chapters in this volume are based on my presentations at various conferences over the past 13 years—especially at the annual meetings of my beloved professional home, the Society for Personality Assessment—and many have been disseminated as unpublished papers up until now. Several other chapters were published previously but are reprinted here because they explicate central points about Therapeutic Assessment and/or are now difficult to obtain.

The book is organized into three sections. Part I describes the history and development of Therapeutic Assessment, including personal experiences that led me to focus on psychological assessment as a potential therapeutic intervention. A major principle of phenomenological psychology is that you must understand a person's context to fully understand their view of the world; I hope these chapters are useful in explaining mine. The longer section of the book, Part II, contains a variety of chapters that illustrate particular techniques of collaborative and Therapeutic Assessment. If you are attempting to learn the "nuts and bolts" of Therapeutic Assessment—for example, (a) how to integrate test findings, (b) how to engage clients in discussing their experiences of a test, (c) how to conduct assessment intervention sessions, or (d) teach Therapeutic Assessment to graduate students—these papers should help you a great deal. In Part III, I draw links between Therapeutic Assessment and two major schools of psychotherapy: intersubjectivity theory and Control-Mastery theory. If time and space permitted, I would also have written about links between Therapeutic Assessment and other psychotherapeutic approaches that influenced me, such as cognitive–behavioral psychotherapy, narrative therapy, systems-centered group therapy (Agazarian, 1997), and self psychology. In the penultimate piece in the book, I explore one of the theoretical claims of

Therapeutic Assessment: that assessors also grow and change as a result of practicing psychological assessment. The final chapter deals with important practical matters: (a) when Therapeutic Assessment is and is not called for, (b) how to bill for Therapeutic Assessment sessions, (c) how to market this type of psychological assessment, and (d) where to find professional support for this kind of work.

Obviously, my thinking about Therapeutic Assessment has continued to evolve over the years. Thus, some of the chapters I chose reflect more current conceptualizations than do others. I have resisted the urge to radically "update" older pieces, believing that readers will find it interesting to see how certain concepts and practices developed over time. However, I have standardized my terminology and eliminated certain redundancies between papers to make the experience of reading them in sequence more enjoyable. Also, in hopes of conveying some of the spontaneity and excitement I felt at the time, I have retained much of the informal language of those papers I first presented in oral form.

My greatest hope for this book is that it will help you "get in your clients' shoes" more completely so that you and your clients may touch each other's lives. A warning label seems appropriate, however: Therapeutic Assessment is not for the faint of heart! As one of my favorite Quaker authors has written:

> For the listener who knows what he is about, there is a realization that there is no withdrawal halfway. There is every prospect that he will not return unscathed. There is no lead apron that can protect his own life from being irradiated by the unconscious level of the one he engages with…each act of listening that is not purely mechanical is a personal ordeal. Listening is never cheap. (Steere, 1955/1985, p. 13).

Most days, I consider what Steere wrote as a challenging but amazing personal benefit of my work with clients. But if you do not wish to change and grow, put this book down immediately and run for cover!

Acknowledgments

Many people contributed directly or indirectly to this book. Barton Evans encouraged me to begin "steering the ocean liner" of my life to a place where I could do more writing. Steve Rutter, my editor at LEA, believed in me and encouraged me to assemble this book; Nicole Buchmann at LEA patiently kept me on track through numerous deadlines. My colleagues at the Center for Therapeutic Assessment listened to early versions of many of these papers, supported me emotionally and professionally, and helped me develop my ideas; I am extremely grateful to them all for their ongoing collaboration: Jennifer Chapman, Marita Frackowiak, Betty Peterson, Dale Rudin, Terry Parsons Smith, and Judith Zamorsky. Millie Smith and Rich Armington held me up with their friendship and love. And above all, this book would not exist without Jim Durkel, who held my hand, read early drafts, and kept our home life together as I spent many hours traveling or in front of the computer.

Many other individuals contributed to the development of Therapeutic Assessment. Connie Fischer, Leonard Handler, and Caroline Purves paved the way with their courage, creativity, and unwavering humanism. Mary Tonsager and Hale Martin helped me test and fine tune many of the methods, and Mary spearheaded the early research. Mary McCarthy added to the theory, took Therapeutic Assessment into new settings, and enthusiastically helped spread the word. Carol Middelberg and Deborah Tharinger added to and improved Therapeutic Assessment techniques for couples and children. Jan Kamphuis helped analyze and make sense of the recent research. The following individuals also worked with me in Austin conducting psychological assessments and were part of the supportive community from which Therapeutic Assessment evolved: Patricia Altenburg, Rosemary Ellmer, Beatrice Gerry, and LaNae Jaimez.

This book is dedicated to my colleagues in the Society for Personality Assessment, who continue to inspire me, teach me, and support me as both a person and a psychologist.

In Our Clients' Shoes

Theory and Techniques
of Therapeutic Assessment

Part I

The History
and Development
of Therapeutic
Assessment

1

Introduction: What Is Therapeutic Assessment?

Definitions and Distinctions

As Therapeutic Assessment has become more accepted in recent years, people are starting to use this and related terms in different ways. For this reason, I find it useful to define my terms and make certain conceptual and practical distinctions. I do this humbly—realizing that my definitions may be different from those of other people who think, write, and practice in this area, and that the distinctions I make are "fuzzy" and do not map precisely onto real life.

Traditional Assessment

In 1997, Mary Tonsager and I published a paper in which we contrasted traditional "information-gathering" psychological assessment and Therapeutic Assessment on a number of dimensions (Finn & Tonsager, 1997). That detailed analysis is still useful, but for my purposes here let me simply define *traditional assessment* as that model where psychological tests are administered to clients primarily for the purposes of diagnosis, treatment planning, treatment evaluation, and/or increased understanding. The main emphasis in traditional assessment is typically on the standard-

Portions of this chapter are drawn from a Master Lecture I presented to the Society for Personality Assessment (Finn, 2006).

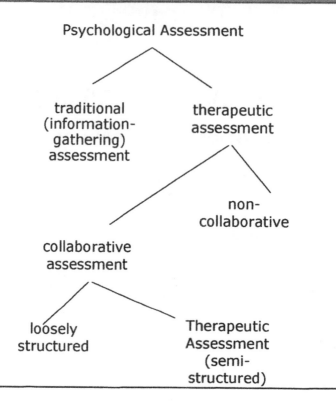

EXHIBIT 1–1
Types of Psychological Assessment

ized data that is carefully collected by the "expert" assessor (or an assistant), who then compares test scores to nomothetic norms in order to derive conclusions that will be useful in understanding, communicating about, and treating a certain "patient," or in monitoring the progress of treatment.

"therapeutic assessment"

Next, let me define *therapeutic assessment* (lowercase). Mainly, I consider this to be an attitude about psychological assessment—where the goal of the assessor is more than collecting information that will be useful in understanding and treating the patient. In therapeutic assessment, in addition, assessors hope to make the assessment experience a positive one and to help create positive changes in patients and in those individuals who have a stake in their lives (such as family, therapists, and employers).

Therapeutic assessment is based on the intent to use psychological assessment to help patients directly, rather than just indirectly, as with traditional assessment. Apart from this intent, from my observations, therapeutic assessment is not tied to any particular set of procedures, clinical techniques, or philosophy. It is practiced in a variety of ways, and I further believe that many clinicians are conducting therapeutic assessments without even claiming to do so! An example of a gifted psychologist who positively impacted clients through his assessments—without ever asserting that they were explicitly therapeutic—was Paul Lerner (2005a, 2005b).

Collaborative Assessment

I also find it useful to distinguish between *collaborative and noncollaborative therapeutic assessment*. One thing probably common to all therapeutic assessment is that assessors generally have some thoughtful way that they communicate information derived from an assessment directly to patients. In my mind, collaborative assessment goes beyond the practice of giving feedback, even if that is done in an interactive way. It involves a comprehensive effort to engage the client in multiple phases of the assessment process—including (a) framing the reasons for the assessment, (b) observing test responses and behaviors, (c) discovering the significance of those responses and behaviors, (d) coming up with useful recommendations, and (e) drafting summary documents at the end.

Collaborative psychological assessment is probably almost always beneficial to clients, and as such I consider it a subset of therapeutic assessment. But collaborative assessment may not always start with the explicit intent to produce positive change. For example, three pioneers of collaborative assessment—Connie Fischer (1985/1994), Len Handler (1995), and Caroline Purves (1997)—were all practicing collaborative assessment for years before they openly acknowledged that their assessments were therapeutic to clients. All three developed their approaches by trying to make the assessment process more humane, respectful, and understandable to clients, or, as Fischer (1985/1994) wrote, by gradually eliminating those aspects of psychological assessment that were dehumanizing or potentially harmful to clients.

Fischer also articulated a coherent philosophy of science, based in phenomenological psychology, which grounds and extends collaborative assessment techniques. My brief summary of this intersubjective model is as follows: "We can never know some external reality in its own right. We inevitably participate in what we see, always using our perspectives, backgrounds, and interests to assign meaning to our observations." (See chap. 17 for a more extensive discussion of Fischer's theory.) This point of view establishes an attitude about psychological test scores and their re-lationship to real-life events that permeates many aspects of collabora-tive assessment. If you grasp and believe Fischer's model, you will never, for example, find yourself arguing with a client over the meaning of a test score (e.g., "What do you mean, you aren't depressed? Your MMPI–2 Scale 2 score is 98!"). Also you will be intrigued, naturally, about the cli-ent's own thoughts about that MMPI–2 score and the match between what psychologists call "depression" and that client's own experiences. If you believe in phenomenological psychology, no one will have to tell you to discuss these matters with the client; you will just do so! For these rea-sons, I believe that Fischer's human–science framework encourages greater consistency in and expansion of collaborative assessment tech-niques, and it therefore underlies much of my own work on Therapeutic Assessment, to which I now turn.

Therapeutic Assessment

I reserve the term *Therapeutic Assessment* (uppercase) for the semistructured collaborative assessment approach—grounded in Fischer's human–sci-ence philosophy—that has been developed by me and my colleagues at the Center for Therapeutic Assessment in Austin, Texas. I call Fischer's, Han-dler's, and Purves's approaches "loosely structured" collaborative assess-ment because there is a systematic method to their work—but it's not spelled out as explicitly as in Therapeutic Assessment. I do not claim that our method produces greater benefits to clients than the less structured forms of collaborative or therapeutic (lowercase t) assessment. However, I do believe it is somewhat easier to teach and to research and that its organi-zation helps guide assessors through the many complex choice points that arise in a collaborative assessment. I've often said—and I'm only half jest-ing—that Therapeutic Assessment is for those of us who are not as cre-ative, intuitive, and quick on our feet as are Fischer, Handler, and Purves. If you follow the structure of Therapeutic Assessment for a period of time, gradually you will know when it is appropriate to deviate from this format and feel confident doing so. I'm reminded of the promise of my childhood piano teacher, who told me that if I practiced my scales diligently, someday

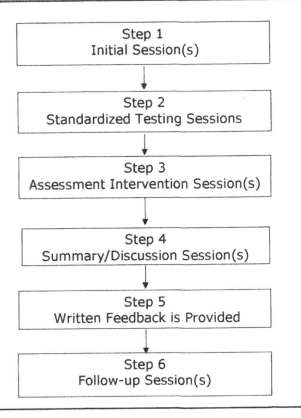

EXHIBIT 1-2
General Flow Chart of a Therapeutic Assessment

Step 1
Initial Session(s)

Step 2
Standardized Testing Sessions

Step 3
Assessment Intervention Session(s)

Step 4
Summary/Discussion Session(s)

Step 5
Written Feedback is Provided

Step 6
Follow-up Session(s)

I would be able to play jazz. Recently I see the truth of this statement in the assessments I do with my clients.

Flow Chart and Brief History of Therapeutic Assessment

So let me review the general structure of a Therapeutic Assessment, explaining, as I proceed, how the different steps developed and were incorporated into the model. Thus, rather than presenting the steps in the order they appear in an assessment, I discuss them in the order in which they found their way into Therapeutic Assessment.

Step 4—Summary and/or Discussion Sessions

I first became convinced of the potential therapeutic value of psychological assessment during my graduate training. During this period, I had several moving and powerful experiences discussing assessment results with clients, and they reported afterwards that their lives were changed. (I relate some of these experiences in chap. 2.) Not surprisingly then, as I became interested in understanding how assessment could be therapeutic and in discovering ways to make it more so, I initially focused on what I then called "feedback sessions" with clients.

One of the things I explored in my early research concerned how to order the information we present in feedback sessions to make those sessions the most useful and beneficial to clients. At first, most clinicians I consulted suggested that one should start by telling clients something positive about themselves. It turns out that this is not always the best practice, especially with clients who have very negative self-images. Instead, my colleague Bill Swann and I demonstrated (Schroeder, Hahn, Finn, & Swann, 1993) that clients are most able to integrate and make use of assessment information when it is presented in the following order:

(1) Begin with what I call Level 1 findings—those that map onto the way clients already think about themselves. An example would be telling a self-labeled extrovert that his very low score on Scale 0 of the MMPI–2 suggests that he enjoys meeting new people, is comfortable in large groups, and would not do well in a job where he worked mainly on his own.

(2) Next, introduce Level 2 findings from the assessment, which reframe or amplify clients' usual ways of thinking about themselves. This might involve telling a client who is concerned about lethargy, lack of motivation, and poor focus, that his Rorschach D score of –4 suggests he is emotionally overwhelmed, rather than just "lazy" as he fears.

(3) Last, if all is still going well, you may introduce Level 3 findings to clients—those that conflict in some major way with their usual conceptions of themselves. Research has shown that in many instances clients continue to consider and assimilate such information long after an assessment is completed.

EXHIBIT 1–3
Ordering Results Presented to Clients
from a Psychological Assessment

Level 1 Findings

Findings that verify clients' usual ways of thinking about themselves and that will be accepted easily in the feedback session. When told this information, a client will generally say, "That sounds exactly like me."

Level 2 Findings

Findings that modify or amplify clients' usual ways of thinking about themselves, but that are unlikely to threaten self-esteem or cherished self-perceptions. When told this type of information, a client might say, "I've never thought about myself quite this way before, but I can see how what you're saying fits."

Level 3 Findings

Findings that are so novel or discrepant from clients' usual ways of thinking about themselves that they are likely to be rejected in feedback sessions. Typically, Level 3 findings are quite anxiety provoking for clients, and thus are likely to mobilize their characteristic defense mechanisms.

Besides collaborating with me on the research that supported this way of discussing assessment results with clients, Swann's own work helped provide an explanation for why this approach works best (Swann, 1996, 1997; Swann, Stein-Seroussi, & Giesler, 1992). His *self-verification theory* posits that people have a drive to maintain the current "stories" or "schemas" they have about themselves and will often discount or push aside information that conflicts with these stories. This is true even if a person's existing self-story is primarily negative, as anybody knows who has tried to pay a compliment to a person with low self-esteem (Swann, Wenzlaff, Krull, & Pelham, 1992). By starting an assessment feedback session with self-verifying information and gradually moving to findings that are less self-verifying, one creates the optimal condition for clients to incorporate new information into the ways they think about themselves and the world.

Once I understood self-verification theory, I began to clarify the most appropriate focus of intervention in a psychological assessment—that is, clients' existing conceptualizations of themselves and other people. I realized that if we could assist clients in changing these stories—which often are vague, inaccurate, and lacking in self-compassion—we could profoundly impact their lives. Around this time, I also had two other insights about feedback sessions. First, I knew that people do not change their beliefs about themselves easily, and that I would need to support people emotionally—in a tangible way—to help them assimilate and accommodate to new information. This spurred me to work on and improve my ability to mirror and connect with clients deeply in a short period of time. Second, experience told me that I could best help clients change their stories by dialoguing with them about the assessment findings and explicitly asking them to agree, disagree, revise, and give real-life examples of what I was saying. Research by Hanson and others has since confirmed that this interactive style of discussing assessment results benefits clients more than a unilateral, assessor-driven presentation of test findings (e.g., Hanson, Claiborn, & Kerr, 1997). For this reason, I no longer talk about conducting "Feedback Sessions" at the end of an assessment, preferring now to call them "Summary/Discussion Sessions."

Step 1—Initial Sessions

The next set of developments in Therapeutic Assessment concerned initial sessions. In listening to clients who voluntarily agreed to participate in psychological assessments, I realized that certain aspects of their self-schemas were more open to change than others. And sometimes, clients themselves were actively searching for new ways of thinking about themselves and the world. This led to the practice of asking clients—in the initial assessment sessions—what puzzles, questions, or quandaries they had about themselves, and then making these questions the focus of the assessment. My initial thought was that such questions would signal me where clients' stories were most flexible, serving as "open doors" through which one could send assessment information during the feedback session. This proved to be true, and my colleagues and I found that Level-3 findings were much more likely to be accepted by clients if they could be related to the clients' own puzzles about themselves. Also, clients' assessment questions often revealed a lot of information about their existing self-schemas, and one could often discover what was Level-1 information by asking clients in the initial session for their best guesses—before any testing was done—about the answers to their questions. Finally, by focusing psychological assessments on clients' personal agendas, we made the whole assessment process much more client-centered, which seemed to lower clients' anxiety, enlist them in the assessment in an active way, and engage their curiosity.

All of these factors seemed to enhance the therapeutic impact of our assessments, but as time has gone on I have become more convinced of the value of helping clients get curious about their problems. By assisting clients in forming questions, we invite them to "climb up" with us, if you will, on an "observation deck" overlooking their lives where we may begin to look jointly for answers. Many clients report that they feel relief immediately after an initial assessment session simply from having translated their inner turmoil into concrete questions. Some clinicians would say the procedure helps engage the observing ego. I believe developmental affective neurobiologists like Schore (1994) and Siegel (1999) would tell us that we are actually helping people engage a different part of their brains, and that this helps them grow and develop.

Step 5—Written Feedback Is Provided

Clients' assessment questions also gave an innovative way to structure written feedback to clients. Rather than provide them with copies of formal psychological reports, we wrote them letters that addressed their questions and that reflected their input during summary/discussion sessions. Although I acknowledge that such letters are time consuming to write, I firmly believe in their value. For example, recent research by Lance and Krishnamurthy (2003) demonstrated that a combination of oral and written assessment feedback was superior to oral feedback alone. We also adopted the process first modeled by Fischer (1985/1994) of inviting clients to comment on or modify drafts of such letters, which again, clearly involves them in co-editing the new story that emerged from the assessment. Sample letters to clients are included in chapters 7 and 10.

Step 2—Standardized Testing Session(s)

In Therapeutic Assessment, in contrast to some types of collaborative assessment, the initial session is followed by one or more sessions in which standardized tests are administered according to standardized procedures. In keeping with Fischer's idea of individualized psychological assessment, there is no predetermined battery of tests. Which tests are administered is determined primarily by the nature of the client's (and/or the referring professionals') questions for the assessment, although, to some extent, they also depend on an assessor's training, experience, and personal preference. For example, clients who ask if they have a learning disability will be given intellectual and achievement testing. A client who asks why he is so angry at his mother may be given the MMPI–2 and the Rorschach.

If you were a fly on the wall watching me during these standardized testing sessions, you'd see very few differences compared to an assessor practicing traditional psychological assessment. The exceptions would be that:

(1) I follow specific guidelines about the order in which tests are administered. I try to administer first those tests that are closest—in their face validity—to the client's central assessment questions. This lowers clients' anxiety by showing them that I am not just a voyeur, but am collecting information that is relevant to our agreed-upon contract. For example, if a client wants to know if he has attention deficit disorder (ADD), I first ask that he complete one of the face-valid screening inventories for adult ADD. Next I might administer cognitive tests of attention and memory. Only after these are completed would I move on to other tests—like the Rorschach or MMPI–2—that are less obviously tied to the client's presenting concerns.

(2) I introduce each test according to its relevance to the client's assessment questions, making a special effort to comment on those tests whose purpose is hard to decipher, for example, "This long questionnaire, the MMPI–2, is a widely used psychological test that will give us information about your anger and a host of other things, like depression and anxiety. I believe it could help us understand why you are so angry at your mother."

(3) After I have completed the standardized administration of each test, I inquire about the client's experience of the task, paying special attention to assessment events that seem related to the client's questions for the assessment. For example, with the client who wondered about ADD, I would likely administer the WAIS–III (Wechsler, 1997) according to standardized procedures, but talk

with the man afterwards about his concentration and attention during the test, and whether it seemed better, worse, or different from his functioning outside the assessment situation. If I gave the man who was angry at his mother the Rorschach, I might ask him to reflect afterwards on his percepts to Card VII: "ice pick," "nutcracker," and "tundra," telling him of the old lore that responses to this card might tell something about a person's relationship with his mother. Alternatively, I might use one of Handler's (2006) techniques for an extended inquiry and ask the client, "If this ice pick could talk, what might it say?" The use of extended inquiries with clients is demonstrated in chapters 10 and 11.

As you can imagine, such opportunities for dialogue during an assessment are useful in helping assessors to understand clients' behavior and test scores. Also, they provide opportunities for clients and assessors to gradually "coedit" the clients' existing stories, rather than trying to make big changes all at once at the end of an assessment. For this reason, in Therapeutic Assessment, we tend to meet with clients once or twice a week for 1–1/2 to 2 hours, rather than administering all the standardized tests in one day in a marathon testing session. We find clients are generally less overwhelmed with this schedule, are more able to participate as active collaborators, and are able to gradually shift their stories, while dealing in small batches with the emotions this brings up.

Step 3—Assessment Intervention Sessions

Assessment intervention sessions were one of the last additions to the Therapeutic Assessment process, and were developed to address several concerns at once. First, in some assessments there seemed to be few clear events or opportunities for meaningful discussions with clients about their standardized testing. For example, for a while, I did a number of assessments using the MMPI–2 as the only standardized test. As you can imagine there are a limited number of relevant things one can explore with clients about their experience of responding to 567 True–False questions, even if those questions are sometimes odd or thought provoking. Second, in spite of our best efforts to "bring clients along" during an assessment, sometimes—when planning feedback—we would find that most of the important findings were Level-3 information that was likely to be quite threatening to clients. Third, I had become firmly convinced by this time that it was much more therapeutic to "midwife" a new story into being for a client than to present it fully formed in a summary/discussion session. Assessment intervention sessions deal with these and other issues.

The main idea behind assessment intervention sessions is relatively simple, that is, to bring into the room those problems-in-living of the client that are the focus of the assessment, where they may be observed, explored, and addressed with various therapeutic interventions. Because these sessions take place after the standardized testing is complete, the assessor can use the results of such testing to help "get in the client's shoes" when imagining how to evoke and then help with the difficult experiences that are targeted. And the assessor has a range of assessment materials and other techniques to use in order to evoke different emotional states in clients that are related to their problems in living. This is the "gestalt therapy" step in Therapeutic Assessment, and I gladly confess that most of the techniques were borrowed from the "Assessment of Process" section of Fischer's (1985/1994) book. I still remember staying up all night the first day I read that book, and in particular being inspired and fascinated by Fischer's creative methods for bringing test scores alive for clients. Assessment intervention sessions are my attempt to "standardize" Fischer's creativity and make it teachable; still, they are the most difficult part of Therapeutic Assessment to learn. Thus, I provide detailed instructions for conducting assessment intervention sessions in chapter 8 and several case examples with different types of clients in chapters 10 and 12.

Step 5—Follow-Up Sessions

Postassessment follow-up sessions were the latest addition to the Therapeutic Assessment model, and quite frankly, my colleagues and I first began doing them because clients asked for them. We now routinely tell clients at their summary/discussion sessions that many people find it useful to meet again in 2 to 3 months, to talk more about their assessment and discuss any questions or developments that have come up. Such an opportunity seems especially valuable for self-referred clients who do not go into ongoing psychotherapy at the end of an assessment. In fact, I now have a number of individuals I tested over the years who come to see me for a few sessions once or twice a year to discuss their progress and clarify their next steps. At first I was skeptical about the value of such an arrangement, but I have become convinced that this model—of an intense assessment, followed by periodic consultations—is a good therapeutic model for some people, and that it provides a reasonable option for those individuals who do not wish to engage in ongoing psychotherapy, for whatever reason.

Conclusion

This then is an overview of Therapeutic Assessment as practiced at our Center in Austin. As you read through the remaining chapters of this book, you will see how the format in Exhibit 1–2 informed my experiences with clients, and how these interactions reciprocally influenced the theory and structure of Therapeutic Assessment. This process is ongoing, and I am certain that in 10 years we will know even more about how to make psychological assessment a transformative experience.

In the meantime, it feels important also to state that every assessment I do is slightly different, and often my colleagues and I find it is necessary to modify the plan I have described to best serve a particular client. For some clients, assessment intervention sessions seem unnecessary or too dangerous (Zamorsky, 2002), and for others it is best to discuss test results as you go along, right after each test is administered. We have even discovered that some clients don't reveal their most important questions about themselves until the very end, when the assessment is nearly completed (T. P. Smith, 2002). So as you read through the remaining chapters, I encourage you to see the structure of Therapeutic Assessment as a heuristic tool that will help organize your thinking, and as an aid to training people how to do collaborative assessment. You may also find that in your own setting—for various reasons—you are not able to implement all the steps of Therapeutic Assessment. Please do not feel bad about this; I encourage you to take what you can and adapt our ideas and techniques to your own clients and personality. Above all, it is important to maintain the therapeutic attitude discussed earlier, to treat clients with kindness and respect, and to remember that we can never know some absolute truth about a client from our test scores. If you keep those things in mind, it is likely that you too will be practicing therapeutic assessment, and your clients and you will benefit.

2

Appreciating the Power and Potential of Psychological Assessment

When I first began speaking to groups of psychologists about the power of psychological assessment, I feared I would be "preaching to the choir." To be sure, I did find that every time I talked, several people in the room had a knowing glint in their eyes and they nodded as I recounted various moving experiences with clients. However, I also learned that many psychological assessors had never thought about psychological assessment as anything beyond a tool for diagnosis and treatment planning.

I now believe that most of us still don't yet fully appreciate the power and potential of psychological assessment. I know this personally, because I keep being surprised—even after all this time—by the mystery and transformative impact of our assessments. I confess that I often begin an assessment thinking, "Oh no, how am I going to help this person?" Then later, as the assessment progresses, I'm amazed at the difficult, meaningful shifts both of us have made. I also know that we don't fully understand psychological assessment when I read our scientific journals, see assessment reports from other psychologists, and attend presentations at professional meetings. Even among groups of experienced and committed psychological assessors I sometimes get the sense that we're groping in a darkened room for a treasure we only see a hint of

This chapter is adapted from my first presidential address to the Society for Personality Assessment (Finn, 2002b).

now and then. And this worries me, for if we don't fully understand the nature of our work, how can we expect those who are skeptical about personality assessment to do so?

I clearly remember the first time I got a peek at the treasure that is psychological assessment. It was at the end of my first year of clinical psychology training at the University of Minnesota, when I did my very first practicum on the adult inpatient unit of Hennipen County Medical Center in Minneapolis. To set the stage, I had just completed a year of assessment training with some incredibly good instructors. We learned the MMPI from James Butcher and Auke Tellegen, intellectual testing from a prominent neuropsychologist, and the Comprehensive System for the Rorschach and the TAT from some excellent adjunct faculty. I had found these courses extremely interesting and arrived at this first practicum with a lot of intellectual curiosity about how psychological tests would be useful in an applied clinical setting.

My primary supervisor, Dr. Glenna Schroeder, took one look at the green and rather intellectualizing graduate student I was, and decided that I should have my first assessment experience with a rather harmless patient, a schizophrenic man named Joe, who was in residence at that time on the unit. Joe was a middle-aged, semihomeless man who was well known to the entire psychology and psychiatry staff. I learned later that he was somewhat legendary for appearing twice a year, exactly 6 months apart, in the hospital emergency room in the middle of an acute psychotic episode. Each time, Joe would be admitted to inpatient psychiatry where he would be stabilized on antipsychotic medication. After about 3 weeks, he would discharge himself and refuse to be involved in aftercare, only to appear again when 6 months had passed.

I saw Joe rather late in his stay, about 1 week before he planned to leave the hospital. He may even have hung around a bit longer then he had planned to help me get some assessment experience. I know I gave Joe the WAIS and the MMPI, but it was the Rorschach that stands out for me now. I think this was the first client Rorschach I ever gave outside the course I had, and I remember Joe rejected Cards II, III, VIII, IX, and X. I came prepared with my memorized instructions for Rorschach administration and assured Joe that if he just kept looking, he would see something. He didn't. I even stopped at one point to ask if he had reservations about doing the testing, and he assured me that he did not, he just couldn't see things on any of those "ugly" cards—only the ones to which he had already given responses. I returned to my supervisor feeling that I had failed my first real Rorschach administration.

Luckily, Dr. Schroeder was a very skilled clinician. She assured me that I had done just fine and told me to go ahead and score what I could of the Rorschach and to come see her in the morning. Joe actually had given a fair number of responses to the cards he hadn't rejected, although the majority of them used pure form. As Dr. Schroeder and I sat with the Rorschach the next morning, she asked me consider what Cards II, III, VIII, IX, and X had in common. "Chromatic color," I offered. "Good," said she. "And what does Rorschach theory tell us about color cards?" "They stir up emotions." "And what might it mean that Joe called the cards ugly?" "He didn't like the emotions they stirred up?" "Exactly! And how did Joe deal with emotions he didn't like facing?" Here, I was stuck. "He denies them," Dr. Schroeder explained. "Joe is ready to leave the hospital again, but he gets there each time by pushing aside a bunch of unpleasant feelings that he can only ignore for so long. Eventually they burst through again, and he ends up back in the hospital."

I remember being amazed at how Dr. Schroeder's interpretation made sense, but the real clincher was when I went to talk about the testing with Joe. Tears rolled down his weather-beaten face as we talked about the Rorschach, and he told me not to worry, it was just that nobody had ever understood him so well before. We talked about what he might do to face the "ugly" feelings that were so hard, and he agreed to check out a few of the aftercare programs that were available. We shook hands briefly, looking deep into each other's eyes (a first for me and perhaps for Joe) and parted.

I left that session deeply moved (and a convinced Rorschacher), but there's more to the story. Thirteen months later, I began my psychology internship in that same inpatient psychiatry ward. It wasn't too long before I heard that Joe had come into the emergency room again, but this time the staff seemed relieved. For as it turned out, Joe hadn't been admitted since that last time I had seen him, and a lot of the nurses were afraid that something bad had happened to him on the streets. Eventually, Joe made it up to unit and when he saw me, he ran across the room, shook my hand, and asked, "Can we do those inkblots again? That was one of the most important things that ever happened to me in my life!!" I was a bit surprised, but assured him that we could, and I asked him how he'd been doing since I last saw him. It came out that he had indeed followed up on the aftercare we had talked about, had been attending a group, had an apartment, and had been taking his medication. He told me he had been working hard to face the feelings he'd been avoiding, and it had helped—he'd just had a setback recently after a friend died. He hoped we could "check out his psyche" while he was there to see if he'd been making progress. And the next week he gave me a Rorschach with responses to all 10 cards.

This experience was so significant to me, in part, because nothing I had learned in my assessment courses had prepared me for it. I remember quizzing my professors and supervisors afterwards. Yes our tests were valid and reliable and interesting, but why had nobody told me that psychological assessment can change peoples lives? Was there anything written about this? Had it ever been studied? And why was this being kept such a big secret?

So let's seriously consider that question: If psychological assessment has the potential to be a truly powerful and life-changing event for clients and assessors both, why don't more people know about that fact? And let's start, as is always good, by turning our focus towards home—on the profession of psychology.

I submit to you that most of psychology bought into a paradigm long ago where psychological assessment is seen as something like a glorified blood test. We have these tools, called psychological tests, which can be used to "extract" information from a semicooperative "patient." Once that is done, we can put our data into a computer, which will analyze it and spit out an interpretation that then can be used to make decisions or direct treatment. And oh, by the way, someone along the way might want to tell the patient what we found, but that isn't really necessary.

This is a harsh characterization, especially of the many gifted, artful clinicians who practice a humanized, nonmechanical form of psychological assessment. But I believe they are largely exceptions! How many assessors do you know who never give assessment feedback to clients, or who mail them a long, boiler-plate report full of technical jargon and other meaningless phrases? How much effort are we putting into developing better and better validity scales—important, to be sure—but instead of researching what things one can do at the beginning of an assessment so that clients want to reveal all they can to a psychologist? And how can we as a profession sit by quietly and continue to let shoddy psychological assessment practices take place that are dehumanizing and even damaging to clients? As best I can tell—this is possible only if we ourselves don't fully appreciate the true power and potential of psychological assessment. And if I'm right here, we need not wonder when so few students want to learn about psychological assessment, or when critical articles get published about us in *The New York Times*, or when managed-care gatekeepers balk at paying for psychological assessment.

I believe we're at a crucial time in the history of psychological assessment and that it's important that we take active steps to get out the secret of what psychological assessment can be. Here are just a few ideas of how we might do this.

First, we have to rid ourselves and our profession of the view of psychological assessment as a semiskilled technical enterprise conducted by slightly schizoid people who would have been therapists if only they liked humans as much as numbers. To do this, we have to stop fooling ourselves—and to realize that every time we give someone an MMPI–2, a Rorschach, or a Beck Depression Inventory, it is an interpersonal event that has the potential to impact that person—for better or worse. Sometimes we want to ignore this, to simplify our jobs, and so we can administer more tests, get more money, and make our bosses happy. But we give both others and ourselves a false message about psychological assessment each time we fail to recognize the import of our work and treat it like drawing blood.

Second, every chance we get, we have to tell people what psychological assessment really can be, and encourage our satisfied clients to spread the word. Do you know that at our group practice in Austin, where we specialize in Therapeutic Assessment, almost half of our referrals now come through word-of-mouth—from people who have heard through other clients how helpful an assessment can be? And, at least in my case, lots of people—middle-class people—pay a fair bit of money for those assessments. Spreading the word is also why, at least once a year, I run a workshop where I do an assessment live—while other psychologists and mental health professionals watch and give me advice. After they have seen what an assessment can do—they never forget. In fact, after one of these assessments I usually get four or five workshop participants calling me to ask if they can do an assessment themselves! I'm delighted that the *Journal of Personality Assessment* is now publishing more case studies of psychological assessment. I hope we can read some examples of how assessment transformed peoples' lives, and perhaps some other examples—where it did not—so we can continue to learn how to improve our methods. For I really don't feel we're anywhere near realizing the true potential of psychological assessment.

To achieve this, I think it's crucial that we shift our focus from researching exclusively test construction and validity, to learning more about what factors make psychological assessment useful and therapeutic for those involved. In 1996 through 1997, I chaired an APA task force, the Psychological Assessment Work Group, whose charge was to review the existing literature on the validity and utility of psychological assessment. You may have read some of our reports about psychological test validity—which were very encouraging (Meyer, Finn, Eyde, Kay, Kubisyn, Moreland, Eisman, & Dies, 1998; Meyer et al., 2001). Regarding test utility, we had disappointing news. Almost no studies existed that had investigated the utility or therapeutic value of psychological assessment. As others had done before us, we issued an urgent call for such studies to be initiated immediately. There still is a great need for such research.[1]

In closing, let me go back to where I started. I love personality assessment. I personally can't think of work that is more interesting, moving, and challenging. I believe that many of you feel the same way too. Now, please join me in letting the world know about the power and potential of psychological assessment.

---

[1]Almost a decade later, it is clear that very few researchers heeded our call. There still are very few published studies of this type.

3

Therapeutic Assessment: Would Harry Approve?

In this chapter I discuss one aspect of my professional development: Harry Stack Sullivan's influence on me and on the evolution and practice of Therapeutic Assessment. Then I point out specific features of Therapeutic Assessment that are consonant with Sullivan's thought. I conclude by discussing how Sullivan's vision of the therapeutic process can inform psychological assessment in general.[1]

My Contacts with Sullivan and Sullivan's Writings

I may be rare in having been exposed to Sullivan's work while I was an undergraduate. My advisor at Haverford College was Douglas A. Davis, a personality psychologist who was quite interested in Sullivan. I remember Davis mentioning Sullivan to me in several discussions while I was a freshman. Two years later, in his Abnormal Psychology course, I read sections of *Schizophrenia as a Human Process* (Sullivan, 1962), while visiting weekly (as part of the course) with a young schizophrenic man hospital-

---

This chapter is drawn from a paper I presented to the Society for Personality Assessment (Finn, 2000). I am grateful to Leonard Handler and David Nichols for their comments on an earlier draft.

[1] As far as I know, Sullivan never mentioned psychological testing directly in his lectures or writings. However, he did make the points "Diagnosis and prognosis cannot be dissociated from therapeutic considerations" (1940/1953, p. 180) and that even history taking is inevitably an interpersonal enterprise.

ized at the Haverford State Hospital. I recall being amazed at the time at the applicability of Sullivan's insights to my experience. Also, as a newly convinced Quaker, I was moved by Sullivan's obvious, profound respect for individuals with schizophrenia, which fit so well with Quaker ideas of the "inner light" shared by all humanity.

When I entered graduate school at the University of Minnesota, we were assigned *The Psychiatric Interview* (Sullivan, 1954) during my first semester. I was struck by Sullivan's statement that a good interview leaves the client changed and "with some measure of increased clarity about himself and his living with other people" (1954, pp. 18–19)—a theme that would become important to me later. I also hungrily read Perry's (1982) biography of Sullivan as soon as it was published; this strengthened my positive identification with Sullivan as I learned that he was probably gay or bisexual and—also like me—came from a poor family in upstate New York.

A crucial phase in my conversion to Sullivanian thought occurred during my internship and fellowship years at Hennepin County Medical Center in Minneapolis. My primary supervisors were Dr. Ada Hegion and Dr. Kenneth Hampton, both of whom practiced psychotherapy and psychological assessment according to interpersonal principles. Through my contacts with these expert clinicians, I learned firsthand the power of authentic relationship between therapist and client, and saw vivid examples of the therapeutic value of psychological assessment with hospitalized schizophrenic clients. Also, through Dr. Hampton and Dr. Hegion, I was exposed to the writings of Frieda Fromm Reichmann (1950), who was, as you may know, one of the core members of the Washington School of Psychiatry.

A final step in my exposure to Sullivan came during my first years as an assistant professor at the University of Texas at Austin (1984–1985). I decided to have clinical psychology students read *The Psychiatric Interview* in their first assessment course. To help me teach this book, I immersed myself in other Sullivan works to develop a broader understanding, primarily *Conceptions of Modern Psychiatry* (1940/1953), *The Interpersonal Theory of Psychiatry* (1953), and *The Fusion of Psychiatry and Social Science* (1964). This was the same period during which I was developing my model of Therapeutic Assessment and beginning to research its efficacy. Therefore, it is no accident that many of the concepts and terms used in Therapeutic Assessment are highly Sullivanian in nature, or that Sullivan features prominently in the discussion of the first empirical study of Therapeutic Assessment (Finn & Tonsager, 1992), done while I was at the University of Texas.

Parallels Between Sullivan and Therapeutic Assessment

There are many direct parallels between Sullivan's approach to treatment and the principles and practice of Therapeutic Assessment. I was conscious of many of these correlations at the time I developed my approach to assessment; others I discovered later, for example while reading Evans's (1996) excellent tribute to Sullivan. Let me explicitly highlight these similarities.

The Importance of Clients' Goals

In many of his writings, Sullivan stressed that the aim of all extended clinical contacts with clients is to help them meet their specific individualized goals. He felt this context was essential to enlisting clients' trust, gathering necessary information, and justifying the whole enterprise of psychotherapeutic treatment. If clients do not expect to benefit from their interactions with the clinician, then—from Sullivan's point of view—one can only address "certain limited objectives" (1954, p.17).

Because psychological testing has traditionally been conceptualized as separate from treatment, psychologists have not tended to emphasize clients' goals, and have instead focused on referral questions from outside sources. I believe this is unfortunate and that it has led to many abuses. In Therapeutic Assessment, I have attempted to reaffirm Sullivan's thinking and emphasize that the primary goal of psychological testing is to help the individual being tested (i.e., the client). In practice, helping the client is accomplished by the assessor and client working to form individualized questions the client wishes to explore during the assessment; these goals then shape all subsequent assessment sessions. By contracting to address clients' personal goals, we enlist them as collaborators in the assessment, and give them a reason, as Sullivan says, to try to be "foursquare and straightforward about [their] most lamentable failures and …most chagrining mistakes" (1954, p.16). Contrast this approach with traditional assessment's focus on developing better and better validity indicators for psychological tests, to tell us whether clients are telling us the "Truth" about themselves. (See chap. 6.)

Respect for Clients' Privacy

In *The Psychiatric Interview*, Sullivan (1954) emphasizes the need to distinguish between relevant and irrelevant data, and cautions the clinician against asking about "matters into which there is no technical reason to inquire" out of habit or simply to satisfy personal curiosity (e.g., see p. 34). Sullivan says that clients appreciate such constraint and that this helps them trust the clinician as an expert working on their behalf.

Unfortunately, such reticence is another factor not emphasized in traditional psychological assessment. It is often assumed that clients should willingly participate in hours of testing or respond—without being given any explanation—to numerous personal questions that have little obvious connection to their goals for the assessment. (The use of large fixed batteries of tests, regardless of the referral question, is a prime example of insensitivity to issues of privacy.) In Therapeutic Assessment, we take respect for clients' privacy even beyond the point suggested by Sullivan, and are wary of asking any questions that are not overtly related to clients' questions for the assessment. I often use the metaphor of the client and assessor agreeing on the blueprints of an "observation deck" to be built over a certain area of the client's life, in order to meet the client's goals for the assessment (Finn, 1996b). All tests and inquiries are connected to this blueprint, especially if their link to the client's goals is not likely to be obvious. For example, recently I asked a client to complete the MMPI–2, and warned him that it contained a lot of questions that appeared unrelated to his assessment questions. I then explained that this test would give me a good sense of his overall personality and emotional condition, which would help address his question, "Why do I have such a hard time meeting people?" As the assessment proceeds, the assessor may suggest that the observation deck be extended, in order to follow up on results that were not anticipated. However, like a good carpenter, the assessor asks the client's permission before altering the blueprints or extending the deck!

The Assessor as a Participant–Observer

Handler (2000) did a beautiful job of elucidating Sullivan's concept of the clinician as participant–observer. Again I would like to contrast this to the logical–positivist view behind much traditional assessment, where a goal is set of the assessors being a "completely objective" observer. This is why standardized data collection procedures are highly emphasized in this model, so that (in analogy to collecting a blood sample), we don't get "germs in the test tube" by introducing any of our stimulus value as a person.

My stance in this area has been influenced not only by Sullivan, but also by Fischer (1985/1994) and other writers in phenomenological psychology and intersubjectivity (e.g., Stolorow & Atwood, 1992). In Therapeutic Assessment, we do not believe in the possibility of complete objectivity in the human sciences, nor do we believe it is advisable if it could be achieved. As Handler so amply demonstrated, the judicious use of our own reactions with clients can greatly further the assessment process. Also, take this wonderfully gruff statement from Sullivan (1954): "…the psychiatrist has an inescapable, inextricable involvement in all that goes on in an interview; and to the extent that he is unconscious or unwitting of his participation in the interview, to that extent he does not know what is happening" (p. 19). If we apply this to psychological assessment, we begin to acknowledge that we are an inevitable part of the context of the client's behavior in sessions. The Rorschach I take from a client is invariably different from that collected by another clinician, and I ignore such factors at my peril.

For this reason, following Fischer's (1985/1994) lead, my colleagues and I write all our assessment reports in the first person and attempt to acknowledge our part in the interpersonal field of the assessment. Here's a quote from a summary letter to a school about an adolescent boy referred because of sexually inappropriate behavior:

> As we went through the Rorschach, Jeff gave more and more explicit sexual responses to the cards, and I was aware of his glancing at me out of the corner of his eye, as if to gauge my reaction. When I later asked about this, he admitted that he wondered if I was "shocked" by his responses. When I said, "No, only curious," I thought he looked a bit disappointed. I inquired and Jeff denied this at first, but then agreed that it was somewhat "fun" to shock people. He then went on

to explain how he normally felt that people rarely noticed him. Shocking people felt good because he could see his impact on them and know that he "mattered."

Although such passages appear to deal only with the assessor–client interaction, you can see how they also could be helpful to a referral source.

The Primacy of Careful Listening and Observation

One thread that weaves throughout Sullivan's writings is his emphasis on careful listening and observation as the primary method of psychiatric inquiry. Sullivan himself was a masterful clinician who learned to pay attention to subtle nuances in language, tone, and body language in part through his groundbreaking work with schizophrenics.

In my view, traditional training in psychological assessment places too much attention on test "scores" and too little on observing how those scores come into being. As we all know, any particular test score can be achieved in numerous ways, and important information is lost if one focuses on the end product of a test to the exclusion of process. In Therapeutic Assessment, we see participant observation in the interpersonal process of the assessment as the primary method of understanding clients' problems in living. Nomothetic test scores are certainly valued as a way of organizing observations and generating hypotheses about clients' problems in living. However, they are not seen as indices of "Truth" about who the client "really is," but as a starting point for discussion with the client. Following Sullivan, we eschew the search for "Truth" and instead seek what he calls "consensual validation"; hypotheses derived from test scores are subjected to "continuous, or recurrent, test and correction" (Sullivan, 1954, p. 121) by both assessor and client.

Skepticism About Standard Psychiatric Terminology

As Evans (1996, 2000) wrote, Sullivan (1954) maintained a firm skepticism about both standard psychiatric terminology (such as diagnoses) and less formalized psychiatric jargon (such as the term, *mother fixation*), which he referred to as "psychiatric banalities" (p. 35). He criticized such language in part because it was vague, easily misunderstood, and not communicative of relevant information about clients. Also, however, he felt that diagnostic labels tend to imply a static, immutable state to clients' problems in living, and to direct the clinician away from what is most interesting: those contextual or situational variables that ameliorate or exacerbate those difficulties.

In Therapeutic Assessment, we follow in Sullivan's steps, attempt to avoid jargon in our discussions with or about clients, and aim to present in written summaries vivid, first-person accounts of our experiences interacting with clients. In this regard, I was influenced not only by Sullivan but also by Fischer's (1984/1994) excellent book on assessment, in which she provides detailed examples of how to replace pseudoscientific terminology with evocative description. Also, like Sullivan and Fischer, I avoid diagnostic labels not just to increase clarity of communication, but because this practice reflects the focus of my attention. I certainly believe in genetically or biologically influenced psychological traits and conditions. However, my goal in an assessment is to identify the necessary and sufficient contextual factors for clients' problem behaviors to occur. If the client and I can discern and label such elements, we can imagine what conditions are necessary to avoid the difficulties troubling the client, and even test out this hypothesis in the assessment sessions. Later, in a report, I record our hypotheses and the results of our experiments, as both a reminder to the client and an aid to other professionals involved in the treatment. Over time, such professionals come to appreciate my focus on context, as they see that it often leads directly to practical interventions after an assessment. For example, I was quite pleased recently when a psychiatrist I have worked with for years asked the following question about a man he was referring for an assessment: "When does Mr. Smith act more schizophrenic and when does he act less so?" Some years ago, this referring professional never would have posed such contextually informed questions.

Far-Reaching Change Occurs Through Changes in the "Self"

One of Sullivan's most famous concepts is what he calls the *self-system*—those thoughts and conceptions that define our identity and protect our self-esteem. Sullivan believed that all of us have an implicit goal of maintaining our self-system (and thereby avoiding anxiety); this then leads to various types of problems, as outmoded conceptions of the self fail to change with shifting life circumstances. For those of you familiar with

Self Psychology, you can hear that this theory of Sullivan foreshadowed that of Kohut (1977, 1984). Like Kohut, Sullivan (1953) also had explicit ideas about how the clinician can facilitate change in the client's self-system. This occurs through an experience of "closeness" and "good will" between therapist and client, in which the therapist "spreads a larger context before" the client, "whereupon, in spite of anxiety...the self-system can be modified" (p. 302).

Sullivan's theory has been integral to my thinking about why assessment can produce lasting and far-reaching change in clients (an idea that some people initially felt was outlandish). You see, in my mind, although psychological assessment is a short-term clinical interaction, it has the potential to directly influence the self-system of the client. By enlisting clients as participant observers in their own assessment and collaboratively discussing our hypotheses and test findings, our goal is to help them modify the existing stories they tell themselves about themselves (i.e., their self-system) so as to more effectively operate in the world. If we are successful at intervening on this level with a client, change occurs across contexts and the client's whole outlook and approach to life is different. I also totally agree with Sullivan's ideas about how to foster such shifts: The client must feel supported enough and safe enough with the assessor and/or therapist to tolerate the anxiety that accompanies such shifts in identity. Or to offer a Sullivanian paraphrase of a recent election slogan: "It's [about] the relationship, stupid!"

Sullivan's "One-Genus" Hypothesis and Psychological Assessment

The *one-genus hypothesis* is Sullivan's elegant postulate, that "everyone is much more simply human than otherwise" (1953, p. 32). I believe that this simple and profound assumption has far-reaching implications for the practice of psychological assessment.

If we adopt Sullivan's point of view, that there is more commonality than difference between our clients and us, it leads to a basic optimism about our work as psychological assessors. We start with the faith the even the most complex and apparently incomprehensible behaviors of our clients can be understood by us because, in fact, we are not so different as to prevent empathic understanding. Also, if we believe Sullivan's statement, it cannot help but bring humility and respect to our interactions with clients because we are aware that "there but for the grace of God go I." Some of the psychological assessment practices I personally find most questionable, such as the failure to provide informed consent or feedback to clients, become almost unthinkable in this Sullivanian framework. For when we are aware of our shared humanity with clients, we find ourselves wanting to treat clients as we would like to be treated.

Sullivan's one-genus hypothesis also leads directly to a challenge that, for me, makes psychological assessment so rewarding and interesting. To fully understand our clients' problems, we must first overcome what Sullivan calls our own "security operations" to find our personal version of their inner struggles, conflicts, and dilemmas. Only then can we effectively help clients or other professionals reach a new level of understanding about their problems in living. For example, in working with Jeff, the sexually provocative adolescent I wrote about earlier, I was required to find that part of me that would rather shock people and bring punishment on myself rather than live with the feeling that I was powerless and did not exist. Once I had identified this set of feelings in myself (and remembered my own version of acting them out), I was able to convey my understanding to Jeff and to those adults in his life who were bewildered and angered by his behavior. From this common framework, we were all able to think of other ways Jeff could feel acknowledged and powerful, and to see if those other ways could successfully replace the solution he had previously achieved through trying to shock others.

Of course, as clients' behaviors become less usual, more shocking, and more socially rejected, we as assessors must work harder to find the parts of us that are more similar to those clients than different. This is what I call the "personal and spiritual growth side effect" of interpersonal assessment and therapy. Through our clients, we come to reclaim parts of ourselves we might otherwise never have acknowledged, increasing our depth, compassion, and vitality as human beings. Or as Sullivan (1962) so aptly said, "There is always interaction between interviewer and interviewed, between analyst and analysand, and from it, both *must* invariably learn if *sound* knowledge of the [client's personality] is to result" (pp. 297–298).

In closing, I assert that if one puts Sullivan's "one-genus" hypothesis into practice in assessment, one inevitably ends up with the techniques of collaborative assessment. On this basis, I believe that Harry would be greatly pleased with the development and increasing interest in Therapeutic Assessment.

4

How Therapeutic Assessment Became Humanistic

(written with Mary E. Tonsager)

This chapter describes the links between Therapeutic Assessment and humanistic psychology, detailing how humanistic practices were gradually incorporated into the methods of Therapeutic Assessment and highlighting those aspects that are clearly compatible with humanistic principles.

The Development of Therapeutic Assessment

The seed of Therapeutic Assessment was Steve's noticing during his graduate training that some clients appeared to have positive life-changing experiences via psychological assessment (see chap. 2.) He became quite curious about how this happened and whether it was possible to enhance the beneficial effects of psychological assessment and increase the proportion of clients experiencing such benefits. In the 1980s, as a faculty member at the University of Texas, Steve began experimenting with different ways of conducting assessments and noticing their results with clients. In the early 1990s, Mary conducted—for her master's the-

This chapter is excerpted from an article that was first published in *The Humanistic Psychologist* (Finn & Tonsager, 2002). I am grateful to Mary Tonsager for her collaboration and friendship over the years.

sis—the first controlled study demonstrating the beneficial aspects of psychological assessment for clients (Finn & Tonsager, 1992). At this point in the development of Therapeutic Assessment, our focus was largely on how to make "feedback sessions" about psychological test results therapeutic for clients.

Looking back now, we see that our methods at that time were largely humanistic in that we emphasized showing respect for clients, reducing the power imbalance between client and assessor, and dialoguing with clients about test results—instead of insisting that test findings were "true" in some objective sense. However, neither of us was highly familiar with humanistic psychology at that point in our professional development, even though to some extent we had both read Maslow, Rogers, May, and other self-identified humanistic psychologists. Thus, it has been interesting for each of us in writing this chapter to muse about the origins of our early humanistic leanings. Clearly, Steve was strongly influenced by being a Quaker and by that group's belief in the "inner light" in every person. Also, Steve felt a great kinship with Harry Stack Sullivan and his view of the psychologist as a consultant and participant observer in the clinical process (see chap. 3). Furthermore, Steve's clinical training at Hennepin County Medical Center in Minneapolis emphasized showing respect for clients' dignity and being open to what they had to teach. Mary had been influenced by her study and clinical supervision in Kohut's Self Psychology and Stolorow's theory of Intersubjectivity (e.g., Atwood & Stolorow, 1984; Stolorow, Brandchaft, & Atwood, 1987). These approaches helped us realize the importance of "accurate mirroring" and empathic attunement, and highlighted the healing power for clients of feeling understood.

In addition to our affinity for humanistic psychology, during the early 1990s we became aware of the writings of psychologists who practiced psychological assessment within an explicitly human science of humanistic framework, primarily Fischer (1970, 1972, 1978, 1979, 1982, 1985/1994; Craddick, 1972, 1975; also Dana, 1982, 1984a, 1984b; Dana & Graham,1976; Dana & Leech, 1974) and others. Contact with these thinkers helped us develop a philosophical underpinning for what we were doing already in assessment. Also, we began to borrow and systematize humanistic practices from these other clinicians—not just because they fit our values and our developing theory of what potentially makes assessment therapeutic—but also because these practices got results. Rather quickly we learned that the more we conducted assessments from a model where clients were integral participants in a collaborative process whose goal was jointly observing, understanding, and rethinking their problems, the more profoundly those clients were affected. To tell the truth, we're not sure that Therapeutic Assessment would be so thoroughly compatible with humanistic psychology today if we had not be so impressed with the positive results of incorporating humanistic principals in our work with clients.

Some specific examples might be helpful. As mentioned earlier, our initial focus was on the process of giving feedback to clients. One initial difficulty we encountered was how to discuss those test results with clients that conflicted with their typical views of themselves. Early on, we found that if clients were first given information that seemed to confirm their self-views, they often were then more open to information that seemed to conflict with those views (Schroeder et al., 1993). Although this insight might be considered empathic, it is not necessarily humanistic. We also learned not to insist upon the validity of a test result, but rather to present it as theory that could be modified, accepted, or rejected by a client. This practice is more in line with a human science view of psychological assessment (cf. Fischer, 2001); however, for us it was more a useful strategy than an expression of an underlying phenomenological point of view.

A next discovery in the development of Therapeutic Assessment was that clients were more accepting of test information that could be tied to their personal goals or "puzzles" about themselves. Thus, we started the practice of asking clients at the beginning of an assessment to form questions about themselves that they wished to explore through psychological testing. At the end of the assessment, these questions provided "open doors" through which to present information that clients might otherwise find overwhelming or difficult to hear. If we could explain how what we were saying was relevant to clients' personal agendas, they seemed to incorporate challenging information more easily and to make bigger life changes after an assessment. This even seemed to work with clients who were referred against their will for an assessment, as is the case for many forensic evaluations.

In hindsight, this simple shift to a client-centered assessment model from a more test-centered model had a profound impact on our view of assessment. As we collected clients' questions and joined them in elucidating their goals, we found our focus shifting from test feedback to the entire assessment process. We became more empathic to clients' dilemmas of change and more attuned to the contextual aspects of behavior. Test results were still important, but we became more interested in how they could help clarify daily problems in living. Finally some of Fischer's emphasis on "life-centered assessment" (e.g., Fischer, 2001) began to make experiential sense.

A next step in the growth of Therapeutic Assessment was our developing "assessment intervention sessions" (see chap. 8). These sessions are a standardized version of what Fischer (1985/1994) called "assessment of process." The assessor elicits—often using test materials—*in vivo* analogs of clients' problems in living and works collaboratively with clients to observe, understand, and shift those problematic thoughts, behaviors, or emotions. For example, a client who is in trouble for "working too slowly" at a job, and who is excessively careful due to a fear of making mistakes, is invited to do the Digit Symbol test of the WAIS–III. The assessor helps the client notice his or her slow pace, name it (e.g., "being careful"), notice the similarity to the job situation, and then experiment with various ways of working faster. Once some success is achieved in the assessment situation (i.e., a quicker pace with the Digit Symbol task) the client is asked to test out similar solutions in the work context itself and report back at the next assessment situation how this went.

Although we have not yet conducted a formal research study on assessment intervention sessions, our clinical experiences have shown us that they often lead to profound, positive shifts on the part of clients. We have even developed a set of interventions that are useful for clients with different types of presenting issues, for example, those clients who believe that they have ADD and are reluctant to consider other alternatives (see chap. 10). And although, once again, our procedures were driven by a desire to impact our clients therapeutically, the end result was a set of practices that allowed us to explore "experiaction" (Fischer, 2001) and that fit extremely well with a human-science model of psychological testing. These and other developments have now led to our articulating an explicit human science basis for Therapeutic Assessment (see chap. 17).

Next we describe some principles and practices of Therapeutic Assessment and how they relate to humanistic psychology and lead to therapeutic benefit for clients.

Some Humanistic Elements of Therapeutic Assessment

Enlisting Clients in Setting Goals for the Assessment

Historically, the goals of psychological assessment have been directed towards meeting the needs of mental health professionals—whether to clarify a client's diagnosis or mental health status, to aid in treatment planning, or to evaluate the effectiveness of interventions that have already taken place. Finn and Tonsager (1997) called this approach the "information- gathering model" of psychological assessment. In contrast, a primary goal of Therapeutic Assessment is to meet the individual goals and/or needs of clients. Typically, this involves identifying, exploring, and answering clients' questions about themselves and/or their relationships with others.

As mentioned earlier, we now typically devote the initial session of an assessment to helping clients formulate these questions and to gathering background information relevant to the questions. In some ways, this process is akin to a first meeting with an architect (the assessor) to discuss plans for an observation deck (the assessment) that will be built over some area of the client's property (life). The two parties decide how large an area the deck will cover and where it will be placed; that is, those aspects of the client's life that are to be examined and in what depth. For example, a recent client asked, "Why do I avoid any situation involving confrontation?" and "Why do I react so negatively to any criticism?" When Steve inquired how it would be helpful to have answers to these questions, the client added the question "How can I become more comfortable with other people's displeasure?"

In assessments of children and adolescents, we gather questions both from parents and the children. For most children and young adults, this is a unique opportunity to have their own goals, frustrations, and concerns addressed and responded to in a meaningful way. Recently, we have been asked the following questions by children we tested: "Who do I get so mad at my mom?"; "How come it's hard for me to fall asleep?"; "Am I good at anything?" Furthermore, with adolescents, we negotiate that the child's questions may be kept private from the parents, although the adolescent will be informed of the parents' questions about him or her.

This practice of working collaboratively with clients to define the goals for an assessment obviously fits with C. R. Rogers's (1951) client-centered psychotherapy and Jourard's (1968) "psychology of invitation" as a means to help people understand themselves better. As theorized by many humanistic writers, we find that collaborative goal setting (a) gives clients a sense of power,(b) heightens their own curiosity and engagement in the assessment process, and (c) ultimately reduces their anxiety during and after an assessment. As such, this practice prepares the ground for clients to undertake revisions in their views of themselves and sets the stage for therapeutic change.

Using Psychological Tests as "Empathy Magnifiers"

In Therapeutic Assessment, psychological tests are not viewed as indicators of some objective "Truth" about clients, even though standardized procedures and nomothetic norms are used as starting points in a dialogue between clients and assessors. Rather, tests are viewed as "empathy magnifiers" that are useful in helping assessors get in clients' shoes (Finn & Tonsager, 1997). In this way, Therapeutic Assessment is in accord with humanistic psychology's goals of "reconciling" the objective and the subjective (Bugental & Sapienza, 1994).

For example, during a recent therapeutic assessment, a client's standardized scores on the Rorschach indicated a tendency to avoid or flee highly emotional situations (Afr = .16, CF + C = 0). (This is the client mentioned earlier who asked, "Why do I avoid any situation involving confrontation?") Immediately after the Rorschach administration, Steve invited the client to reflect on one of his responses to Card VIII: "These two creatures are scurrying away from a bad situation...It looks like an explosion could happen at any minute and they're running like hell to save their lives." The following dialogue ensued:

> *Steve:* Do you identify with those creatures at all?
> *Client:* (Smiling) I sure do! That's what I'm doing all day long at work. I guess I think I'll get killed if I stick around. The explosion these two are running from is a bad one.
> *Steve:* And is that true for you?
> *Client:* Not that bad, really. But I never really realized before that it feels like I'll die.

> *Steve:* Yes, that seems like an important insight into why you avoid confrontation.
>
> *Client:* I'll say. No wonder I've had such a hard time with all this.

As Fischer (2001) noted, this is essentially a hermeneutic approach. The assessor cycles (in a disciplined way) between the client's goals, the nomothetic test data, the assessor's own associations, and the client's interpretation of his test response. Gradually, a deeper understanding of the client's dilemma emerges—for both client and assessor—yielding a moment of greater self-awareness and self-compassion on the part of the client. This fits our experience of the therapeutic benefit of a successful psychological assessment: Both assessor and client come away with a deeper understanding of the client's dilemmas of change, an understanding that heals shame and points towards new ways of being for the client.

Sharing Our Reactions With Clients—Including What We Learned

In Therapeutic Assessment, we acknowledge the contextual basis of all knowing, and reject the positivist goal of being "objective observers." Throughout an assessment, when relevant, we share our reactions and personal context with clients, acknowledging our biases so that they may take them into account in forming their own opinions. For example, here is an excerpt from Steve's final session with the client who avoids confrontation, when the two of them were discussing ways the client could become more comfortable with "other people's displeasure" (one of his assessment questions).

> *Steve:* So from what we've discussed so far, do you see any way to get more comfortable confronting other people?
>
> *Client:* I guess I just need to learn that I won't die if other people are mad at me.
>
> *Steve:* That sounds right to me. Any ideas how to help yourself with that?
>
> *Client:* Perhaps I could start with some people who aren't that important to me. That would make it less scary.
>
> *Steve:* Great idea! I remember starting with store clerks and people like that when I was working on this same issue.
>
> *Client:* Oh, did you have problems with this same thing?

Steve: Oh, yes. I used do to all kinds of things to keep people from getting mad at me. You should have seen me!

Client: And now it's better?

Steve: Yes. I'm not so scared of confrontation anymore.

Client: That makes me feel better—like there's hope for me too.

Steve: I'm having a similar reaction—that both of us are getting better at this anger stuff, and it's going to make our lives a whole lot better.

We believe such interchanges are in keeping with humanistic principles of authenticity, modeled so powerfully by Perls and others (cf. Barton, 1994). In their feedback to us at the end of our assessments, many clients have referred to such moments as turning points in their regaining hope for themselves. Also, many clients feel enlivened when they feel they have impacted the assessor. For this reason, we make it a practice to tell clients at the end of an assessment specific ways that we have been touched or have grown through working with them.

Believing in an Innate Healing Potential

When we lecture about Therapeutic Assessment, one frequent question we are asked is "Do you really believe that such a brief procedure has the potential to change someone's life?" We do, and typically we explain how psychological assessment potentially can have lasting impact because it addresses the "story" individuals tell themselves about themselves and the world. In preparing this chapter, we came to see the humanistic thread in our optimism, for we too view human beings as "resourceful, free, imaginative, creative, integrative, symbolic, perspectively gifted, [and] temporally flexible person[s]..." (Barton, 1994, p. 228).

In contrast to traditional relational psychotherapies, which attempt to bring out such qualities in clients through an ongoing relationship with a therapist who is more "self-actualized," Therapeutic Assessment operates in a more incisive way. By engaging clients in an intense process of self-exploration and using psychological tests to quickly gain empathy for clients' problems in living, we attempt to decrease shame and assist clients in seeing and testing out new ways of being. Clinical experience and controlled research now bear out the healing potential of this approach.

One client recently reflected this aspect of Therapeutic Assessment in her written feedback at the end of an assessment:

> I realize now that I started this not really thinking it could help since 4–5 therapists had already given up on me. But part way through, your constantly asking me to think about what I was saying and doing hit me. If you thought I could change, maybe I could if I just started paying attention to my assumpshuns [sic]. Now I know there are different ways to see things and its [sic] already starting to work.

In closing, we are pleased and bemused to report that by searching for ways to conduct psychological assessments in ways that are helpful to clients, we ended up with practices and principles that are clearly humanistic. This provides fresh validation for the principles of humanistic psychology and speaks to common truths that may be discovered by any open-minded clinician through deeply listening to clients.

Part II

Specific Techniques
of Therapeutic Assessment

5

Testing One's Own
Clients Mid-Therapy
With the Rorschach

During my training, I was taught, as most psychologists were, that seeing a client in therapy whom one had previously assessed was an iffy enterprise, at best. Such an arrangement was said to distort the transference in the therapy, and I was encouraged to refer all clients I had assessed to someone else for treatment. Even more flawed, my instructors and colleagues told me, is the procedure of testing one's own clients in the middle of ongoing psychotherapy, for it (a) produces skewed test results that are impossible to interpret and (b) can be destructive to the psychotherapy relationship. I would like to set this second issue—the effects of testing on the therapy relationship—aside for a moment, to focus on the first issue: the question of test validity.

A well-known study by Exner, Armbruster, and Mittman (1978) directly examined how Rorschach protocols of clients are affected if the clients are tested by their own psychotherapists. Two groups of clients were randomly assigned to be administered the Rorschach either by their own therapists or by therapists previously unknown to them. The latter arrangement resembles most clinical assessment situations and also paral-

This chapter is drawn from a paper I presented to the Society for Personality Assessment (Finn, 1994). I was amused at the time that my presentation was placed in a session called "Misuses of Psychological Testing." I am pleased that collaborative assessment practices are now more accepted.

I am grateful to Constance Fischer for her comments on an earlier draft of this paper.

lels the procedures by which the normative data for the Comprehensive System (Exner, 1993) were collected. All clients had participated in 20 to 40 sessions of psychotherapy when they were tested.

Exner and his colleagues found that clients tested by their own therapists gave longer protocols with more Blends and more color and human movement (M) responses than did clients tested by clinicians with whom they had no previous relationship. Clients tested by their own therapists also gave more sex responses (Sx), fewer popular responses (P), and responses of lower form quality. These results suggest that clients tested midtherapy by their own therapists do produce different, perhaps more revealing, protocols and that an assessor could possibly overpathologize when interpreting one of these protocols by comparing it to either formal or subjective normative data alone.

These data impressed me the first time I saw them and let me know that the cautions of my supervisors were not without some empirical backing. But they were not enough to convince me that it would never be wise to give the Rorschach to a client of my own during psychotherapy. First I was greatly influenced by Fischer's (1985/1994) writings on individualized assessment and by her arguments that standardized test procedures could be departed from when nomothetic scores were not necessary for individual classification. Second, I felt one might even be encouraged by Exner et al.'s (1978) results. If my client's protocol were "more revealing" if I administered the Rorschach, might I learn even more about the client than if I referred to another clinician? And although there might be alterations in the client's Rorschach due to our relationship, couldn't I adjust my interpretation of the Structural Summary based on the significant differences reported by Exner and his colleagues? Finally, in my own thinking I was coming to believe that assessment is a possible therapeutic intervention with clients, as well as an information-gathering procedure (cf. Finn & Tonsager, 1997). If this were true for the Rorschach, I did not want to miss the opportunity to use it with my own clients.

On the basis of these thoughts, I was ready to go ahead and give several of my own clients the Rorschach but I was given pause by the other, previously mentioned admonition—that by doing so I could damage a well-functioning therapy relationship. I carefully thought through the concerns of my instructors and colleagues. As best as I could understand, the gist of these was that the assessment situation often pulls for transference projections from clients. Most commonly clients will attribute to assessors what Shafer (1954) called voyeuristic, autocratic, oracular, or saintly traits. The introduction or exaggeration of such transference elements in an ongoing therapy could derail the normal development of the therapy relationship, I was told, and lead to therapeutic impasses or premature terminations. This seemed possible to me, but I am a person who wishes to learn from my own mistakes. Thus, I decided to go ahead and see what it was like to give the Rorschach to some of my own clients midtherapy. I have now done this approximately 75 times over the course of 20 years, and I'm going to share with you four brief case histories that illustrate what I have learned. All the clients I discuss had never taken the Rorschach before I administered it and many were asked to complete the MMPI–2 at about the same time. All had completed at least 25 sessions of individual, psychodynamically oriented psychotherapy with me before the testing.

Case 1—Chad: Using the Rorschach to Introduce Material into Psychotherapy

Chad was an attractive intelligent 26-year-old man who sought psychotherapy because of difficulties with his studies at a prestigious medical school. He had previously done well at an elite liberal arts school where he had majored in philosophy and literature, but was failing several courses in medical school. At first, I believed that Chad's academic difficulties were mainly due to intense performance anxiety based on his need to gain respect in a family that had always belittled him. As the therapy continued, however, I became impressed with what appeared to be a subtle thought disorder, which grew more obvious when Chad was anxious. I came to believe that disrupted thinking was interfering with Chad's cognitive performance and I sought for a way to introduce this hypothesis into the psychotherapy. I decided to ask Chad to take the Rorschach with me.

Chad produced a long (R = 43) protocol with many Blends and few popular responses (P = 4), just as Exner et al. (1978) found. In addition to numerous shading responses (Sum Shading = 24), Chad's protocol had significant indicators of thought disorder (WSUM6 = 62) including two contamination responses (CONTAM = 2) and three Level–2 fabulized combinations (FABCOM2 = 3). As there was no evidence in the Exner et al. (1978) study that increased familiarity with the assessor leads to higher scores on indicators of ideational disturbance, I felt comfortable that my informal observation of Chad's thought disorder had been confirmed.

It took several weeks before I felt ready to discuss Chad's test results with him and during that period, he experienced intense anxiety about what I had "found out about" him. It appeared that the oracular aspects of the transference had indeed intensified, as my supervisors and colleagues predicted. Although this period of the therapy was intense, it certainly was not impossible to manage. I told Chad that I knew he had revealed a great deal of himself in the Rorschach and that I was taking time to be clear about the results. When I finally told him in the feedback session that it appeared that his thinking style was quite different from others, and I wondered if it interfered with his academic performance, he became quite tearful at first. After a few moments of sobbing, he then expressed relief, saying this was a characteristic he recognized about himself and that he had been working hard in therapy for months to hide his "different thinking" from me. In the next several sessions, Chad told me that his father had the same type of "different thinking" as he. We also began to explore under what circumstances Chad came up with a thought that was unique or unusual. Chad stayed in therapy for 28 months after the testing, and we continued to mark the Rorschach administration as a turning point in our relationship. He showed an appropriate idealized transference to me, but this transference did not continue longer than usual or interfere with termination.

Case 2—Barry: Taking Advantage of the Regressive Pull of the Rorschach

Barry was a 41-year-old African American man who had seen me weekly in psychotherapy for about 2 years when we decided to do the Rorschach together. Barry's presenting issue was his failure to ever have a successful heterosexual relationship. He had had few interpersonal sexual experiences at all and was quite frustrated that he was so successful in his career and so unsuccessful in the social and/or sexual realm of his life. In the first several sessions, Barry revealed that his mother was diagnosed with bipolar disorder and had regularly been hospitalized throughout his life. Over the next 2 years we periodically explored her erratic temper and occasional severe beatings of Barry and his siblings. We came to understand that these beatings were in part connected with the anxiety Barry suffered when he considered approaching women for a date. Still Barry seemed unable to take behavioral steps towards confronting his anxiety. Finally during one session, Barry almost casually reported an early memory of his mother standing over his crib and fondling his penis until he got an erection. He had no other memories of sexual contact with his mother. Several sessions later I asked Barry if he would take the Rorschach with me.

Barry's opening response was of two wolves in the D7 area of Card I. In the inquiry he commented on the texture of the wolves' fur and their eyes. In sequence, his following responses were (2) "two hands reaching up to the sky" (D1). [Inquiry: "They're in mittens—you can't see the fingers—they're reaching for help."] Then, (3) "two breasts" (Dd22). [Inquiry: "They're here. I'm looking down at them from above."] (4) "The more I look at it I see a whole body with a waist and a skirt. The first thought I have is maybe this is my mother with a skirt here. She's lunging at me. It gets more ominous as I look at it. If that whole figure is a woman, this light spot (Dd27) is the womb. It's a little high, but that's what it is."

The Card II content seemed even more significant: 5) "Two elephants sort of joining together" (the Popular), 6) "blood stains (D2) because of the red," 7) "a rocket ship blasting off" (DS5 + D3), and 8) "bloody finger prints" (D2 again). Here is the inquiry for the latter response: "They're here and here. Somebody just put finger prints down there." [Me: What makes they look like finger prints?] "It's all messy, like somebody put their fingers in blood and put them down again. I have a recollection of the one and only time I had my house broken in. They cut themselves. I saw blood on the door and was nauseated that not only did they violate my house, they left their blood behind."

Barry went on to give 14 responses with sexual content, most of which were percepts of vaginas or anuses involving a Vista determinant. Even adjusting for the increase in Sx responses found by Exner et al. (1978), I felt this was a highly significant finding, and it made me wonder if Barry had been sexually traumatized. Of course, I was careful not to suggest this possibility to Barry. Even more significant than the test feedback session was a series of dreams Barry began to have even before test feedback was given. The first of these occurred several nights after the Rorschach administration. In the dream Barry had an image of his mother punishing him by rubbing his face in a soiled sanitary napkin. When Barry got the nerve to ask his older brother about this image, the brother confirmed that this incident had in fact happened. Over the subsequent months of therapy Barry began to recover more images of sexual traumas, many of which were confirmed by his brother. To my best understanding, the regressive pull of the Rorschach had opened a door for Barry that proved very important in his healing from his sexual difficulties. I don't know if the same series of events would have occurred if I had referred Barry to a consulting psychologist for his Rorschach, but I tend to believe that the trusting relationship we had built prior to the Rorschach was important to what happened.

Case 3—Stephanie: Transference Crisis Following the Rorschach

The next case also concerns sexual abuse and recovered experience. I share it because it temporarily shook my confidence and taught me a great deal about the power of administering the Rorschach to one of my own clients. Stephanie was a 23-year-old woman who came to see me after she completed the allowed number of sessions at her university counseling center. Stephanie's history was significant in that she had been sexually and physically abused by her father from ages 7–11, until one day she reported the abuse to a teacher at school, who notified authorities. Stephanie was removed from the home while the case was investigated, her father spent some time in jail, and the family was reunited after Stephanie's mother pressured her to say that all was forgiven and that she wanted to go home with her father. Stephanie came to therapy with her memories of the abuse intact, but with a noticeable lack of emotion about any of the events. She was quite loyal to her family and even to her father, and she mentioned quite frequently that she felt she was responsible for the abuse. One year into the therapy, I asked Stephanie to participate in the Rorschach.

Stephanie gave an extremely rich protocol containing much useful information, but I mainly want to focus on the events after the test administration. Let me explain first that I administered Stephanie's Rorschach in the standard side-by-side seating format. Also, she gave such a lengthy protocol (64 responses) that I had only a few minutes to talk with her after the test, because I had another client waiting to meet with me. The morning after the Rorschach administration, Stephanie called to say she urgently needed to see me. When we met several hours later, she tearfully reported being furious at me ever since the Rorschach. She said that I had treated her badly, barely spoken to her or looked at her during the test administration, and then left her alone afterwards. She said she felt angry, dirty, used, and hurt. She had thought I was a kind man who was interested in her well-being, but now she saw I was evil and uncaring and she never wanted to see me again.

Although I was greatly taken aback at first, I listened quietly to Stephanie until I understood what was occurring. I then told her that I had inadvertently recreated a situation that felt like the many times her father had sex with her. She now was experiencing many of the feelings that she had previously been unable to remember. Stephanie recognized almost immediately that what I said was true and became calmer. She was then able to listen as I apologized for not telling her beforehand about the seating arrangement used with the Rorschach administration and for not making sure that we had time to talk after the test administration. Stephanie and I were able to work together over the next several months on the parallels between her experience during the Rorschach and the abuse by her father. One day she told me she said she saw the painful experience of the Rorschach as serendipitous and as crucial for her in opening up to the emotions surrounding her sexual abuse. I learned how important it is for the therapy relationship to be strong enough to handle any transference disruptions if I continued to administer the Rorschach to my own clients.

Case 4—Robert: An Example of Projective Counseling

In a now overlooked paper, Harrower (1956) described a technique in which projective test results are shared with clients after an assessment, and clients are invited to share associations with the therapist, much as might be done with a dream fragment. Harrower called this method "projective counseling" and I used it with Robert, a 43-year-old psychotherapy client. Robert was a gay man who sought psychotherapy to explore recent difficulties establishing lasting intimate relationships. He had been in several long term relationships in his twenties and thirties, but these had ended and he currently reported little luck getting beyond the first or second date with potential boyfriends. After 14 months of psychotherapy, I was convinced that Robert had a deep ambivalence about intimacy. He seemed consciously aware only of the part of him that longed to be in a close relationship. He rejected my suggestion that there might be ways he was inadvertently pushing potential lovers away. We were able to broach this hypothesis in a new way during the Rorschach feedback session.

For example, Robert and I reviewed all his pair (2) and human movement (M) responses, as I suggested that these might tell us something about his perceptions of relationships. We started with Robert's opening response to Card III: "two people in formal clothes facing each other and bowing while tipping their hats" (D1). As we discussed this percept, Robert recognized his own somewhat formal interpersonal style and his desire to "look good" for others. He realized that sometimes this might make him seem distant to men in whom he was interested. We then moved on to Card IV, to which Robert had reported, "Some sort of scary monster coming out at you. He's about to come out and stomp you...It's a big figure. You are seeing it from a worm's eye view. It looks like it's about to land on you" (W). I guided Robert slightly by telling him there was old clinical lore that people's responses to Card IV reflected their feelings about men. With this help he associated to times neighborhood bullies had taunted him as a child and the fear he still sometimes felt around groups of loud men. We wondered together if some remaining fear of being taunted or humiliated made him anxious when he approached a potential boyfriend.

On Card IX, Robert had seen, in sequence: ". . .two little pink babies lying there with their feeding hands up" (D6) and then "...a guy riding on a motor cycle with exhaust coming out of the back" (Dd99). At this point in our discussion Robert was on to himself, looked up at me and grinned, saying: "I guess I'd sure like to leave the baby part of me behind in the dust." This led to a fruitful discussion of how uncomfortable Robert was with his longing and need for closeness and how he worked hard to hide this part of him from others. For weeks afterwards, Robert and I continued to review his Rorschach responses and he raved about the insights he received about his approach to relationships. Some time later, Robert started dating a man who seemed quite suitable for an intimate relationship, and years later they are still together.

Conclusions

In summary I have learned that it is possible and useful to give the Rorschach to my own clients mid-therapy. The findings of Exner et al. (1978) seem to be confirmed in that I get longer, more revealing, and more disturbed looking protocols from my long-term clients than from clients who are in the beginning stages of a relationship with me. For this reason, I would not administer the Rorschach to a client of mine who needed testing to appear in court or for the purposes of employment screening. However, as part of the ongoing exploration of therapy, it can be useful to administer the Rorschach to one's own clients. As I have illustrated, the Rorschach can confirm impressions that a clinician has already begun to form in a therapy relationship and then provide a way to introduce such impressions into the therapy. The regressive pull of the Rorschach testing situation can also unearth unconscious material that then emerges either in clients' associations or dreams. In some cases, a mid-therapy Rorschach administration can temporarily intensify transference from the client and perhaps even present a crisis in the therapy. Although I have never again experienced as big a disruption as I did with Stephanie, I have had clients temporarily go through increased fear that I will judge them or try to hurt them with test findings. However, I have found that such crises can be managed and even harnessed to produce significant breakthroughs in therapy. Last, the Rorschach may be used mid-therapy in the collaborative enterprise of projective counseling, where the client not only learns new insights but also discovers the power of the Rorschach. For these and other reasons, I suggest that we continue to explore the uses of the Rorschach mid-therapy and that we stop condemning the testing of one's own long-term clients. A more reasonable admonition is that assessors should also consider the context of an assessment whenever interpreting test data. This principle applies not only to testing one's own clients, but to every other assessment situation as well.

6

Giving Feedback to Clients About "Defensive" Test Protocols

I believe that, in many ways, how we think about and deal with clients who have MMPI–2 L, S, or K scores over 65 or Rorschachs with less than 14 responses reveals a great deal about how we view the assessment process in general and our role as assessors specifically. In addition, this topic highlights a number of conundrums we encounter in the practice of clinical assessment as a result of the different internal and external pressures we face.

In this chapter, I highlight the complex context of clinical assessment by proposing five different guidelines regarding guarded or "defensive" test protocols. These suggestions also apply to protocols that are possibly exaggerated or malingered, but I focus most of my examples on guarded protocols. Although I focus on how to talk about "defensive" protocols with clients, I also discuss how I think about such assessment events; as you know, how we interpret an event greatly influences how we respond to it. A final caveat is that these guidelines are from my personal experiences interacting with clients who produced "defensive" or invalid protocols. I have no illusions that these guidelines apply to all assessments settings.

This chapter is drawn from a paper I presented to the Society for Personality Assessment (Finn, 1999). I am grateful to Ronald Ganellen for encouraging me to write about this topic.

GUIDELINE #1:   DON'T believe that a guarded test protocol
means you have no information about the client with which to address the goals of the assessment. DO realize that a guarded test protocol is an important assessment event that can contribute to your
understanding of clients' problems in living, dilemmas of change,[1]
and of how others react to them.

In making this point, I'm thinking of one of my first assessment experiences, which involved a client on an adult inpatient unit, recently admitted after a serious suicide attempt. As I remember, the nursing staff
and team psychiatrist found the client close-mouthed and quite puzzling
and had asked for an MMPI to clarify the diagnosis. I was looking forward to practicing my newly learned MMPI interpretive skills and also
had fantasized about making an incisive contribution to the case. Therefore, I was quite dismayed when the client produced an MMPI with elevations on the validity scales L and K, and no elevations on any of the
clinical scales. After scoring the profile, I confirmed—through reading
my MMPI books—that it was "invalid" and "uninterpretable," and I
complained to my supervisor, "Now I'll never be able to address the referral questions!" He smiled and patiently asked, "Is that so?" He then
helped me get curious about how the "defensiveness" on the client's
MMPI might relate to the staff's confusion about the client—which of
course was the case. As the assessment unfolded, I gradually learned that
the client was in great distress, but feared telling anyone about his concerns because he believed that the CIA was involved in a plot against
him. The MMPI accurately reflected the dilemma he found himself in, of
wanting help, but not knowing whom to trust.

I now realize that my error—of viewing a "defensive" test protocol as
conveying no information about the client—is a common one and reflects the logical–positivist, information-gathering model of assessment
(Finn & Tonsager, 1997) in which I was trained. An invalid MMPI was
the same as a dirty test tube in a blood test; it precluded finding out what
was "really" wrong with the client. My disappointment also reflected the
pressures I felt to fulfill what Shafer (1954) called the "oracular" role of
the assessor. Once I realized that my job was not to "scoop" the other

---

[1]*Dilemmas of change* is a term used by family therapists (e.g., Papp, 1983) to describe those situations in which clients are "stuck" in a certain pattern, because they perceive all their options as
leading to painful, undesirable outcomes.

members of the treatment team, I relaxed and set about forming a relationship with the client. As he got comfortable on the unit, he gradually revealed his fears to me and to others, and even eventually retook the MMPI, producing a valid profile.

> GUIDELINE #2:   DON'T think that you can interpret a single validity indicator as always meaning the same thing. DO remember that—as with any test result—validity indicators must be interpreted in light of other test scores, the client's history, and the context of the assessment.

Here I'm thinking about a custody situation I was involved in some years ago, where another psychologist had concluded—almost entirely on the basis of an MMPI–2 K score of 70T—that a father was "unable to admit to faults," "highly defensive," and "personality disordered." Clearly this conceptualization was faulty, for the psychologist seemed unaware that elevated MMPI–2 K scores are almost typical in custody assessments (Ben-Porath, Graham, Nagayama Hall, & Hirschman, 1995). The psychologist's error reminds us, however, that how clients understand the purpose of an evaluation may greatly influence their test performance. This general point is sometimes easy to forget.

Likewise, an MMPI–2 F score of 100T will mean different things for an inpatient than for an outpatient, and there are many factors that can contribute to a low R or a high Lambda on the Rorschach. Any good assessor knows that there are no guaranteed, fixed rules about interpreting single test scores. But we don't always remember this when interacting with clients whose test protocols deviate from traditional guidelines for test validity. With the guideline I've given in mind, we can stay humble and curious in discussing supposedly "defensive" test responses with clients. Such assessment events may not indicate defensiveness in the usual sense at all.

Again, I suspect that our desperate search for fixed rules to interpret test scores reflects a way to deal with the anxiety of the clinical assessment situation. The pressure on the psychologist in the information-gathering model of assessment—to interpret test results unilaterally (i.e., without input from clients or others) in a way that yields the "Truth" about the client—is so great that we long for simple rules that help us appear "scientific" and "hard-minded." Unfortunately, when these rules are used rigidly, they often result in conclusions that are less valid and reliable than do other methods that are more practical and based in common sense. For example, in collaborative or Therapeutic Assessment, we are likely to discuss with clients any test score whose meaning is ambiguous, thereby enlisting them as "co-investigators" in the assessment and keeping us from reaching erroneous conclusions.

> GUIDELINE #3:   DON'T take clients' "defensive" or "invalid" test responding "just personally," that is, as necessarily indicating their distrust of you or as a sign that they are unwilling to collaborate with you during the evaluation. DO, in such situations, consider whether you adequately developed a relationship with a client before beginning testing and/or whether you fully appreciated the dilemmas facing the client in the evaluation.

In coming up with these suggestions, I'm grateful to another supervisor who patiently helped me sort through my narcissistic injury as a beginning assessor when a client—with whom I thought I was working well—gave me a Rorschach record with R = 12 and Lambda = 2.4. I believed that if the client trusted me, as I had thought, surely she would have given a longer, less "defensive" protocol. I later discovered that the client's constriction on the Rorschach had more to do with her terror of interpersonal situations where she didn't "know the rules" than it had to do with anything about me. However, at the time, I felt embarrassed and insecure about my abilities as a clinician, and was angry at the client for "fooling me" into thinking we were getting along well together. Despite whatever my reaction says about my own personality struggles at the time, it also relates to the context in which I was operating.

I had been taught that a good assessor establishes enough "rapport" with a client to ensure an unguarded test protocol. (In other respects, one's relationship with the client wasn't really emphasized during my early training; it simply had to be adequate to get good "data.") When this woman's Rorschach appeared "defensive," I believed there either had to be something wrong with her or with me. Given these two options, I did what many of us do—I blamed her! I submit to you that this kind of self-protective externalization is often at work when we label our clients as "defensive," "deceptive," "uncooperative," "resistant," or "uninsightful." I believe this process also explains what the psychologist did in the custody evaluation I mentioned earlier, when she labeled the father with high MMPI–2 K score as "personality disordered."

Besides taking the client's test responses just personally, we also can make the other mistake—of never examining whether we contributed to a constricted or guarded test result. This is why I use the phrase "just personally"—we should always consider our personal contribution to the field of assessment. I remember a number of years ago when the chief psychologist of a private psychiatric hospital asked me to consult about the high number of invalid MMPIs being generated by the facility's psychiatric inpatients. The first thing I did was to watch how the MMPI was being administered to patients. I discovered that the nursing staff or a psychometrist would approach clients, give them an MMPI booklet, answer sheet, and a pencil and say, "Your doctor wants you to do this." Then clients would complete the MMPI in the middle of the day room, while other clients were sitting near them and milling about. The number of invalid and defensive protocols dropped drastically as soon as clients were allowed to complete the MMPI in their rooms, and when the nurses and psychometrists were trained to spend time with clients discussing the reason for testing and answering their questions.

This solution may seem obvious, but again, I don't view the hospital psychologists as having been stupid, poorly trained, or lacking in common sense. Rather, they had simply learned a way of thinking about assessment that emphasized "getting the data" over establishing a relationship with clients. When we all realize that psychological testing is more than a "blood test" in medicine, we will automatically put most of our attention on helping clients feel safe and trusted during an assessment, rather than on their simply completing certain tests. As I discuss later, those of us practicing Therapeutic Assessment have developed a number of ways to enlist clients' cooperation.

> GUIDELINE #4:   DON'T accuse clients who produce invalid test protocols during feedback sessions of "not cooperating," "holding back," "lying," "exaggerating," or "faking bad." DO, instead explore with clients any dilemmas or "Catch–22s" they faced regarding the assessment, and whether these dilemmas were recognized and adequately discussed prior to testing.

Perhaps some of you, like me, have encountered clients who have been criticized during previous evaluations for not cooperating adequately or for attempting to influence the results of the assessment. I've been struck by how deeply such criticisms are felt and how damaging they can be to clients' attitudes about psychological assessment. For example, I remember a client we once worked with at our Center who was reluctant to take the MMPI–2. On further inquiry, we discovered that his memory of a previous MMPI feedback session was of being told that he himself was "invalid." I've always wondered if this was his distortion or an accurate reading of the attitude of the previous assessor!

But if we're not going to target clients who produce guarded or invalid test protocols, and also not target ourselves (although we may consider our contribution to the interpersonal field of the assessment), what are we to do instead? I believe that what is called for in many of these situations is empathy about the client's "dilemma-of-change" (Papp, 1983) as reflected in the assessment, that is, those apparently unresolvable conflicts or Catch–22s that manifest sometimes in elevated scores on validity indicators. Unfortunately, if we assessors are in what Agazarian (1997) called a "barrier experience"—of taking clients' test behaviors just personally or blaming them for not responding as we wished—it's very difficult to be empathic or curious about an invalid or guarded test result.

As one example of how we can conduct an assessment differently, let me return to the custody assessment I mentioned earlier. When I discussed with the father his high K score on his MMPI–2, he told me about his approach as he filled out the test. He felt it was important to cooperate fully with whatever he was asked to do by the court-appointed assessor, as he recognized that she could play a major part in whether he had future contact with his daughter. On the other hand, he wanted to put his best foot forward during the evaluation because his ex-wife was accusing him of many things he felt were distorted, unfair, or just not true. When confronted with the MMPI–2, with all its socially undesirable items, the man did what seemed reasonable to him in the situation, that is, to emphasize his strengths as a person and as a father and downplay those factors that would leave him open to his wife's accusations. As he explained to me, "When I apply for a job, I tell them what I do best and in what areas I'm trying to improve. I don't give them a long list of every difficulty I've had with jobs in the past. Here I was being interviewed for a job as a father, and I approached it the same way."

When I told the client I thought his strategy was reasonable, but that it left him open to accusations of having covered up deep-seated problems, he asked if he could take the MMPI–2 again or whether there was another test that was less vulnerable to these kinds of interpretations. We agreed to do the Rorschach together—which had not been administered in the previous evaluation—and he produced a very unguarded protocol with some indications of oppositional tendencies, but no other deviations from the general norms. In my court testimony, I suggested that rather than indicating a personality disorder, the father's MMPI–2 K score might reflect his good judgment and his desire for continuing involvement with his daughter. After all, what we would think of a parent who deliberately revealed all his faults during a custody evaluation? I also acknowledged the man's tendency to "dig in his heels" when he felt unfairly blamed, and said that although I didn't see this as a major personality flaw, the client and I agreed that it had certainly affected his ability to deal with his ex-wife. The client was quite happy with my testimony, and the jury concluded that he should have ongoing contact with his young daughter.

Client conflicts of interest are quite easy to understand in assessments where clients are being tested in part against their will, for example, in forensic situations, disability evaluations, assessments done as part of the treatment of another family member, or in inpatient settings where clients' personal desires to be admitted or released from a hospital sometimes are in conflict with those of staff or of their larger interpersonal system. However, it is my experience that similar dilemmas of change often are involved when clients who are being tested voluntarily produce invalid or guarded test protocols. Once, I assessed a 15-year-old girl who had voluntarily asked for psychotherapy for severe depression. Her symptoms had gotten no better after a year of treatment by an excellent psychologist and following several trials of different antidepressant medications. The treating therapist was quite puzzled and suggested an assessment, to which the client readily agreed.

During the assessment, the young woman generally was quite open and forthcoming with me, except when I asked about her family situation, when she appeared more anxious and reserved. Her therapist reported that the girl had refused repeatedly to involve her parents in her therapy, and when I contacted the parents during the evaluation, they seemed reluctant to come in for an interview as part of the assessment. I grew even more intrigued when the client produced an extremely guarded MMPI–A protocol, and a Rorschach with R = 14 and Lambda = 1.2. Her last response on the Rorschach was this: "Here's a person who has been caught in an awful situation. He doesn't know what to do because if he moves one way or the other, someone will get hurt. Finally, out of desperation, he jumps off this cliff. He may die, but at least he'll be free from trying to decide what to do."

In a subsequent session, with her therapist present, I told the girl that I wondered if this response reflected some way she felt trapped in

her own life. After first saying "No," she eventually broke down crying, and told her therapist and me that her father had been sexually
abusing her for 4 to 5 years. Understandably, she was depressed miser-
ably but also terrified of telling anyone about the abuse because she
feared her mother's anger and worried that her father would be put in
jail. Her "defensive" test protocols were a perfect expression of the
Catch–22 she found herself in her life and in the assessment.

> GUIDELINE #5:   DON'T think that the final solution to defen-
> sive testing responding is for psychologists to develop better validity
> scales or statistical corrections to compensate for response styles or re-
> sponse sets. DO recognize that there's no better way to get reliable
> and valid test data than to enlist our clients' curiosity, motivation,
> and willingness to explore their problems in living during an assess-
> ment.

I want to be careful here, in that I don't mean to disparage the work of
my talented colleagues who continue to do excellent work on the development and interpretation of test validity indicators. Such research is extremely valuable, especially to psychologists working in settings where
clients are assessed routinely assessed without their full consent. However, I continue to believe that the best solution to the problem of test in-
validity is for assessors to mitigate the dilemmas of change facing clients
in typical assessment situations.

In Therapeutic Assessment we work to reduce clients' reservations
about the assessment process in various ways. Before we begin an assessment, we give them detailed information about psychological assessment in general and about their evaluations in particular and then attempt to answer all their questions. We solicit clients' goals for the
assessment—even if the clients are referred to us by another mental
health professional, the court, or an insurance company—and promise to
make those goals a primary focus of our evaluation and to give clients
feedback at the end of the assessment. We also inquire whether clients
have encountered psychological assessment in the past, and if so, how
they felt about those experiences. If the previous experiences were negative, we attempt to negotiate with clients an assessment contract with
specific terms that preclude our repeating the previous trauma. As the

assessment takes place, we explain the purpose of each test in terms of its relevance to the clients' goals, and we involve clients in making sense of their test behaviors and experiences during the evaluation. Finally, we check our assessment findings with clients during the feedback session, ask them to comment on early drafts of written reports, and offer a follow-up meeting 2 to 3 months after the assessment for them to ask further questions and give us additional feedback.

It is our experience that the combination of these various steps—many of which are based in common sense or basic rules of respectful relationships—greatly decreases the number of guarded or invalid test protocols we encounter. When guarded or invalid test protocols show up, which they do, I now find it easier to be curious and nondefensive myself, and to trust that this assessment finding—like all others—is a useful and important communication from the client. If I am surprised by this communication or am unable to imagine what it might mean, I ask clients to help me understand it and to tell me what I still have not grasped about their lives or their view of the assessment.

There is a corollary to this last guideline that may seem provocative, but I mention it because I believe it deserves serious discussion as we think together about the future of psychological assessment. If a client's full cooperation and motivation cannot be gained during an assessment, because of inevitable Catch–22s embedded in the assessment process, perhaps we should think twice about whether it is appropriate to conduct the assessment at all. Just as clients have the right to not incriminate themselves in court, perhaps they also should have the right to not participate in any psychological assessment whose findings could be used against them and to know about this danger beforehand. This consideration would require us to give serious scrutiny to some types of forensic assessment, to preemployment evaluations, and to other evaluations where it seems unlikely that one can obtain unambiguous informed consent, such as assessments of adolescents who are referred against their will.

I have done all these types of evaluations myself, and I do not mean to say that they cannot be conducted in ways that are respectful to clients. I am heartened greatly by the serious attention given to client informed consent by many forensic examiners. Also, at our Center we are experimenting with ways to modify assessments containing inherent conflicts of interest for clients, to see if they can be made less problematic and more therapeutic. For example, we have developed a protocol for "therapeutic custody evaluations" that so far has resulted in a large number of out-of-court settlements in extremely polarized postdivorce situations.

Nevertheless, I believe many psychologists are not trained adequately to discuss the pros and cons of "involuntary" assessments fully with clients before they begin testing. Or, the complex pressures we feel to fulfill our roles and make a living lead us to gloss over the intricacies of getting informed consent from clients. Again, I think these problems stem from our emphasis on the traditional model of assessment, which views psychological testing as a neutral, objective way to gain information about a client, rather than as a vulnerable and potentially profound relational experience that can deeply affect—for better or worse—clients' lives. Perhaps as we begin to appreciate the true power of psychological assessment—as I think is now happening—we will find that invalid and guarded test protocols become less frequent.

7

Assessment Feedback Integrating MMPI–2 and Rorschach Findings

Recently, there has been increased interest in the process of giving feedback to clients about personality assessment results, and a number of excellent resources exist to guide clinicians in sharing results with clients about their MMPI–2 profiles (e.g., Butcher, 1990; Finn, 1996b; Lewak, Marks, & Nelson, 1990). Although many clinicians often use a battery of tests rather than a single assessment instrument, to date little has been written about how to talk with clients about findings from multiple personality tests. This void in the literature is significant for several reasons. First, the current ethical principles of the American Psychological Association (1992) make it clear that clients should be given feedback—in language they can understand—about tests that are administered to them. Presumably, if multiple instruments are used, clients should be given feedback about all of them. Second, recent research suggests that clients therapeutically benefit from hearing about their MMPI–2 results when such feedback is presented in an empathic, collaborative way (Finn & Tonsager, 1992). If a method can be developed to provide feedback to clients about both self-report and performance-based personality tests, it is possible that even greater therapeutic benefits could be achieved.

In this chapter, I first propose a model for integrating results from the MMPI–2 and Rorschach, depending on the pattern of clients' MMPI–2

This paper was originally published in the *Journal of Personality Assessment* (Finn, 1996a).

and Rorschach scores. I have developed this model over years of conjoint use of the two tests with clients and have come to believe that the two instruments complement each other extremely well in applied clinical situations. Next, I use this conceptual model to suggest ways of discussing findings from these two tests with clients. The guidelines I present have proven to work well with many clients and were developed with the goal of providing therapeutic feedback to clients about their MMPI–2 and Rorschach results. Last, I illustrate this feedback approach with a single case example.

Understanding MMPI–2 and Rorschach Results

Before we can discuss test findings with clients, we must first understand them ourselves. Unfortunately for the practicing clinician, there is still considerable disagreement among experts about how to integrate results from the MMPI and Rorschach (e.g., Archer & Krishnamurthy, 1993a, 1993b; Exner, 1996; Meyer, 1997). Based on my clinical work, I have come to believe that both the MMPI–2 and Rorschach provide reliable, valid, and clinically useful information. In many cases, the two tests largely confirm each other, and this is useful in giving me more confidence about the assessment results and hence making me more sure-footed in my interactions with clients. I believe that in other cases, the MMPI–2 and Rorschach should be expected to disagree, and I use a model that has been in part articulated by others (Ganellen, Wasyliw, Haywood, & Grossman, 1996; Lovitt, 1993; Meyer, 1997; Weiner, 1993) to resolve those apparent contradictions. This model bases conjoint interpretation of the MMPI–2 and Rorschach on the different characteristics of the two tests.

The MMPI–2 is a highly structured test that is typically administered in a noninteractive fashion. Its response format draws on intellectual mechanisms, such as reading and filling in dots on an answer sheet or pushing buttons on a computer keyboard—tasks that are now fairly familiar to a large number of adults in the United States. The MMPI–2 has the potential—because of the empirical correlates of its test scores—to reveal traits and problems of which clients are not fully aware. In general, however, its scores reflect clients' self-presentations and their conscious views of themselves at the time of testing. Also, clients who use intellectual defenses and who function well in structured, noninterpersonal situations can easily produce benign MMPI–2 profiles, without significant elevations on its validity scales.

In contrast, the Rorschach administration takes place in an interpersonal, relatively unstructured situation. The nature of the task is largely unfamiliar to most clients and thereby generally produces more anxiety for clients than does the MMPI–2, in part because it is harder for them to know what they are revealing about themselves. As is well known, the shadings and colors of the Rorschach blots often stir up emotional responses in clients. In general, then, the test excels at revealing problems in cognition, perception, and affect that arise in unstructured, interpersonal, emotionally arousing situations. Some clients excel at avoiding such situations in their day-to-day lives; hence Rorschach results can be especially important in predicting the kinds of difficulties clients will encounter in unusually stressful situations, such as during the middle of a long-term uncovering psychotherapy.

Patterns of MMPI–2 and Rorschach Responses

Exhibit 7–1 shows a schema for broadly classifying combinations of Rorschach and MMPI–2 results into five patterns, according to (a) the level of disturbance revealed on the MMPI–2, (b) the level of disturbance revealed on the Rorschach, and (c) the level of engagement of the client in the Rorschach. The two convergent cells (Cells A and D), where both the MMPI–2 and the Rorschach show either high or low levels of disturbance, are relatively easy to interpret. The two discrepant cells (Cells B and C), where the MMPI–2 and Rorschach appear to disagree on the level of the client's disturbance, are more complex. Let us now consider the meaning of each of these test patterns.

Cell A—High Disturbance on Both the MMPI–2 and Rorschach

In this cell fall clients whose psychological functioning is disrupted in both structured and unstructured situations. The MMPI–2 and Rorschach agree because there is no hidden "underlying" disturbance; that is, the clients' problems in living are quite evident in their day-to-day functioning, they are aware of these problems, and are willing and able to report them on the MMPI–2. This pattern of test results is common

EXHIBIT 7–1
Patterns of MMPI–2 and Rorschach Results

	High Degree of Disturbance on MMPI–2	Low Degree of Disturbance on MMPI–2
High Degree of Disturbance on Rorschach	Cell A[a]	Cell B[a]
Low Degree of Disturbance on Rorschach	Cell C, Case 1[a] .... Cell C, Case 2[b]	Cell D[a]

Note. MMPI–2 profiles in all cases are considered to be consistent (i.e., VRIN and TRIN within normal limits), valid, and unguarded (i.e., with no significant elevations on L, K, Fp, and S).

[a]Rorschach protocols in these cells show adequate engagement on the part of the client (i.e., R is average or above and Lambda is < 1.0); [b]These Rorschach protocols are constricted (with low Rs and/or Lambdas greater than 1.0).

among inpatients and outpatients who are voluntarily seeking help because of an emotional crisis. In my experience, clients with this pattern of test results have histories that are consistent with their test results. Such clients are not surprised by feedback about the assessment findings.

Cell B—Low Disturbance on the MMPI–2, High Disturbance on the Rorschach

When the Rorschach and MMPI disagree, this is the most frequent type of discrepancy. In clinical settings, clients with this pattern have underlying pathology that emerges in emotionally arousing, regressive, interpersonal, unstructured situations (such as the Rorschach administration). However, they function relatively well in familiar, structured situations when they can use intellectual resources to deal with anxiety (such as when taking the MMPI–2). Such clients are often unaware of the full nature of their difficulties and hence, are unable to report them on the MMPI–2. They often present for mental health services puzzling over certain problems in living that do not fit with their usual self-concepts. In my experience, this pattern of test results is most common in outpatient settings, especially those settings where clients have been preselected for a certain level of adaptive functioning (e.g., university counseling centers, employee assistance programs.) In our outpatient clinic, such clients are often referred by therapists who are puzzled at their lack of progress in treatment, or who are concerned because the clients have begun to exhibit disturbing, atypical behaviors or characteristics in the middle of a long-term uncovering psychotherapy. In my experience, a careful history often reveals several unusual events in these clients' pasts that seem out of character, and that occurred when the clients were under severe stress. Giving assessment feedback to such clients is complex, for they may be surprised when an assessor talks about their underlying pathology. Such clients have the potential to become flooded, confused, or defensive when the full extent of their problems is discussed.

Cell C—High Disturbance on the MMPI–2, Low Disturbance on the Rorschach

This is the least frequent discrepancy between the MMPI–2 and Rorschach in inpatient and outpatient settings; this pattern is most frequently found among clients applying for psychiatric disability or being tested for forensic purposes. Two distinct interpretations are possible:

Case 1—Client Shows Adequate Engagement on the Rorschach. In this instance, clients are adequately engaged in both the MMPI–2 and Rorschach, and the disagreement between the two sets of test findings reflects the greater control clients have over their self-presentations on the MMPI–2 as compared to the Rorschach (Ganellen, Wasyliw, Haywood, & Grossman, 1996). The disturbance shown on the MMPI–2 represents a conscious attempt on part of clients to endorse psychopathology, whereas the lack of disturbance on the Rorschach is inconsistent with this presentation and raises the possibility of malingering, exaggeration, or a "cry for help." In such instances, clients typically produce a very high score on Scale F of the MMPI–2, and the F(p) scale developed by Arbisi and Ben-Porath

(1996) may be useful in distinguishing conscious malingering from more characterologically based symptom exaggeration.[1] Malingering should also be considered when this test pattern occurs in assessment situations where clients are clearly motivated to present themselves as more psychologically disturbed than they actually are (e.g., when applying for psychiatric disability or claiming "insanity" in a legal proceeding). As might be expected, assessment feedback with clients in this cell is often anxiety provoking for assessors, as it involves discussing the possibility of clients overreporting symptoms.

Case 2—"Constricted" Rorschach. The pattern of a highly disturbed MMPI–2 and a relatively "normal" Rorschach also occurs in situations where clients have no motivation to feign psychopathology (e.g., in outpatient and inpatient settings where clients are voluntarily seeking treatment). In such instances, this pattern results from a defensive reaction of emotional withdrawal or constriction on the part of clients in response to the regressive pull of the Rorschach administration. These clients are able to reveal their problems in living on the MMPI–2 because it is impersonal, less arousing, and less overwhelming. However, during the Rorschach, these clients "shut down" because they are overstimulated and confused by the interpersonal, emotionally arousing test situation. An assessor will typically sense that such clients have made a sincere attempt to cooperate with the Rorschach; nevertheless, their protocols typically show a high Lambda and/or low R. Meyer (1997) labeled this response style as "Style 2-R," and reminded us of another term, "coarctated," used by Rapaport, Gill, and Schafer (1968) to describe such Rorschachs. Feedback with such clients can be disastrous if an assessor mistakenly asserts that they have overreported symptomatology on the MMPI–2.

Cell D—Low Disturbance on the MMPI–2, Low Disturbance on the Rorschach

Clients in this cell function well in both structured and unstructured situations. This pattern of test results is rarely seen in clinical settings and is

---

[1]Meyer (1997) referred to these two response styles as "Style 4-M" and "Style 5-M," respectively.

more common when assessments are performed for employment screening or research.

Feedback to Clients

Exhibit 7–2 takes these understandings about MMPI–2 and Rorschach patterns and applies them to the task of giving feedback to clients. As you can see, when the Rorschach and MMPI–2 agree in their assessments, it is relatively easy to discuss them with clients (Cells A & D). In such situations, I generally tell the client that the two tests largely agree in their conclusions, and that I will use the MMPI–2 profile to illustrate the assessment findings. I structure my feedback around the MMPI–2 because its dimensional scales are quite understandable to clients and the profile provides a better visual aid than does the Structural Summary. I then explicate the general absence or presence of different traits or problems in living, making modifications from the Rorschach results whenever appropriate.

In such situations, the Rorschach is still extremely valuable in the feedback, by providing a metaphorical language in which to word assessment findings. For example, a client may have a score of 80T on Scale 4 of the MMPI–2, as well as a significant elevation on the Anger Content Scale. The Rorschach Structural Summary shows an elevated number of S and AG responses, and the content includes five percepts of volcanoes ready to explode. When discussing Scale 4 with this client, I would label it an "anger scale," and tell the client that he appears to be so angry that he feels like a "volcano ready to explode." Although the MMPI–2 has provided the visual aid, the Rorschach gives me the exact words to use with the client in describing his subjective experience.

Similarly, a recent client with an MMPI–2 F score of 80T, the Anxiety content scale at 91T, and a D of –4 on the Structural Summary gave the following as her last percept on Card X of the Rorschach:

> "These pink things are cliffs and you can see these little creatures hanging on, trying not to fall off. There's been a terrible earthquake, or a storm or something, and this one in the middle couldn't hang on and is dropping. But these ones are still holding on for dear life."

Without the Rorschach content, I might have told this woman that the testing revealed that she was under a great deal of emotional stress. Instead, during the feedback session I told her that the recent events of

> **EXHIBIT 7–2**
> **Sample Feedback Statements to Clients With Different**
> **Patterns of MMPI–2 and Rorschach Results**

Cell A (Both MMPI–2 and Rorschach Show High Level of Disturbance)

"Both the MMPI–2 and Rorschach agree in showing that you are having significant difficulties in your coping right now. Your difficulties appear to be so severe that they are even troubling you in familiar, low stress situations."

Cell B (MMPI–2 Shows Low Disturbance; Rorschach Shows High Disturbance)

"The MMPI–2 shows how you generally think of yourself and how you appear to most people in your day-to-day life. The results suggest that you have learned how to manage emotional pain and are able to deal with a great deal of inner turmoil that might be unbearable to other people—as long as you stay in familiar, structured situations.

The Rorschach taps a different level of your personality, which is not visible to most people, and of which you yourself may sometimes be unaware. This test suggests that you are having some significant underlying struggles and turmoil. These difficulties may arise only occasionally, when you are in highly emotional, interpersonal, or unfamiliar situations. You may even avoid experiencing such inner turmoil for long periods of time by isolating yourself and staying out of uncomfortable situations."

Cell C (MMPI–2 Shows High Disturbance; Rorschach Shows Low Disturbance)

Case 1

"On the MMPI–2 you reported a great deal of distress and disturbance. It appears that you wanted to make sure that I knew about your troubles and you may have downplayed some of your strengths.

The Rorschach gives a good picture of these strengths, and shows that you function well even in unfamiliar, unstructured situations, where most people have more difficulties."

Case 2

"On the MMPI–2 you let me know about the great number of problems you are having at the current time. It appears that you

EXHIBIT 7–2
(Continued)

were able to tell about these when you were left alone and asked to respond by paper and pencil.

The Rorschach gives a less clear picture of your difficulties. It appears that you might have closed up in the unfamiliar, interpersonal situation of the inkblot test. When you close up, your distress is less visible to others."

Cell D (Both MMPI–2 and Rorschach Show Low Level of Disturbance)

"Both the MMPI–2 and Rorschach showed that you are functioning well and not reporting a great deal of distress. Even the unfamiliar situation of the Rorschach did not cause you difficulties. You appear to be a highly resilient, stress-resistant individual."

---

her life had so upset her that she seemed to feel as if she were "hanging on for dear life" and might "fall off the edge of a cliff any moment." My words resonated with her deeply and she seemed to feel profoundly understood. (Incidentally, like most clients, she appeared not to realize that the wording of my feedback came from her own Rorschach response.) Alternatively, I could have read this woman's final response to her so that we could discuss it together, in the style of Molly Harrower's (1956) "projective counseling" or Constance Fischer's (1985/1994) "individualized assessment."

Giving feedback is most difficult when the Rorschach and MMPI–2 diverge, that is, when one of the tests shows much more disturbance or distress than the other. When the Rorschach shows more distress and/or disturbance than the MMPI–2 (Cell B), I typically invoke the concept of *levels of personality*—telling clients that the MMPI–2 depicts the way they typically think of themselves and are usually seen by others. I then explain that the Rorschach taps a "different level" of personality functioning, that is not as visible in day-to-day life, and that is revealed in unfamiliar, stressful, emotionally arousing situations. Clients typically readily understand and accept this explanation, and we then go on to discuss how their coping mechanisms help them manage the stresses of everyday living. After this groundwork has been laid, I suggest to clients that more serious difficulties tend to get put aside but may arise to plague them and confuse them from time to time. With these clients, I think it is important that I interpret the MMPI–2 as reflecting real strengths, and do not try to insist that the Rorschach findings are more "real" or "important." In this way clients feel affirmed, rather than shamed, for the ways in which they have managed underlying problems.

When the MMPI–2 depicts more distress and/or disturbance than the Rorschach (Cell C), I talk with clients about how they clearly want help or acknowledgment and have used the MMPI–2 to communicate this message to me. Again, by seeing both sets of test results as "real," I avoid accusing clients of exaggerating or lying for primary or secondary gains. In Case 2, where the lack of disturbance on the Rorschach is the result of the client's constricting during the performance-based test situation, I talk with clients about how difficult it may be at times for others to see how much inner turmoil they are experiencing.

In both divergent situations, I again compile the test findings first and then look through the Rorschach for metaphors to use in wording feed-back statements for clients. Especially in the case of Cell B—where clients are sometimes unaware of underlying levels of distress—using met-aphors will often allow clients to resonate with what I am saying.

Case Example—Harry[2]

As an illustration of some of these principles, let us consider the case of a 56-year-old man, Harry. Harry was an attractive, successful businessman who had recently divorced and fairly quickly begun a romantic relation-ship with another woman. He was puzzled by feedback he got from this woman, close friends, and his ex-wife that he was "emotionally unavail-able." In contrast, he was quite proud of his fierce independence and emotional resilience. At the suggestion of his new girlfriend, he sought a personality assessment to get "an outside opinion" on himself. He posed two main questions to be answered by the assessment:

(1) Others say I'm closed and don't open up emotionally. I think I am very self-sufficient and self-controlled. Am I just a pompous ass?

---

[2]The client's name and other identifying information have been changed to protect confiden-tiality.

EXHIBIT 7–3
Harry's K-Corrected MMPI–2 Profile

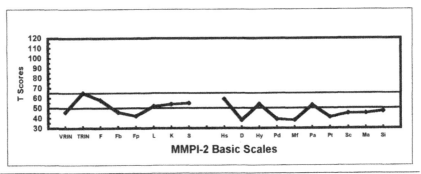

MMPI-2 Basic Scales

Notes. VRIN = Variable Response Inconsistency Scale; TRIN = True-Response Inconsistency Scale; F = Infrequency; Fb = Infrequency Back Page; Fp = Infrequency Psychopathology; S = Superlative Self-Presentation; Hs = Scale 1, Hypochondriasis; D = Scale 2, Depression; Hy = Scale 3, Hysteria; Pd = Scale 4, Psychopathic Deviate; Mf = Scale 5, Masculinity—Femininity; Pa = Scale 6, Paranoia; Pt = Scale 7, Psychasthenia; Sc = Scale 8, Schizophrenia; Ma = Scale 9, Hypomania; Si = Scale 0, Social Introversion.

Source. This figure is excerpted from the *MMPI–2™* (*Minnesota Multiphasic Personality Inventory–2™) Manual for Administration, Scoring, and Interpretation, Revised Edition,* Copyright © 2001 by the Regents of the University of Minnesota Press. All rights reserved. Used by permission of the University of Minnesota Press. "MMPI–2" and "Minnesota Multiphasic Personality–2" are trademarks owned by the Regents of the University of Minnesota.

Am I really controlling and closed, or are others so insecure that it makes them uncomfortable that I have my ducks in a row?

(2) Why am I so ambivalent about getting close to people?

MMPI–2 and Rorschach Results

Exhibit 7–3 shows Harry's basic MMPI–2 profile (Welsh Code 136/0897:425# FKL/). As you can see, there were no significant elevations on the validity scales, and only one mild elevation on the clinical scales—on Scale 1 ($T = 59$). Consistent with my impressions of him in the interview, Harry presented himself as free from any significant emotional problems. The physical distress on Scale 1 appeared in line with Harry's reports of joint and muscular pains, which he attributed to injuries suffered while he was a Green Beret in Vietnam.

EXHIBIT 7–4
The Structural Summary for Harry's Rorschach

LOCATION FEATURES	DETERMINANTS		CONTENTS	APPROACH
	BLENDS	SINGLE		Card: Locations:

LOCATION FEATURES	DETERMINANTS BLENDS	DETERMINANTS SINGLE	CONTENTS	APPROACH
			H = 2,2	
Zf = 21	Fma.FC'	M =2	(H) = 1,0	I : W.D
ZSum = 69.5	Ma.FC=2	FM =0	Hd = 0,1	I I : WS.WS
ZEst = 70.0	FC'.CF	m =1	(Hd) = 0,0	III : WS.D.D
	mp.FT	C =0	Hx = 0,0	IV : W.W
W = 18	FMa.FT	Cn =0	A = 4,2	V : W.W
(Wv = 2)	Fmp.FY	CF =1	(A) = 0,0	VI : W.D
D = 4	FD.FT	FC =1	Ad = 0,1	VII : W.W
Dd = 1	FY.FV	C' =0	(Ad) = 1,0	VIII : W.W.Dd.W
S = 4	Fr.CF	C'F =0	An = 0,0	IX : W.W
	ma.FC.Ma	FC' =0	Art =7,0	X : W.WS
DQ	FC'.C.ma.Ma	T =0	Ay = 0,3	
....	(FQ-)	ma-p.FC'.C	TF =0	Bt = 1,1	SPECIAL SCORES
+ = 16 (6)	VF.ma	FT =0	Bl = 0,1	Lvl-1 Lvl-2
o = 4 (0)	ma.CF	V =0	Cg = 1,4	DV= 2 0
v/+ = 0 (0)		VF =0	Cl = 0,0	INC = 0 1
v = 3 (2)		FV =1	Ex = 0,0	DR = 2 2
		Y =0	Fd = 0,0	FAB = 0 0
FORM QUALITY		YF =0	Fi = 0,1	ALOG= 1
		FY =0	Ge = 0,0	CON = 0
FQx FQf MQual SQx		rF = 0	Hh = 0,2	Raw Sum6 = 8
+ = 0 0 0 0		Fr = 0	Ls = 0,1	Wgtd Sum6 = 29
o = 13 0 2 1		FD = 0	Na = 1,3	
u = 2 0 1 1		F =0	Sc = 5,4	AB = 6 CP =0
- = 8 0 3 2			Sx = 0,0	AG = 3 MOR =3
No= 0 0 0		(2) =8	Xy = 0,0	CFB = 0 PER =0
			Id = 0,0	COP = 2 PSV =0

------------------RATIOS, PERCENTAGES, AND DERIVATIONS------------------

R = 23	L =0		FC:CF+C = 4:6	COP =2	AG = 3
			Pure C = 2	Food =0	
EB =6:8 EA =14		EBPer = -NA	SumC':WSumC= 5 : 8	Isolate/R = .48	
eb =10:13 es =23		D =-4	Afr = 0.53	H:(H)+Hd+(Hd) = 4 : 3	
Adj es =8		Adj D = -1	S =4	(H)+(Hd):(A)+(Ad) = 1 : 0	
			Blends:R = 15 : 23	H+A:Hd+Ad = 11 : 3	
FM = 3 SumC' = 5		SumT =4	CP =0		
m =7 SumV =3		SumY =1			

		P =7	Zf =21	3r+(2)/R = .48
a:p = 13 : 4	Sum6 =8	X+% = .57	Zd = -.5	Fr+rF =1
Ma:Mp = 5 : 1	Lv2 =3	F+% = NA	W:D:Dd = 18: 4: 1	FD =1
2AB+Art+Ay = 22	WSum6 =29	X-% =.35	W:M = 18: 6	An+Xy =0
M- =3	Mnone =0	S-% =.25	DQ+ = 16	MOR =3
		Xu% =.09	DQv = 3	

SCZI = 6	DEPI = 5	CDI = 2	S-CON =7	HVI = No	OBS = No

Exhibit 7–4 shows the Structural Summary from Harry's Rorschach.[3] As you can see, this revealed a great deal of distress and disturbance that was not visible on the MMPI–2, including ideational difficulties, depression, strong needs for affection, and a great deal of underlying anger.

[3] I am presenting the fourth edition of the Structural Summary (Exner, 1995), as this is what was available at the time I was working with Harry.

Thus, Harry's test results are a good example of the pattern found in Cell B of Exhibit 7–1. The Rorschach also illustrated Harry's overreliance on intellectualization as a coping mechanism [2AB + (Art + Ay) = 22], which, as mentioned earlier, is typical of someone with his pattern of discrepancy between the MMPI–2 and Rorschach. Note also that Harry had an elevated score (.30) on Armstrong and Lowenstein's (1990) Trauma Content Index.

One of Harry's responses to Card V is illustrative of the complex and highly informative content of his Rorschach protocol. Referring to the whole blot, he said:

> "This looks like a bat. Here is the tail, head, wings...I guess it's possible that there is a significant growth on the wings that's not normal. It's carrying fungus, dust, or something instead of being fluffy. I don't see it as a burden, but it could be. A bat struggling along in spite of gradually accumulating stuff. It needs to be cleaned away or it will follow a natural process and slow down. I sense a hesitance in me to accept this idea that this bat might be in trouble, or be overburdened, or have developed a cancer that will overcome it. But I have this realization that it may not be as good as it looks like. It's more sad."

Assessment Summary/Discussion Session

When I discussed the assessment results with Harry, I first showed him the MMPI–2 and praised him for his emotional resilience and general good coping. I enumerated his many strengths and said that I thought that in many ways, he did have his "ducks in a row." He seemed relieved and proud as I confirmed the ways that he thought about himself. I then told Harry that I thought more was going on in him than met the eye and I talked about the underlying difficulties revealed on the Rorschach—the depression, powerlessness, neediness, and thinking problems. As I continued, Harry began to weep silently, and slowly a story emerged of the multiple severe traumas he had suffered in Vietnam, including one mission where all the men in his company had been killed, except for him. Harry had never discussed these experiences with anyone, and had coped by pushing them out of his mind. It also came out that Harry had been physically abused severely as a child by his father.

Again, he had never discussed this abuse with anyone, but had coped as a child by excelling both academically and in sports at school. Harry seemed to feel touched and grateful at the end of the feedback session.

Feedback Letter

The following are excerpts from the letter I sent Harry after our feedback session, summarizing the assessment results and answering his questions. These comments are very like those I used with Harry during the summary/discussion session:

> Dear Harry,
>   This letter is to summarize the results of your psychological assessment, which we reviewed in our feedback session last week....
>   One of the major findings of the assessment was that you have extremely strong and varied coping mechanisms that allow you to function under circumstances that would emotionally disable a majority of people. One of these coping mechanisms is your ability to push painful feelings to the side and keep on going....Three other very useful coping mechanisms that you have are:
>   (1) *Self-reliance*: a strong ability to take care of yourself if need be. The testing indicates that you do enjoy being around people, but you have learned to meet your own needs and survive on your own. This ability allows you to exit from bad situations and relationships if you need to, instead of being stuck there because of fears of being alone.
>   (2) *Rationality*: a strong ability to analyze and rationally approach problems, putting feelings aside so that you can think clearly and not get overwhelmed by emotions.
>   (3) *Forgetting*: an ability to forget painful events from the past so they don't continue to bother you.
>   The Rorschach test allows us to look "below" your coping mechanisms to see what is going on at a deeper level of your personality. The results from this test suggest that more is happening in you emotionally than at first meets the eye. There may even be a level of emotional experience in you that you are not fully aware of and that is burdening you. Some of these feelings, which are nearly invisible to others, include depression, powerlessness, intense longings for affection and nurturance, and anger....
>   Your strong coping mechanisms have allowed you to function well in catastrophic situations in the past and to escape the worst consequences of those traumas in the present. However,

using those mechanisms to the extent that you do probably slows you down and is psychologically costly....

The biggest cost of your unresolved distress may be the effects it has on your intimate relationships. Your test scores predict that you will have strong ambivalence about getting close to others. You are likely to worry about getting hurt and getting in over your head. This fear is not unreasonable, since...getting too close could open up a Pandora's box of feelings inside you and leave you overwhelmed, distressed, and feeling crazy.

Harry, we now have enough information to understand your "dilemma of change"—the costs and benefits you have to weigh in deciding whether to keep your life as it is now, or try to change it.

Your dilemma begins with the strong hunger inside you to be close to others and your obvious desire to continue to open up and grow emotionally. Opposing this is the reality that your level of closeness with others is currently limited by the need to protect your inner distress. On the one hand, the major traumas in your life are now past and it is much safer to explore your feelings about these situations. However, to do so would be painful and you may decide that it's better to leave things the way they are, especially since you are functioning quite well and learning to open up some on your own. Trying to go faster in your opening-up process would require quite an investment in yourself to get through it safely. You would need to work with a psychotherapist who is highly skilled in working on trauma and who can support you as you explore "beneath" your strong coping mechanisms and work through some of the pain that has been accumulating gradually....

Let me now answer the questions you posed for the assessment:

(1) Others say I'm closed and don't open up emotionally. I think I am very self-sufficient and self-controlled. Am I just a pompous ass? Am I really controlling and closed, or are others so insecure that it makes them uncomfortable that I have my ducks in a row?

Some of both appears to be true. You do appear on the outside to be self-sufficient and self-controlled and to have no needs for other people. We know the latter is not true from the Rorschach testing, but your appearance may make others feel insecure and uncomfortable about their own needs. Another thing that may be happening (which is common to most people) is that your coping mechanisms may become a bit harsher and more exaggerated when you feel threatened by internal emotions or by others' demands or criticism. When this happens, you may have a tendency to look like you're full of yourself and insensitive to others. Clearly, from our assessment, the opposite is true.

(2) Why am I so ambivalent about getting close to people?"
As described, the testing indicates that you do want to be close to others and that you have a strong desire for affection and companionship. But intimacy is going to be a mixed bag for you right now. As you get closer to others, you will probably fear getting in over your head. As of yet, you still aren't able to set secure limits when you sense that other people want things from you. Also, getting closer to others could bring up a lot of painful feelings in you. For the time being, you'll probably feel both pulled towards others and like you want to run away.

The reader will note how I incorporated the language of Harry's Rorschach responses into many of my comments.

Harry's Response

Shortly after I sent my letter, I received a note from Harry, from which I quote:

> Thank you for your perceptiveness and gentleness during our last session. I realize now that I have been carrying a lot of junk around with me that is slowing me down and that I better do something about it before it's too late....I have made an appointment with a psychologist near where I live. He has some experience with Vietnam himself and seemed to understand what you and I discovered in the testing.

Conclusion

The MMPI–2 and Rorschach are sometimes difficult to integrate in an assessment, and there is still controversy about their conjoint interpretation. However, I believe that the two tests tap important and potentially different aspects of clients' life experiences and that apparent contradictions can often be resolved by a conceptual understanding of the inner workings of the two instruments. Further research needs to be done to investigate the interpretive model proposed in this article. In the meantime, my colleagues and I at the Center for Therapeutic Assessment have found this model to enrich our understandings of clients. By using the Rorschach and MMPI–2 in conjunction, we find that we have better empathy for our clients' subjective experience and can reflect their inner worlds back to them more accurately. Our clients feel more understood and "held" in the assessor–client relationship, which often allows them to explore new alternatives to their familiar problems in living. In the current discussions of whether the MMPI–2 and Rorschach are worth using together—based on incremental validity and diagnostic efficiency—psychologists should also consider whether the two tests have incremental therapeutic utility.

8

Assessment Intervention Sessions: Using "Softer" Tests to Explore "Harder" Test Findings With Clients

Sometimes, as in the case of Harry in chapter 7, it is possible to go directly from standardized testing to an effective collaborative summary/discussion session with a client. Research has shown that summary/discussion sessions—when they are conducted according to the principles of collaborative and therapeutic assessment—can produce significant decreases in clients' self-reported distress and symptomatology, increases in self-esteem and hope about the future, and improved treatment compliance (Ackerman, Hilsenroth, Baity, & Blagys, 2000; Finn & Tonsager, 1992; Newman & Greenway, 1997).

In other instances, however, an assessor realizes that in spite of his or her best efforts to "bring a client along" through the early stages of an assessment, particular challenges are presented by a summary/discussion session. It may be that there were few opportunities for collaborative discussion during the standardized testing, perhaps because of time constraints or the nature of the tests used (such as paper-and-pencil invento-

---

This chapter is based on a paper presented at the 28th Annual Symposium on Recent Developments in the Use of the MMPI, MMPI–2, and MMPI–A (Finn, 1993).

ries). Or, the client may not have been very open to new ways of viewing himself or herself and the world. Whatever the reason, sometimes an assessor approaches a summary/discussion session with the sense that "the bulk of what I want to talk about with the client is probably Level 3 information!"—that is, "Most of my hunches and tentative answers to the client's questions are very different from how the client already conceives of things, and are likely to produce a lot of anxiety and/or be rejected by the client." As explained in chapter 1, my colleagues and I developed a set of procedures that we call "assessment intervention sessions" to address such situations and to help clients get the most out of an assessment.

Goals of Assessment Intervention Sessions

To borrow a phrase from psychodynamic psychotherapy, in part, assessment intervention sessions help avoid the dangers of "premature interpretations" by giving clients the opportunity to discover assessment findings on their own that assessors have formulated from standardized tests. In this way, such sessions help clients become aware of and explore findings that might otherwise be rejected in a summary/discussion session, and they help clients "rewrite" their own stories about themselves and the world—rather than having revisions suggested entirely by the assessor at the end of the assessment. Also, assessment interventions help the client and assessor explore and test out hypotheses the assessor has derived from the standardized testing. Concepts and hunches that might come across as dry when tied to formal test scores can become vivid and alive when enacted in an assessment intervention session. Such enactments help clients understand and hold onto new understandings achieved through the assessment process and provide memorable, shared moments that assessors and clients can refer to throughout the rest of the assessment. Finally, because assessment intervention sessions attempt to bring clients' problems in living into the assessment setting and then solve them in that context, they help assessors and clients develop empathy for clients' dilemmas of change, and also provide opportunities to more adaptively address such problems in the outside world.

EXHIBIT 8–1
Basic Steps in Conducting Assessment Intervention Sessions

Step 1—Plan Beforehand

• Select a focus
• Ask yourself, "How can I elicit the problem behavior *in vivo?*"

Step 2—Introduce the Session to the Client

• Set the stage by telling the client you will be exploring a particular question

Step 3—Elicit, Observe, and Name the Problem Behavior

• Elicit the target problem behavior several times
• Invite the client to observe the problem behavior and adopt the client's words
• Draw connections to versions outside the assessment setting

Step 4—Explore the Context Leading to the Problem Behavior

• What evokes it, maintains it, reinforces it?

Step 5—Imagine Solutions to the Problem Behavior and Test Them Out In Vivo

• Let the client go first in suggesting solutions
• Test them out and jointly observe the results
• Keep revising proposed solutions until the client feels some success

Step 6—Discuss How to Export Successful Solutions to the Outside World

• Envision difficulties and plan how to address them
• Ask the client to be curious, "give it a try," and report back at the next session

Basic Steps in Conducting Assessment Interventions

As discussed in chapter 1, assessment intervention sessions take place after the assessor and client have completed the standardized testing that is relevant to the client's questions for the assessment, and before the summary/discussion session. Exhibit 8–1 summarizes the basic steps in planning and conducting assessment intervention sessions with clients. I discuss each step in detail and then illustrate it using the example of Jim, a 24-year-old man I assessed several years ago. As mentioned in chapter 1, these steps are derived from Fischer's (1985/1994) procedures for "assessment of process."

Step 1—Plan Beforehand

Select a Focus.   This is the most important step. You will want to choose one major focus for each assessment intervention. (You can do several interventions if you wish, each targeting a different problem behavior.) And it is best to select a focus that is related to one of the client's assessment questions. First, ask yourself, "What are the most important things I think I know from the standardized testing about this client's problems in living?" Then ask, "Would I like to explore any of these hypotheses further with the client?" and "Which of these points is going to be most difficult for the client to accept or understand?" Finally, "Which of the client's questions can I relate to this issue?"

Case Example.   Jim was a shy, gentle man with a long history of achievement difficulties. His major question for the assessment was "Why can't I succeed at anything?" and he explained that he had barely graduated from high school due to poor grades and spotty attendance. Since high school, he had lived at home with his parents and had been unable to hold a steady job or finish a single course at the local community college. He had registered for and dropped different courses numerous times.

Intellectual and achievement testing confirmed that Jim had a severe verbal learning disability, which had been diagnosed when he was 7 years old. His Performance IQ on the Wechsler Adult Intelligence Scale–III (WAIS–III; Wechsler, 1997) was 124, but his Verbal IQ was only 92. His composite scores on the Wechsler Individual Achievement

Test–II (WIAT–II; Psychological Corporation, 2002) were as follows: Reading = 88, Mathematics = 89, Written Language = 87, and Oral Language = 99. What struck me most in administering these tests was Jim's constant stream of self-denigration, for example, "I won't be any good at this one," "I can't write well," "Stupid, stupid, stupid!" (when he made a calculation error during the WAIS–III Arithmetic subtest). This self-targeting took place even when Jim was doing well on a subtest. For example, after earning a scaled score of 14 on Block Design, Jim said, "That was pretty hopeless, wasn't it?" When I countered that in fact he had done quite well, he seemed to brush off my comment. Not surprisingly, Jim also had a tendency to give up easily and would have earned much lower scores on many of the WAIS–III subtests if I had not encouraged him to "keep trying."

Jim's basic MMPI–2 profile had a 2–7–8–0 code type (with all elevations close to 90T), and I was struck once more by the evidence of his extremely low self-esteem. For example, his score on the Low Self-Esteem (LSE) Content scale was 97T—the highest possible—and suggested that he saw himself as inept, defective, and unable to succeed. I knew that Jim would not be surprised by interpretations of his depression and anxiety, or of his learning disability, all of which were certainly contributing to his inability to achieve. I also had important things to say to him about his enmeshed relationship with his parents, and how I thought that prevented him from "launching." Again, I thought this fact would be no surprise to Jim. What I believed would be more difficult for Jim to see and accept was how he unconsciously sabotaged any chances of succeeding in his areas of strength, by giving up or not even letting himself try things because he was so very certain that he would fail. I knew I would have to present Jim with a vivid example of this phenomenon for him to grasp it, and I had the "open door" of his assessment question ("Why can't I succeed...?") to help set the stage. Thus, I chose Jim's pervasive tendency to give up before he started as the focus of my assessment intervention.

How Can You Elicit the Problem Behavior In Vivo?   Once you have a focus, the next task is to use your empathy, and a deep understanding of the standardized test results, to "get in the client's shoes" and strategize how to evoke—right there in the assessment room—the problem behavior you are interested in exploring. At this stage, you might ask yourself, "What are the necessary and sufficient contextual cues to produce the problem behavior I want to focus on?" and "What test materials or other activities can I use that will provide these cues?" Your options are to use (a) standardized tests you haven't yet used (perhaps in unstandardized ways); (b) role plays, art projects, psychodrama, or other less-structured activities; or (c) nonstandardized, or even out-of-date assessment materials that you will not score or attempt to interpret by comparison to nomothetic norms. Many of my assessment interventions use this third strategy, and for this reason I titled this chapter "Using 'Softer' Tests to Explore 'Harder' Test Findings With Clients."

Case Example.   I knew from the WAIS–III that Jim would likely judge himself inept at any cognitive or performance task I asked him to do. I also knew from his high Performance IQ that he was skilled at tasks involving visual memory and visuospatial integration. My plan was to present Jim with some such task and elicit the self-denigration and desire to quit that he showed during the WAIS–III, then confront him with irrefutable evidence of his success to help him realize how distorted his self-perceptions were. I considered various tests and opted to use the Bender Visual Motor Gestalt Test (BVMGT; Bender, 1938), because it is so face valid and easy to administer. I was also thinking of the many creative ways Fischer (1985/1994) uses the Bender- Gestalt in her interactions with clients. To highlight Jim's negative self-views, I decided I would not only use the copy procedure, but also the immediate recall for the BVMGT.

Step 2—Introduce the Session to the Client

As in the standardized testing sessions, you should begin an assessment intervention session by checking in with clients (e.g., "How are you today?") and asking about their reactions to the previous session. Then, introduce the current session by telling clients which of their assessment questions you hope to address that day. This helps lower clients' anxiety and reminds them that your main goal is to meet their personal agenda for the assessment. By mentioning one or more specific questions, you also "prime" the client to be thinking along certain lines as you conduct the intervention.

Case Example.   Jim had completed the MMPI–2 in the previous session and said he had not thought about it since we last met. He looked even more down than usual on the day of the assessment intervention, and said his father had been "hassling" him that morning about not having found a job. I listened and reflected that such interactions seemed to make him feel more hopeless. He agreed and said he didn't know why he couldn't get himself to apply for jobs. I said maybe what we did that day would help shed some light, and told him that I hoped to explore his question, "Why can't I succeed at anything?" He said that would be helpful and that he was ready.

Step 3—Elicit, Observe, and Name the Problem Behavior

Elicit the Problem Behavior Several Times.   Next, conduct your planned experiment and see if your chosen strategy elicits the problem behavior you want to explore with the client. If it does, try to get a large enough sample of the problem behavior so that the client will have a chance to observe it and connect it to contextual variables.

Case Example.   When I gave Jim the standard instructions for the Bender-Gestalt copy, he immediately said, "I'm no good at drawing." I encouraged him to do what he could, and as I expected, he then proceeded to copy all nine of the figures almost perfectly, sighing throughout, and erasing several times to get them "just so." He looked pretty miserable and ashamed the whole time. When he finished, I asked how he was doing and he said he was "angry at himself" that he had so much difficulty with something that "simple." I then took away his sheet of copied designs, gave him a blank piece of paper, and told him that I wanted him to draw as many of the Bender designs as he could from memory. He looked quite panicked and said he was sure he wouldn't be able to remember any. I told him to do the best he could, and after a few minutes, he drew excellent versions of the last four designs presented, then pushed the paper towards me and said that was all he could remember. I thanked him and told him that was fine, then asked if he would take just a few more minutes to see if he could remember any more. I thought he would refuse, but he did not, and as he sat there he remembered two more designs, again tried to bail out, and then with my encouragement remembered and drew two more, recalling a total of 8 out of 9 of the designs.

I thanked Jim and looked over, expecting to see some relief or satisfaction on his face, but to my surprise he still looked miserable. I wasn't sure what was happening, but was inspired to ask, "Well, how do you think you did?" Jim replied with real anguish, "Terrible! I'm so stupid I couldn't remember any of them." It began to dawn on me that I had underestimated the extent of Jim's distorted self-appraisal, and I asked him, "How many do you think there were?" "I don't know," he replied, "14 or 15." Again, I was quite surprised and had to pause for a minute. "No, Jim," I said, laying the cards out on the table, "there were only 9 cards, and you got almost all of them. Most people only remember 6 or 7, and you got 8. And your copies of the cards are also excellent—much, much better than most people's. Really! I'm telling you the truth."

Jim looked shocked and confused and sat there immobile and speechless. I began to talk in a soft voice,

> You see, Jim, you feel so negatively about yourself that you can't tell what you're good at or what you're not. Like most of us, you don't want to attempt anything you think you'll fail at, but you don't believe you can do anything well—even when you can. This is partly the answer to your question, "Why can't I succeed at anything?" You *can*, but you don't believe in yourself, so understandably you don't even try. If I hadn't encouraged you, you would have given up after four designs, but I was pretty sure you could do this, so I asked you to keep going. Also, even when you do something well, you'll see it negatively. So that just reinforces that idea that you can't do anything well.

At this point, Jim was weeping, and put his head in his hands to hide his face. I put a hand on his shoulder and kept quiet, handed him some tissues, and then got up to get him a glass of water, which he accepted and drank.

Invite the Client to Observe the Problem Behavior and Adopt the Client's Words. Draw Connections to Versions Outside the Assessment Setting.   Once the problem behavior is in the assessment room, your next step is to bring it to the attention of the client. Ask the client what he or she calls that way of acting, and if possible, see if the client recognizes versions of the behavior in other contexts. I try to adopt the client's language from that point on, although sometimes I will offer alternate wordings if I think they will lead to a more useful understanding of the client's problem. To return to the metaphor used in chapter 1, all of this is a way of inviting clients to climb up with you on an "observation deck" over agreed-on aspects of their lives. From there, you can collaboratively discuss what you both see and come to better understand clients' dilemmas of change.

Case Example.   It might have been useful if I had stopped to discuss the Bender-Gestalt with Jim before I showed him how well he did on the recall portion of the test. This would have allowed us an opportunity to talk about its similarity to other types of achievement situations and for me to hear Jim's thoughts about what I viewed as his tendency to give up. Instead, once Jim calmed down, I asked him if we could talk about what had happened and what he was feeling. He said yes, and I gestured for him to start. He then explained, "I was crying because nobody has ever told me that I did something good. I just couldn't believe it at first, but then you explained how I don't know what I can do anymore, and I saw that it is true. I started wondering what else I can do that I don't know about." I said I was thinking the same thing and I wondered what we might call Jim's tendency to undersell himself. He said he didn't know. I said it was almost like he saw himself through a distorted "lens." He agreed and said he saw himself as "loser." We then began to talk about his "loser lens" and how it influenced a lot of his behavior. He agreed it kept him from looking for jobs, led him to give up easily—as on the Bender-Gestalt—and made him really self-critical about anything he did. I pointed out how he had been seriously "off" in his estimation of the number of designs he had failed to recall. I asked if there were other times he could think that he had really underestimated himself to that extent. He told of going away to camp when he was 9 years old and of a counselor who had taught him how to toss horseshoes. At first Jim hadn't wanted to try and was sure he couldn't learn the game. By the end of the week of camp, he was beating everyone—even the counselor who had encouraged him. He glowed as he told me about this series of events.

Step 4—Explore the Context Leading to the Problem Behavior

Sometimes it is enough to elicit, name, and connect a problem behavior to the outside world, and you should stop an assessment intervention at that point. Mainly, I attempt to judge whether the client is emotionally overwhelmed after we do that work or can take part in further discussion. If the client can proceed, my next step is to learn more about the context of the problem behavior. What factors are necessary and sufficient to elicit it? What is its history? What reinforces or maintains it? Clients typically are not at all aware of such contextual cues, so it can take careful questioning by the assessor to get this information.

Case Example.   I asked Jim if there were any situations where he did-n't have the "loser lens" on, and he took a few minutes to think about this. Eventually he replied, "When I'm playing my guitar in my room all by my-self. Then I don't worry about how I am doing and I just play for myself and for the fun of it." So would that change if he knew someone was listening to him? "Oh sure. That would ruin the whole thing. I wouldn't be able to play at all." And did he ever think he played well? He admitted that sometimes he played OK, and gave a small smile. Jim then spontaneously recalled his father sitting with him in elementary school at the kitchen table, attempt-ing to tutor him on various subjects and ending up berating Jim instead. I said that sounded really awful and I wondered if those events were part of how he developed the "loser lens." Jim said that might be true, but that it was still going on, like that morning when his father criticized him for not looking for jobs. I asked if he thought the morning's events had influenced his approach to the Bender-Gestalt. He said he wasn't sure, but admitted he had arrived feeling pretty "hopeless." "So," I said, "these lectures from your parents—which they may see as trying to motivate you—actually make it less likely that you'll succeed." Jim agreed that was true. He then suggested we should find a way to tell them that, and I said that seemed like a very good idea.

Last I asked Jim if there was anything he got out of "giving up" early—some way it helped him, even though it made him feel ashamed of himself. "Sure," he said, "I don't have to feel scared about how I'm do-ing." "So shame is preferable to anxiety in your book?" I asked. Jim paused, and slowly said, "Nooo...I guess I just never thought it through before." I said I was sure that was true and that many of us seemed to prefer pain that was familiar (like shame) rather than pain that was new and unknown (like anxiety).

Step 5—Imagine Solutions to the Problem Behavior and Test Them Out In Vivo. Keep Revising Proposed Solutions Until the Client Feels Some Success

Once the problem behavior is in the room and you and the client have some understanding of what evokes it and reinforces it, you can begin to imagine what might block it or keep it from occurring. You then can run little "experiments" together to see if you can make it go away. In keep-ing with the collaborative approach, I'm careful to let clients generate solutions first, then I make additions or completely new suggestions if necessary. I draw on my knowledge of different therapeutic strategies in imagining possible solutions.

Case Example. At that point, I checked in with Jim to see if he needed a break or could keep on talking. He assured me that he was doing well and was very interested in what we were discussing. We then had the following interaction:

> *Steve:* I wonder if you're willing to do a little experiment with me?
>
> *Jim:* What's that?
>
> *Steve:* I'd like to give you another achievement task that would normally pull for the loser lens, and see if we can keep it from happening.
>
> *Jim:* OK. How would we do that?
>
> *Steve:* Do you have any ideas based on what we talked about?
>
> *Jim:* Well, I guess first I should just keep going, no matter how badly I think I'm doing.
>
> *Steve:* Good idea. And what might that be like?
>
> *Jim:* I guess I'll feel anxious.

We then discussed how to deal with the anxiety and Jim suggested he just try to "ignore it." I seconded the idea and proposed that he try to remember there was nothing to fear; we were just doing a little experiment.

I then asked Jim to try one more time to draw the Bender-Gestalt figures from memory. I told him this would give us a measure of his long-term recall. (At this point, it was about 40 min since the immediate recall.) Jim started to say that he wasn't sure he could remember any, caught himself, stopped, and deliberately said, "I'll do the best I can." He then started to draw. After several figures, he said he didn't want to stop but was having a difficult time ignoring the anxiety he was feeling. I asked if he could approach the task like he was playing his guitar. He pondered this, and then he asked if I would be willing not to look at him while he drew. I said I would, and suggested that I step outside the office for a minute, which he agreed to.

When I returned after refilling my water glass, Jim was sitting at the table beaming. He looked so different from the man who had walked in my office earlier and met my eyes, smiling. "How did you do?" I asked. "Good," he said, and proudly showed me his paper on which he had drawn all nine of the original BVMGT figures. I said, "That's great, Jim," and asked him to tell me about his experience. Jim then told of doubting himself and almost stopping several times, but getting himself to "just take a few more minutes to see if [he] could remember any others" (as I had coached him previously). He was clearly overjoyed with how well he had done, and also with his success at holding off the "loser lens." I mirrored his excitement and said I was really impressed at what a "quick study" he was. I asked if he could now answer his question of why he couldn't succeed at things, and he said, "Because I don't believe in myself and give up too easily!" I affirmed that was the biggest reason, and that we could talk about more possibilities when we met next week to go over all the test results.

Step 6—Discuss How to Export Successful Solutions to the Outside World

Over the years I have learned that some clients become easily deflated when they try to implement solutions we have discovered in assessment intervention sessions in their daily lives. Clearly, different contexts have a host of different cues and demands, and without the presence of the assessor/coach, it can be difficult for clients to successfully remember and export adaptive strategies they have experienced one time. For this reason, before ending an assessment intervention session, I often ask clients to join me in doing "thought experiments" about what it will be like to take the strategies we explored and try to use them in their lives outside the assessment office. As clients and I envision and discuss this possibility, sometimes we can then make further refinements to the solutions we have discovered so they will be more generalizeable. I also suggest clients "see what they can do" with what we have learned and report back to me at our next meeting. As discussed in chapter 1, I believe such instructions help reinforce clients' curiosity, which sets the stage for therapeutic change to occur.

Case Example. Towards the end of our session, I asked Jim, "What do you think it would be like to try some of what we learned today when you go home and want to look for a job?" He said it would be "interesting" and "different," and I proposed that we think about what things would be similar and what would be different so we could plan for any difficulties. We agreed that job hunting was hard because it pulled for the "loser lens" and that Jim had trouble even getting started because he was sure he was going to fail. He suggested that he would have less performance anxiety if his parents didn't know he was making applications, because otherwise they asked lots of questions and it would be harder, like when I was watching him do the Bender-Gestalt drawings. I wondered if he could just try to ignore the anxiety that would inevitably come up—as he had done in our session—and just consider the next week "a little experiment." He smiled with recognition at that phrase and said he would see if he could fill out four applications before we met next week. I offered that he could call if had any questions before then, or if he wanted to share the results of his efforts. He said he might, shook my hand, and thanked me for the session saying it had been very useful. After he left, I made detailed notes and began to think more about my plan for the summary/discussion session the following week.

Conclusion

As I hope you see from this case example, assessment intervention sessions are powerful tools for impacting clients' stories about themselves and the world and helping them begin to see previously blocked solutions to their chronic problems in living. Such sessions work because they illuminate for clients how they (like all of us) actively participate in constructing their own worlds, thereby limiting themselves unintentionally. By making new sense of characteristic behaviors, assessment intervention sessions help clients see new options and move beyond learned helplessness to thoughtful action.

Assessment intervention sessions also help assessors become more empathic to clients' dilemmas of change and really grasp the idiographic meaning of nomothetic test results. For example, I thought I understood the degree of negative distortion in Jim's self-concept from his MMPI–2 profile, yet I was quite surprised when he said he had done "terribly" on the Bender-Gestalt recall and that there were "14 or 15" designs in total. This brought to life Jim's score of $97T$ on the MMPI–2 LSE scale, and I will never see a score like that again without remembering Jim and his view of the Bender-Gestalt.

Last, I must acknowledge that assessment intervention sessions can seem a little "magic" when you first start hearing about them or watching videotaped examples. In this chapter, I have attempted to demonstrate that in fact, they are logically and systematically structured, and can be done even by clinicians who are new to Therapeutic Assessment. I have taught first-year clinical psychology graduate students to do successful assessment interventions (see chap. 15). And my colleagues and I have now developed a number of "standard" assessment interventions for different types of problem behaviors. The following references provide detailed examples of some of these interventions: Finn and Martin (1997); Finn and Kamphuis (2006); Finn (2003, in press); Tharinger, Finn, Wilkinson, and Schaber (in press). Clearly, assessment interventions are one of the most "artful" pieces of Therapeutic Assessment, and you will benefit from reading about then, practicing them, and getting supervision over time. For now, however, I encourage you to "give them a try" and "see what you find." Then feel free to let me know how it goes.

9

One-Up, One-Down, and In-Between: A Collaborative Model of Assessment Consultation

Over the years, I have come to appreciate that it is quite complicated to assess a client already in treatment with another mental health professional or with a team of professionals. Relatively little has been written about this topic, although there are some notable exceptions (e.g., Allen, 1981; Berg, 1986, 1988; Cohen, 1980, Shafer, 1954). In chapter 9, I present a detailed account of my consulting with a client and therapist via Therapeutic Assessment. In this chapter, I discuss assessment consultation more generally and outline the collaborative principles and techniques that my colleagues and I employ.

In fact, in our practice at the Center for Therapeutic Assessment, about half of the assessments we do are of clients whose treaters find them to be puzzling, frustrating, frightening, and/or boring. Typically, we are asked to test such clients to help understand them and aid in their therapy. Sometimes, the referring professional (henceforth referred to as the RP) has just started to work with the client. At other times, the treatment has gone on for some time but is in some kind of crisis at the time of the referral. In many instances, we are asked to address important refer-

This chapter is adapted from a paper I presented to the Society for Personality Assessment (Finn, 1997b). I am grateful to Jim Durkel and Steve Smith for their comments on an earlier draft.

ral questions, such as: "Should I refer this client to another therapist?," "Does this client need a higher level of care?," "Have we done all we can do for this person and should we terminate therapy?," or "Why are the client and I so stuck in therapy?" Other times, the RP isn't explicit about such questions and instead simply refers for "diagnosis and treatment planning."

My experience and the existing literature show that there are many potential pitfalls in such assessments. Let me start by mentioning just a few.

The Referring Professional Doesn't Think Systemically About Treatment Impasses

After years of consulting to other mental health professionals and also treating my own clients I have come to the following conclusion: In most instances, when a treatment is stuck, or a client or therapist feels anxious, frustrated, confused, or despairing about their interactions, both individuals play a part in that predicament. I say this humbly, and with the advantage of hindsight about the many times I have gotten into conundrums with clients because of my own "stuff." Now if you think systemically or intersubjectively about your relationships with clients, my statement will seem completely self-evident. However, the fact is that many mental health professionals do not think about treatment as an interpersonal enterprise that inevitably affects both people. And even those of us who generally do can lose that perspective when we are in the middle of a difficult impasse with a client.

A nonsystemic view is often reflected in the referral questions one receives from the RP at the beginning of an assessment. For example, contrast these two questions (actually given by RPs in recent assessments): "Why do I feel so disgusted with John in our sessions over the last two months?" versus "Why won't Sara do what I tell her and what she knows is good for her?" In the first instance, the referring therapist was quite open to considering her role in the treatment difficulties; in the second, the treater blamed the client for the lack of progress and seemed closed to the idea that he [the treater] might be part of the problem. As Cohen (1980) noted, in some such instances, the RP simply sends the client for a diagnostic assessment, and never acknowledges at all to the assessor that the treatment is in trouble.

We have found that when RPs are open to thinking systemically about treatment impasses, assessment consultation is easier and more effective. Assessors are then able to use an assessment to "get in clients' shoes" and then help treating clinicians become more empathic to those clients' dilemmas of change. Often, this then helps RPs understand how and/or why they were blocked in their understandings, and which factors had more to do with them than with the client. As mentioned earlier, sometimes a RP normally thinks quite systemically, but loses that view temporarily in the middle of treatment; an assessment can help the person shift from blaming the client to a more complex understanding.

Unhelpful Triangulations

Related to the aforementioned point: When an RP and a client are at an impasse, and when neither of them has a systemic view of the situation, the potential for the assessor to get triangulated in an unhelpful way is quite high. Sometimes, in these instances, both the RP and the client hope (consciously or not) that the assessment will show that the other is at fault. There is a pull for the assessor to "take sides" and put the other person in their place. In extreme situations, if the assessor avoids taking sides, the RP and/or client may feel betrayed and furious! Luckily, this level of splitting is rare, in my experience.

More frequent is the situation where the client and RP both seem to agree that the client is the sole problem. For example, the client, Sara, I referred to earlier—whose therapist wanted to know why she wouldn't do what he "told her"—began her assessment completely echoing her therapist's framing of the therapy, for example, "I know I should do what my therapist tells me; he has my best interests in mind, but I always screw things up and don't know why." Assessors can have different reactions to this kind of referral, but one common one—especially when the assessor is aware of shortcomings in the treatment—is to feel protective of the client and frustrated with the RP. This kind of experience can be intensified by the fact that psychological assessment is different in many ways from (especially long-term) therapy. In collaborative assessment, it is easy for clients to develop idealizing transferences towards assessors, and for assessors to feel more compassionate toward clients than toward RPs. Then, if the assessor experiences the RP as blaming or failing to understand the client, it is easy to be pulled towards "rescuing" the client.

Not infrequently, in these situations, assessors will fantasize "I could do better with this client," and clients will think, "Maybe I should change therapists and work with the assessor instead." I have seen instances where these fantasies were carried out (sometimes with the cooperation of the RP), the assessor and client start psychotherapy together, and before too long they too are at a therapeutic impasse that resembles the original one between the client and RP!

I do not mean to imply that there never are times when it is appropriate for an assessor to assume treatment of a client referred for assessment by another clinician. However, I believe that these are very rare. As I discuss later, in most instances, the RP, client, and assessor will all benefit the most if the assessor can use the triangular format of the assessment to help the RP and client repair their relationship and move on with a deeper understanding of why they were stuck.

The Vulnerability of the RP

I don't think I'm just projecting my own issues in believing that most mental health professionals are not great at asking for help. Many of us in caregiving professions are more comfortable giving than receiving, and this has a number of important implications for our work with clients. One thing I've noticed over the years is that many of us will wait until we are completely stumped, confused, or exasperated by a client until we ask for a consultation from a colleague. And then, when we do finally admit that we can't figure out and resolve a difficult treatment situation on our own, we have to battle shame and a loss of face. For these reasons, I always appreciate the courage of any RP who refers a client for an assessment, especially if that person has been working with the client for some time.

A related place of vulnerability for most clinicians is that we all base at least some of our self-esteem on our skill and ability to be helpful to clients. With some RPs, this leads to a "Catch–22" about assessment consultation: They want the assessor's help, but also fear being exposed or "shown up" by the assessor. As Allen (1981) noted, such competitive feelings can produce a dilemma for assessors: If they learn new things about the client, the RP feels diminished; if the assessment confirms what the RP originally thought, it may be dismissed as "not really that helpful." As I discuss later, if assessors are blind to this dilemma, they may become competitive themselves and make matters worse. Or in extreme cases, they may not realize that the RP actually wants the assessment to fail and is subtly sabotaging it from behind the scenes.

Oracular Transference in the Referring Professional

The anxiety of RPs may also be heightened if they are a nonpsychologist, or otherwise not very familiar with psychological assessment. This can lead to a number of misconceptions about the purposes of psychological testing, for example, the belief that psychological testing will reveal the final "Truth" about the client. This idea is an example of what Shafer (1954) called the "oracular" view of assessment. Although this misconception may initially generate referrals for assessment, my experience is that assessors who play into it (or believe it themselves) will eventually be hurting for business! Typically some RPs will be disappointed that psychological assessment did not give them what they hoped and will stop referring. In other cases, RPs will feel intimidated by psychological assessment and will only refer in dire circumstances. In Therapeutic Assessment, we try to remember that there is no absolute "Truth" in the human sciences; rather, we look for overlapping insights that each are shaped by the context in which they were drawn, for example, assessment versus long-term therapy. In my experience, this attitude leads to more successful assessments.

Hidden Agendas

Sometimes, it becomes clear that an RP wants to use an assessment to make a point to the client, rather than to genuinely explore some set of questions. This is often apparent in the initial consultation between assessor and RP, when the latter—either openly or subtly—seems to be dictating the assessment results the assessor should "find." Sometimes this is rather blatant, as in the case of the therapist who made it clear that I was to use an assessment to prove to his client Sara that what he said about the cause of her depression "was really true."

Another type of hidden agenda occurs when difficult things need to be said to clients—and this is already patently clear to everyone involved—but the clients are referred for an assessment in hopes of "passing the buck" to the assessor. For example, some years ago I was asked to evaluate a mother of two—who was extremely psychotic and depressed—to see if she was "capable of caring for her children on her own." My sense was that everyone involved in the treatment already knew the answer to this question; they just didn't want to make the decision! Along these lines, I have learned to pay special attention when an RP poses a referral issue that seems totally obvious, simply on the basis of the client's history. I don't immediately assume the RP is trying to shift responsibility to me; sometimes he or she is truly confused. But I always ask the RP why an assessment is needed to address that particular question. Also, I firmly believe that even when some matter is already fairly clear, an assessment can be helpful in preparing a client to accept difficult information. The important distinction here is whether this reasonable goal is on the table at the beginning of the assessment, and whether both the RP and assessor are responsible for helping the client assimilate emotionally charged material.

Splitting Among a Treatment Team

Yet another kind of hidden agenda occurs when a client is involved with multiple professionals who have very different views of the client and disagree about what approach to take in treatment. In some instances, the different treaters agree to refer the client for assessment in order to find out "who is right." A classic example of this is mentioned by Berg (1988), where a client with borderline traits was being assessed on an inpatient unit to determine appropriate treatment, and the staff split into two major groups: one that advocated for a "tough love" approach, and another that felt the client needed more "compassion and support." I have seen this kind of situation develop in outpatient treatment also, when a client is involved with multiple professionals, for example, a psychiatrist, individual therapist, family or couples therapist, and/or group therapist.

In private practice situations, splitting in a treatment team can be even more difficult to navigate if the treaters involved do not know or rarely have contact with each other. I find this situation is all too common among busy mental health professionals who are not reimbursed for time to talk with each other. Another complication in such situations is that one professional (typically the individual therapist) sometimes refers a client for assessment without consulting with or even letting the other treaters know this is happening. Naïve assessors can find themselves caught in the middle of major power struggles within a treatment team, especially if they don't make an effort to talk to all the professionals working with the client.

Anxiety in the Assessor Leads to Role Enactments

Given what I've already discussed, is it any wonder that assessors may also feel anxious about consultative assessments? Such assessments often are very delicate situations that pose great challenges for assessors. In a relatively short period of time, assessors are called on to (a) connect with clients, (b) establish a collegial relationship with one or more RPs, (c) be honest with each individual, and (d) try to make the consultation a useful, positive experience for people who may not be getting along very well with each other!

We all have our own habitual ways of dealing with such anxiety, but my experience is that there are two major troublesome patterns of responding on the part of assessors and RPs. Both occur when—out of their anxiety—assessors and RPs go into stereotyped, hierarchical role relationships, where either: (a) the assessor goes "one-up" to the RP (e.g, "I am the expert who will tell you the Truth about your client") and/or the RP goes "one-down" (e.g., "Please look in the crystal ball of your testing and tell me what to do with this difficult client"), or (b) the assessor goes one-down to the RP ("I will do your bidding; all your ideas about the client are perfectly accurate; what do you want me to say to the client to support you?" and/or the RP goes one-up ("You are a minor technician whose job is to do what I tell you, soothe my anxiety, and mirror my brilliance to me and the client").

Of course, I've exaggerated these positions in describing them here. My experience is that one rarely gets full-blown role-enactments like this; and clearly, when they happen it is not good for clients, RPs, or assessors. I do think, however, that some flavor of these roles may be present in many consultative assessments, and such patterns—even when subtle—interfere with the usefulness of psychological assessments in facilitating therapy. This brings us to the following questions: How can we assessors avoid such hierarchical roles—not take sides, or go "one-up" or "one-down" to an RP or treatment team? How can we stay "in-between," if you will, during a consultative assessment and maintain the most relational, effective, way of being?

Suggestions

The following proposals are based in my experience conducting, supervising, and receiving consultative assessments:

Maintain Empathy for the Referring Professional

First, when I am in the role of the assessor, I make a conscious effort to be empathic to the RP, as well as to the client. I try to remember how scary it can be when I refer my own clients for consultation to let another professional see the details of my work, especially when a therapy is not going well. I also review in my mind all the clients I have struggled with in treatment, and how difficult it was for me to ask for help. Finally, when sitting with a client that another professional has found difficult, I try to "feel my way into" those difficulties, for example, in what ways do I find the client frustrating, confusing, or difficult? And if I don't feel this way towards the client during the assessment, can I imagine how I might if I saw the client in another context, such as long-term treatment?

When the experience I have with the client parallels in some way the difficulties experienced by the RP, I am quick to share that fact with the RP, for example, "Dr. Smith, I sure see what you mean about Ms. Atkins's guardedness! In an hour interview, I wasn't able to get her to do more than answer Yes or No questions!" I find that RPs greatly appreciate this kind of joining, and typically feel relieved to know "it is not all them." I then can help lead them away from blaming the client by asking such questions as, "What have you noticed about when Ms. Atkins seems more or less guarded?" I have also found that RPs who began an assessment scapegoating a client, sometimes become more willing to examine their own part in treatment difficulties once I have affirmed the challenges presented in working with the client.

Be Aware of Your Own Anxiety

I find I am less likely to get triangulated or to get caught in unhelpful role enactments if I am aware of my own anxiety and take steps to deal with it directly (through a variety of ways I have learned over the years). Also, I know now—as the result of my own therapy, self-observation, and feedback from others—the kinds of behaviors I'm likely to exhibit when I'm anxious and overwhelmed. (My personal favorite is to go "one-up" and become an "authority.") This self-knowledge helps me to keep a lookout for such behaviors during an assessment and to interrupt them in myself (hopefully) before they get out of hand. If I find myself wanting to quote research and give books to an RP to get the person "up to speed," I realize I am more allied with the client than the RP, and I work hard to get back to an equidistant place. I also accept that there are limits to self-awareness. For example, in chapter 13, I tell about a couples assessment I did that ended badly. In retrospect, one major factor that contributed to the outcome was that I was unaware of how anxious I felt about various aspects of the assessment. I have come to accept that I did the best I could at the time.

Build a Collegial Relationship From the Beginning

In most instances, the success of a consultative assessment relates directly to the strength of the relationship between an assessor and a RP (and also, of course, between the assessor and client). For these reasons I extend myself with RPs I haven't worked with before; for example, going to their office to discuss a referral and inquiring about their training, treatment philosophy, and even (if appropriate) their personal lives. Over time, as the RP and I work together on more assessments and come to know one another better, such contacts can be shortened and/or may take place over the phone. But initially, I find it helps to have face-to-face contact with a RP before an assessment gets too far along. Also, in our beginning contacts, I try to inform the RP about my particular approach to assessment, the ways I think I can help, and how they can assist during the assessment. I also have developed an information sheet for RPs about Therapeutic Assessment, which I send them when they first inquire about a consultation. (See Exhibit 9–1.)

EXHIBIT 9–1
Information Sheet for Referring Professionals

Center for Therapeutic Assessment

4310 Medical Parkway, Suite 101, Austin, TX 78756-3335
Phone: (512) 329-5090   Fax: (512) 329-6765

Information Sheet for Referring Professionals

What is Therapeutic Assessment?

Therapeutic Assessment is an approach developed by Stephen Finn, Constance Fischer and others. It uses psychological tests and a collaborative assessment method to help clients re-conceptualize their lives and move forward in their healing. Research has demonstrated that after a therapeutic assessment, many clients exhibit less distress and have higher self-esteem. In addition valid and usable test data are collected, which may be used for diagnosis, treatment planning, or documentation of change after treatment.

How is Therapeutic Assessment Different from Traditional Assessment?

In the Therapeutic Assessment model, psychological testing is seen as a potential intervention, as well as a method of gathering information about a client. We involve clients and referring persons in all stages of the assessment process, as collaborators, co-observers, and co-interpreters of certain test results. We always give verbal feedback to clients about test results and provide a written report when it is desired. At the end of an assessment we solicit written feedback from clients about their experience of the assessment.

When Should I Refer for a Therapeutic Assessment?

We welcome referrals for psychological assessment when you feel this process will be useful to you and your client. Common times for making such a referral are 1) at the beginning of therapy to help in treatment planning, 2) when you and/or your client are puzzled about the client's history or experience, 3) when therapy is "stuck" and you wish an outside event to move it forward, 4) when you feel a client is planning to terminate therapy prematurely, and 5) as part of the termination process to document change and plan for the future. Our collaborative assessment methods are often particularly better than traditional procedures for clients who have strong reservations about being tested. We never proceed with an assessment until we have a client's cooperation.

What Types of Assessment Do You Do?

We accept referrals for outpatient individual assessments, including intellectual testing, learning disability evaluations, personality testing, diagnosis and treatment planning, and neuropsychological screening with clients ages 4 and above. If we determine that more extensive neuropsychological testing or educational testing is needed, we will make a referral to an allied professional. We also perform innovative evaluations of couples and families, which include the production and analysis of a consensual Rorschach protocol. Except in rare instances we do not accept referrals for forensic evaluations.

EXHIBIT 9–1
(Continued)

What Can I Expect from You, the Assessor?

We will address the questions you and your client pose for the assessment, or let you know beforehand if the assessment is unlikely to provide the information you seek. We will keep in contact with you during the assessment and discuss findings with you before they are shared with the client. We will provide you and your client with a written report, if desired. We will remain in contact with you and/or your client until the assessment results have been fully explored and integrated into your work. We are available to meet with your client months or even years after an assessment to again discuss test results.

What Will You Expect of Me as a Referring Professional?

We ask that you prepare your client for the assessment by discussing the specific questions you would like answered by the assessment and helping the client to form his/her own questions. Early in the assessment, we will contact you to get background information on the client. While the assessment is taking place, your client may need emotional support and/or help describing the experiences of the assessment. If you notice a change in your client's behavior in or outside of therapy during an assessment, please let the assessor know as soon as possible. If possible, we ask that you attend the feedback session where the assessment results will be presented to the client, and we welcome your comments before the feedback session about how to best discuss the assessment findings with your client. If we can, we will come to your office for the feedback session, as your client is likely to feel most comfortable in this setting. After the assessment is completed, we will ask you for feedback about our work, so that we may better serve you and other referring professionals in the future.

How Much Does an Assessment Cost?

The fees for a therapeutic assessment vary depending on the complexity of the referral questions. After the initial interview with a client, we quote a fee for the entire assessment, including interviews, testing sessions, test scoring and interpretations, written reports, and feedback sessions. We ask that, if possible, your client pay half this fee at the beginning of the assessment and half at the completion. Typically, we can fairly accurately estimate our fees from talking with you about your client.

How Long Will It Take to Have My Client Assessed?

Because of the high demand for our assessments, we generally have a 3-5 week waiting period between the date of a referral and the beginning of an assessment. Once an assessment has begun, we typically provide the feedback session within 4 weeks, except in very complicated assessments. Although we prefer to test clients over 2-3 weeks to allow us to see them in different contexts, we can perform assessments within short periods of time (e.g. 3-5 days) if you so desire.

How do I refer my client?

Please contact Stephen Finn at (512) 329-5090 to discuss your particular client or if you would like more information about our approach to psychological assessment.

Forestall Triangulation

I find that there are a number of ways I can prevent triangulating with clients and RPs to minimize the possibility of "splitting." For example, I make it clear to clients that I will be communicating with the RP throughout the assessment and I ask the client to sign a permission form (if this has not already taken place) for me and the RP to talk freely. Occasionally, clients balk at this request, saying that they came to me for an "independent second opinion." I assure clients that my job is to do just that but that it will be helpful for me to talk about their treatment with the RP. So far, this has always resulted in the client allowing the RP and me to collaborate.

Also, typically I let clients know early in an assessment that my job is to facilitate their treatment with the RP and that I will not be available for treatment after the assessment, although I will be open to future consultation. And although I accept that clients often develop very positive transferences to me during an assessment, and I try not to interfere with this process (believing it facilitates—in many instances—the therapeutic outcome of an assessment), I also make an attempt to avoid taking clients' idealization of me "just personally." By this I mean that I take pride in my ability to comprehend the dilemmas of challenging clients and to help them feel understood; but, I am also aware of the particular features of the assessment situation that allow clients and me to develop a very positive alliance.

As mentioned earlier, I generally consider it disadvantageous for an assessment to end with the client's transferring from the RP to the assessor for ongoing treatment. Not only is this is a good way for an assessor to lose sources of referrals, it also can be destructive for all the parties involved. Clients may feel rejected by the RP and as if they "failed" the previous treatment. RPs may feel relieved at first, but also inadequate that they were not able to work through an impasse with their client. And assessors, I believe, are likely to be enacting omnipotent rescue fantasies that will only get them into trouble later!

In addition, I believe that clients and therapists learn the most and make the most progress in their work by repairing breaches or empathic breaks in their treatment relationship. I believe the best outcome of an assessment is for the assessment to facilitate such repairs and help the RP and client understand the context of any struggles they have had together. And if it becomes clear that a RP lacks some expertise or skill that would benefit the client (e.g., Eye Movement Desensitization and Reprocessing (EMDR), sex therapy, Dialectical Behavior Therapy) I find it oftentimes works to involve other professionals as "auxiliary therapists" after the assessment, rather than for the client and RP to terminate their relationship entirely.

If continuing treatment is not possible—because of limitations in the RP or the client, or because irreparable harm has already occurred to their relationship—it is important for the assessor to acknowledge this reality and discuss it with both client and therapist. In such instances, if the two parties decide to terminate their treatment relationship and the client wishes to continue therapy, I recommend the client be referred to someone else than the assessor. The assessor—if asked—can help find the new therapist and share with that person what was learned through the assessment.

One other—fortunately infrequent—scenario is when the assessor realizes that a treatment impasse is related to unethical practices of the RP, such as a dual relationship, or sexual misconduct with the client. I imagine that generally, RPs who take part in such behaviors are unlikely to seek consultation; however, I have found myself in this situation several times. Once I was asked to test an adolescent boy who had grown very noncommunicative in therapy. Before long, I discovered that the therapist was a close friend of the boy's parents, and the client understandably didn't feel safe talking to him! I recommended that the boy have a different therapist, but again, resisted the invitation to see him in treatment myself. A challenge in such situations is for the assessor to confront such ethical lapses—and in some cases go as far as facilitating a report to the RPs licensing agency—while still not going into a "one-up" judgmental place. I'm happy to say that I was able to maintain a relationship with the therapist I just mentioned and that he continued periodically to seek consultation from me after that initial assessment.

Collaborate With the RP

Perhaps the most important thing a consulting assessor can do to ensure a positive outcome is to involve the RP—as much as possible—as an active collaborator in the assessment. This can be done in a number of ways:

Work With RPs to Clarify Their Goals.   I collect specific referral questions from RPs and share with them assessment questions posed by the client. Through this process, I educate RPs about what an assessment can and cannot do. For example, the referring therapist in the case in chapter 9 wanted an assessment to know if her client had been sexually abused. I told her that psychological assessment could not definitively answer such a question, but that I would be happy to explore this issue as part of the assessment. Also, I never accept a referral simply for "diagnosis and treatment planning." Fischer (1985/1995) details ways to help a RP expand such referral questions. For example, if a RP says he mainly wants a diagnosis, the assessor can ask, "What diagnoses are you considering, and how will it affect your treatment plan if the assessment supports one diagnosis over the others?"

As mentioned earlier, RPs' assessment questions also provide information about whether they are scapegoating or overpathologizing a client. If I believe this to be true, I "test the waters" in an initial meeting, to see if the RP can regain empathy for the client. For example, after listening to one RP complain for 20 min about his client, I gently asked, "What's your sense of how your client views the difficulties the two of you are having?" This led the therapist to immediately shift to thinking more compassionately about the client, which helped the two of us work together as the assessment proceeded.

Ask the RP to Help Prepare the Client for the Assessment.   Unfortunately, many RPs say little to their clients about their reasons for requesting an assessment consultation. If this happens, clients often arrive for their initial assessment session with a variety of fantasies of what prompted the assessment, for example, "My therapist is really sick of me and is getting ready to fire me," "I'm so crazy that even my therapist can't figure me out," or "I'm hurting my therapist with my anger." Sometimes there is some truth to what the client is thinking, but even then, there are helpful ways for RPs to discuss such matters with clients. When RPs call me to make a referral, I often ask if they have already discussed the assessment with their clients. If not, I tell them it would facilitate the assessment if they would explain to clients their reasons for making a referral and tell them what is entailed in an assessment. I offer to send RPs an information sheet about my assessments that they can share with their clients. Some RPs will then ask for help framing what they will say, and I'm able to coach them in wording their rationale systemically, for example, "I want help understanding why our work hasn't been more helpful to you" versus "We need to figure out why you won't do what I tell you." I mention to RPs that clients often need to discuss a possible assessment several times before they are ready to call me. Again, many of these details can be skipped if the RP and I have worked together on a number of assessments.

Besides revealing their own reasons for requesting an assessment, it can also help for RPs to work with their clients before my initial assessment session to help identify those clients' own questions for the assessment. I often learn a great deal about the relationship between an RP and client by how such efforts fare. Some clients arrive at their first session with a number of questions that seem to have been dictated by the RP and that they clearly don't understand. This sets the stage for me to explore the clients' confusions and questions about treatment, and to share those with the RP after the initial assessment session.

Stay in Contact With the RP During the Assessment.   Given that I typically assess outpatient clients over a number of weeks, rather than just on 1 day, I give RPs periodic updates—often in the form of short messages on their answering machines. I make a special effort to talk with RPs after particularly significant sessions with clients, and I ask them to share information with me about how their clients are experiencing the assessment. (Most clients continue to meet with the RP during an assessment.) As mentioned earlier, if I find myself struggling with a client, I share such experiences with the RP, and I ask for advice from the RP about how to handle difficult interactions. This approach reinforces the idea that I am not an expert with all the answers and that the RP and I can best help the client by working together.

Involve the RP in Interpreting Test Data and Planning Feedback to the Client.   I make it my practice, whenever possible, to meet with RPs to review assessment findings and answer their questions before they meet with me to discuss the assessment findings with clients. This is beneficial in several ways. First, RPs are often quite helpful in interpreting test data, and I generally seek their associations to clients' Rorschach responses, MMPI–2 scores, and Thematic Apperception Test (TAT) stories (among other assessment information). Nonpsychologist RPs often seem especially gratified that I would share such information with them and are very interested in how psychological tests work. "Demystifying" the assessment process seems to facilitate our collaboration. Second, I find that RPs have excellent insights as to how I should present certain assessment findings to clients. They and I can work together to identify Level 1, 2, and 3 information (see chap. 1), choose specific words that will be most useful to a client (e.g., should we use the term *depression* or simply talk about "painful feelings"), and make decisions about how much to say. Given that it is never possible to tell clients everything I have learned from an assessment, it helps me to have another person hold information that must be "contained." Last, in our meeting, the RP and I can discuss what our respective roles will be in the summary/discussion session with the client. I typically ask RPs to help track clients' emotional reactions, slow me down if necessary, and intervene if they think clients are confused about what I am saying. They can also help clients tie assessment findings to real life examples, for example, "John, I think what Dr. Finn just described from your MMPI is what happens between you and your boss at work. Do you agree?"

Help RPs "Depersonalize" the Helpfulness of an Assessment.   As discussed earlier, some RPs tend to feel "shown up" by an assessment, or will blame themselves for "not having figured things out" earlier on their own. In truth, sometimes a consultation does highlight an area of deficit for the RP (e.g., a lack of knowledge about a certain condition), and if so, I do not minimize that fact, nor do I draw inordinate attention to it. Generally, however, I see such reactions as reflecting the shame (I mentioned earlier) that many mental health professionals seem to feel about ever needing help. Therefore, I try to assist RPs in not taking the usefulness of an assessment "just personally." I might say to them (if I believe it's true) that this was a complex client who was difficult to understand without testing, or I might join RPs in lamenting the inevitable truth that none of us can know everything! Again, I do all this not just to be kind, but because I believe if the RP goes "one-down" that it will interfere with our collaboration.

Treat Differing Views of Clients as Opportunities for Synthesis, Discovery, and New Understanding.   Given my belief that there is no absolute "Truth" about a client, and that all insights are perspectival, I see differences in how RPs and I experience clients as interesting puzzles to be understood. For example, one client I assessed was quite sadistic with his female therapist, but gentle and kind with me. When the RP and I discussed this with the client, he admitted that he "had a lot of anger at women"—a conclusion that was supported by his Rorschach and TAT responses. Identifying such "interaction effects" is of-

ten key to achieving a deep understanding of clients, and in helping them overcome problems in living. For example, with the aforementioned client, the RP and I recommended that he shift from his female work supervisor to a male one; this change almost completely eliminated the work problems that had prompted the assessment referral.

Clearly, I would never argue with an RP about an assessment finding or insist that my view of a client is "better" or "right." If an RP and I cannot achieve a consensual integration of our perceptions, I generally back down, or suggest that we "agree to disagree," or propose that we bring up our different understandings with the client. Berg (1986) suggested that the nature of the relationship between an assessor and RP may be highly informative about the client. Thus, when I find myself wanting to argue with an RP, I ask myself (or the two of us) what this might tell me about the client. Even if I felt that a RP had a seriously distorted view of a client—and was not open at all to alternative conceptualizations—I most likely would not push my own perceptions—unless I felt the client was being harmed. Instead, I try to calmly raise my differing point of view and then let it go, hoping that if the RP feels respected, he or she may be open to further discussion at some later date.

Ask the RP to Attend the Client's Summary/Discussion Session.
As you will have surmised, whenever possible I conduct my summary/discussion sessions with the client with the RP present; in fact, I like to do these at the RP's office. (Some RPs charge clients for these sessions; others do not.) Such sessions are a chance for real healing if the client and RP have been at odds, as the three of us discuss the previous treatment difficulties and put words to a common understanding. Also, if the client and RP have been working well together, the RP's presence helps the client feel "held" during such sessions, which typically are somewhat overwhelming and anxiety provoking for clients. Finally, as clients see the RP and me working together, they typically feel safer—sensing that there now are multiple individuals who have their best interests in mind. I often suggest to RPs that they book a little extra time to sit with a client after I have completed my work and left. This arrangement signals to all of us that I am "handing things back over" to the client–RP dyad—although I make it clear that I am available for future consultation and/or sessions. Also, in most instances, I remind the client and RP that I will be sending a written summary of the assessment findings.

Ask the RP to Review the Written Summary Before It Is Sent to the Client.   Regarding the written report or letter to the client, I often ask RPs if they are willing to review and comment on an early draft before I send it to the client or collateral professionals. Again, I do this not only to help RPs feel included, but because I have found their insights and comments about such documents to be invaluable!

Follow-up With the RP After the Assessment.   I typically talk with RPs soon after each summary/discussion session—or exchange phone messages—to compare notes and thank them again for their referral. I also seek feedback from RPs in several ways about my work—for example, during our discussions before or after the summary/discussion sessions, or by asking them to fill out and return a simple feedback form after the assessment. This form consists of six open-ended questions:

(1) "Briefly, what were your hopes and expectations when you referred this client for a psychological assessment?";
(2) "Did the assessment meet your expectations?";
(3) "What part(s) of the assessment were most useful to you and your client?";
(4) "What parts were least useful?";
(5) "What would have made the assessment more useful?"; and
(6) "What would you tell a colleague who was considering referring a client to me and/or us for this type of assessment?"

I provide a self-addressed stamped envelope when I send this form to the RP.

A Few Caveats

I have two remaining caveats before closing. First, some RPs do not seem interested in close collaboration with assessors. This may be because they are busy and do not want to devote the time to discussing assessment results, attending summary/discussion sessions, and/or reviewing letters to clients. If this is the case, in some instances, I suggest the RP discuss with the client the possibility of billing for such professional time. Also, some RPs are simply unfamiliar with the collaborative model of assessment, especially if this is the first time we have worked together. Their previous experiences led them to believe they would simply "send" the client to me for testing, and I would then simply mail back a report at some later date. As mentioned earlier, I handle such situations by educating new RPs about how I approach psychological assessment; then we jointly decide if my approach will meet their needs and those of the client. Yet other RPs resist collaboration because they aren't interested in being affected by the assessment themselves or don't think they have anything to learn. They may not view psychological assessment as a potential form of consultation, but rather as something akin to ordering a blood test, and this is the way they want to keep things. It is up to each assessor to decide whether they wish to work with RPs who maintain this kind of stance.

This leads to my second piece of advice: If possible, be thoughtful about which RPs you choose to work with. (I realize that many assessors work in settings where they have no choice about such matters.) I myself don't enjoy doing assessments for RPs who won't work together with me—whatever the reason for their lack of collaboration. And I tend to decline assessments where I sense a potent hidden agenda on the part of the RP or treatment team, although I may confront that agenda first to see if it shifts. Remember also, if you believe in intersubjectivity, it follows that we assessors will be personally and professionally affected by our interactions with RPs. When such relationships function well, they involve no small degree of professional intimacy. Hence, I tend to turn down referrals from people I don't care to know, and accept those from people who interest me or who I think have something to teach me. And I recognize that I must limit the number of RPs I can work with because I only have so much time and emotional energy. Again, I must acknowledge that not every assessor has this type of freedom.

Conclusion

In closing I want to recognize that a collaborative model of assessment consultation can also feel daunting to assessors. In some ways, things may seem easier if we consider (a) our psychological tests as ways to uncover absolute truths, (b) clients as objects of scientific study, and (c) RPs as consumers who simply need us to provide them with factual information. Also, who wouldn't feel good about being an infallible oracle? So given all this, why adopt an interpersonal, collaborative model in your work? First, I think it is a more humble way of viewing psychological assessment, and more accurate. Second, a collaborative approach will lead you to be more helpful to clients and RPs. I just don't believe it is possible to help decipher complicated treatment situations without developing relationships with all those involved. Third, you'll learn more about psychological tests, yourself, and the world. And last, perhaps it's not so bad to trade in our reputation and identity as oracles for those of experts whose job it is to facilitate healing relationships between people! Most of us could feel pretty good about doing that kind of work.

10

Therapeutic Assessment of a Man With "ADD"

This chapter represents the first complete published case study of a psychological assessment conducted by the methods of Therapeutic Assessment. I hope that a detailed, comprehensive example of Therapeutic Assessment in action will help those psychologists attempting to use this approach on their own. I've chosen this case because it represents a common scenario in my practice whereby I use psychological assessment to consult to a therapist–client pair who are feeling "stuck" in psychotherapy (see chap. 9). Also, I believe this particular case illustrates certain strengths of collaborative psychological assessment.

Case Study

Referral

Elizabeth S, a master's-level therapist who had been in private practice for 4 years, initiated the assessment after hearing about my work from a colleague. She called and explained that she had been working in art therapy for several years with David, a 28-year-old man, primarily focusing on his desire to be more successful at work and in his romantic relationships with women. Both David and Ms. S felt that therapy had

---

This chapter is excerpted from a paper previously published in the *Journal of Personality Assessment* (Finn, 2003b).

helped him but that recently it lacked a clear focus. Ms. S said that sessions often "meandered" and covered many topics. She reported that David had been diagnosed with attention deficit disorder (ADD) when he was a child but that privately she wondered if he had bipolar affective disorder or a dissociative disorder or had been sexually abused. She asked if a psychological assessment could address these issues and give direction to the floundering therapy.

I replied that no test could say for certain whether someone had been abused or had bipolar disorder but that I could investigate these issues as part of an assessment. I also told Ms. S that often a midtherapy psychological assessment helps document progress to date and define new goals. We agreed that she would ask David to call me to discuss the assessment and that I would get back in touch with her if he called. I said I would mail her two information sheets about Therapeutic Assessment—one for referring professionals (see Exhibit 9–1) and one for adult clients—and asked her to pass the latter on to David when she talked to him about doing the assessment. Last, I asked if she had shared her questions for the assessment with David; she said that she had and would do so again when discussing the referral with him.

David called about a week later saying that Ms. S had given him the information sheet and that he was very interested in pursuing the assessment. I asked about his goals for the assessment, and he told a similar story to Ms. S. He had been in therapy for over 2 years, felt it had helped him get to know himself, but he was still struggling with two major issues: relationships with women and disorganization. He attributed the latter to his ADD, diagnosed when he was a child. He wondered why he had never responded well to Ritalin™ or other psychostimulant medications and asked if the assessment could help explore that question. I said I believed it could. We discussed the cost of the assessment and set a time for an initial meeting. I asked David to think about specific questions he wanted the assessment to address; he agreed to do this and said he would bring them to our meeting. I then called and left a message for Ms. S, letting her know that David had contacted me and promising to call her after his and my initial meeting.

First Session

When I greeted David in the waiting room the first time, he bounced up quickly from his seat and shook my hand vigorously. I was struck by his youthful appearance and his high energy. We walked back to my office where he threw himself on the couch. He said he was looking forward to the assessment, and he talked quickly and animatedly throughout the first 15 min of the 90-min session. During the meeting, we worked together to develop questions he wished to address in the assessment, and I collected background information relevant to each of his questions:

(1) Do I really have ADD and if not, why do I have trouble concentrating and remembering things?
(2) Why can't I break up with girlfriends when they're treating me badly? What in me is too weak to do this?
(3) Why is it so hard for me to be alone?

Regarding the first question, David explained that he had been diagnosed with ADD at age 10 after his teachers complained that he didn't pay attention in school and or complete homework assignments. He also mentioned being tested at age 14 because of his "complete disorganization" but knew nothing about the results or the person who evaluated him. David now experienced similar organizational difficulties in his work as a computer technician and had been denied promotions because he was not as productive as his co-workers. When I asked for an example of how his ADD showed up, he said he struggled to remember instructions from his supervisors. Typically, after meeting with one of them, he couldn't remember what they had told him. When I first inquired, David could identify no contexts under which his memory and attention problems were better or worse. When I urged him to think more, he concluded that on days when he felt "agitated," he had more trouble paying attention, but he did not know what caused him to feel agitated. David's doubts about the ADD diagnosis—reflected in his first assessment question—stemmed from comments Ms. S had made in therapy and from his own recognition that the medications he took for ADD "rarely did any good." However, if ADD was not responsible for his attention problems, he did not know what was. He explained that currently he was not taking any psychostimulants; his current psychiatrist had prescribed Luvox™, but he said he often forgot to take it and did not know if it helped.

Regarding his romantic relationships, David explained that he had a series of girlfriends who treated him badly, yet he hung on to the relationships because he "was in love with them" and felt "it was better than being alone." He described a common pattern. Initially he would start dating a woman to whom he was not that attracted thinking, "It's not the greatest thing in the world, but I can leave her if I meet someone better." Then, within several months he would find himself feeling insecure and possessive and would accuse his girlfriend of being unfaithful. Eventually he would discover he was unable to break off the relationship even if the girlfriend were treating him terribly. For example, his most recent girlfriend had been sexual with David's best friend and then told him about it. He forgave her for this; then she went on to have sex with yet another of his friends. Once again, David was willing to continue the relationship, but the girlfriend ended it, saying that she was tired of David's being "so needy."

Although this comment stung, David said he recognized the truth of it—hence his third assessment question, "Why is it so hard for me to be alone?" He explained that typically he worked hard to find a new romantic relationship as soon as one ended. At the time of the assessment, he had not dated for 2 weeks—his longest period since age 18—mainly at the urging of Ms. S. He found this situation near intolerable in that the "pursuit of a woman" distracted him and kept him "out of bad feelings." He said he hated being alone because he always felt "lost and empty." He coped by (a) planning activities that involved others, (b) watching television, and (c) frequently moving to new cities where he would get caught up in the excitement of meeting new people. In fact, recently he had been considering another move. I asked David what he would feel if he didn't do these things. He replied, "Chaos, lost, blackness, panic." I remember thinking at this point in the session that he looked like a lost, small boy. Finally, I asked David how he would answer his own assessment question (about being alone) if he had to make his best guess before we did any testing. In reply, he told me about his early history.

When David was 7 years old, his parents divorced. He had no idea at the time that his parents were having marital problems and was extremely surprised by the separation. Following the breakup, David lived first with his father and saw his mother 1 day each month. His father was quite depressed during this period, had severe financial problems, dated a lot of women, and smoked marijuana a great deal. Because of these issues, David eventually went to live with his mother, who also was "very confused and sleeping around." When he was 10 years old, David's mother married his stepfather, a "very strict man" who "didn't like children." When he was 11, David began experimenting with marijuana and got in trouble for stealing liquor from his parents. In high school, he "calmed down" and was able to graduate both high school and college.

David explained that Ms. S thought all he had gone through as a child made it hard for him to be alone. He said this was possible, but he was not sure what the exact connection was. He did wonder if he was "always expecting girlfriends to break up with him because his parents had gotten a divorce." We also discussed Ms. S's question about whether he had been sexually abused as a child. He said he himself had no inkling of this but that Ms. S had come up with this idea from some drawings he had done during therapy. We agreed to keep his childhood experiences in mind as we explored his questions for the assessment.

At the end of the session, I read aloud the questions David and I had developed together. He said he liked them and that he was excited about the assessment. He agreed to help me track down the professional who had tested him at age 14, saying that he would ask his mother for her name. He also signed a release for me to talk with his current psychiatrist and gave me permission to talk more with Ms. S about him and his therapy. Finally, we set up several appointments over the next several weeks for David to come in for testing.

Contacts With Collateral Sources

Prior to my next meeting with David, I worked to gather background information from other health professionals who had worked with him. First, I scheduled an appointment to meet Ms. S at her office. I often do this when consulting with therapists I have not worked with before, finding that it helps the two of us work as collaborators rather than as competitors during the assessment (see chap. 9). Ms. S served me tea and seemed to appreciate the opportunity to talk about her work with David. It was clear to me that she cared about him a great deal and was concerned about whether she was helping him. She worried that she was "missing something" and confessed that she was not very sophisticated in psychodiagnosis. I asked for more information about her three questions: (a) Does David have bipolar disorder? (b) Does he have a dissociative disorder?, and (c) Was he sexually abused as a child? She explained that the first question came from talking to David's current psychiatrist, Dr. K, who had mentioned this possibility. Ms. S wondered about the dissociative disorder because David so often had trouble remembering things. I asked if she had ever seen him in a dissociative state or whether he ever reported depersonalization, dere alization, amnesia, or evidence of separate identities. Ms. S said that he did not, nor had she witnessed any of these phenomena. Finally, she showed me several drawings David had produced in therapy sessions and explained how the colors and placements of various objects in the drawings fit with art therapy theories about sexual abuse. I listened respectfully and asked if anything else had made her wonder about abuse. Again, she said she was concerned that she was missing something with David and that she was confused why he let girlfriends "abuse" him so. We parted with a good feeling between us, agreeing to stay in contact as the assessment progressed and to meet again when I had completed the testing with David.

Next, I called Dr. K, the psychiatrist who was treating David, and learned that he had seen David only two times. He explained that various physicians had prescribed a number of psychostimulants over the years for David, with little positive result. Dr. K said David was "hard to get a read on" and that he wondered if the ADD symptoms weren't due more to a bipolar or cyclothymic process. Dr. K had prescribed Luvox™, an antidepressant known to decrease anxiety, but David had not been on it long enough at their last meeting to know if it was helping. Dr. K said David was due for a follow-up appointment very soon in which he would assess the success of the Luvox. He asked me to let him know the results of the assessment as soon as I could.

Several days after our initial session, David called to say that his mother had located a copy of the report from his evaluation at age 14. He said it was interesting and that he would drop it by my office. The report described an achievement and language evaluation done by a PhD speech–language pathologist. At the time, David's individual achievement test scores were high in math and reading, both at the level of a high school senior. However, his spelling and written language skills were much weaker and the report concluded "David's ability to organize his written work...is quite poor. It is quite likely that many of David's behaviors which are characterized as 'irresponsible' are actually a result of his difficulties in the area of organization."

Standardized Testing Sessions

Second Session.   When David returned for his next session, I noticed immediately that he seemed calmer. He said it had been good for him to ask his mother about the earlier assessment and that she had expressed guilt about ways her parenting might have affected him. He had not known how to respond and he expressed hope that Ms. S and I could help him think this through. I said I would be glad to help. We looked at the report from the assessment together and agreed that it supported his belief that his problems with organization went way back. I asked if the evaluation had made much difference in the way his teachers responded to him; he remembered getting some coaching on study skills but said he felt teachers still thought his poor school performance was his "fault."

In Therapeutic Assessment, the assessor begins standardized testing with those instruments that seem most related—on the basis of face validity—to the client's main concerns (see chap. 1). Thus, I asked David to complete a self-rating scale (the Attention Deficit Scales for Adults; Triolo & Murphy, 1996) for adults regarding ADD symptoms. When he finished, I quickly scored and plotted the results, and David and I examined them together. His scores indicated that he saw himself as having long-standing problems with attention, concentration, organization, and short-term memory, and that these problems caused him distress and affected him negatively in his social and work relationships. I explained to David that although these results were consistent with ADD, they did not prove it. I then showed him a diagram I had copied from a professional article (Forness, Kavale, King, & Kasari, 1994), depicting how attention and concentration problems can have many sources other than ADD. David found this quite interesting, and our discussion provided a good segue to the next part of the session in which I interviewed him about symptoms of bipolar spectrum disorders, asked about his current drug and alcohol use, and had him complete the Dissociative Experiences Scale (Bernstein & Putnam, 1986).

David did describe some discrete periods of hypomanic mood, often lasting several days, when he felt "on top of the world" and that he could "do anything." During such times, he would sleep 4 to 5 hours a night, engage in some impulsive buying, and contact old friends around the world. However, none of these behaviors was ever severe enough to cause him social or financial difficulties. Typically, these periods would end with a "crash" after 2 to 3 days, but David said he had never had a prolonged episode of depression because he always "got [himself] out of them" by being busy or hanging around people. As far as he knew, no one in his extended family had highs like he described or had ever been treated for bipolar disorder. He believed his mother had been on and off antidepressants, but he had never discussed this with her. Interestingly, David said he believed his attention and concentration were actually better than usual during his "highs." On this basis, I hypothesized that such periods were unlikely to be the major cause of his memory problems.

Regarding drug and alcohol use, David said that at the time of the assessment he drank two to four beers a week but several times a year would "tie one on." He no longer smoked marijuana, in part because his job required periodic drug screens. On the Dissociative Experiences Scale, David scored very low and we discussed the few items he endorsed at all—one indicating occasional memory difficulties and one in which he said he could occasionally do things with ease that were typically difficult for him. When I asked about the latter item, David explained that when he felt on top of the world, it was easier for him to approach women at parties. At the end of the session, David and I discussed what we had learned so far that day: He had long-standing problems with attention, concentration, and organization, but those problems were not due to drug and alcohol use nor to "phasing out" (the words we used for dissociation). He did have some periods of hypomanic mood, had never had a major depression, and at least by his report, the hypomania didn't account for his ADD-like symptoms. At the end of the session, David seemed thoughtful and grateful for my having included him in my thinking. We set up a time for him to complete the Minnesota Multiphasic Personality Inventory–2 (MMPI–2; Butcher, Dahlstrom, Graham, Tellegen, & Kaemmer, 1989) under the supervision of my testing assistant, then reaffirmed our next appointment together. Following the session, I called Ms. S and left a message on her phone machine describing the session and what I thought David and I had learned.

Third Session.   At the beginning of our next session, David talked about his experience of the MMPI–2. He joked about being attracted to my female testing assistant, then described doing the MMPI–2 in one sitting with no breaks, saying he found it remarkably easy to concentrate while he was doing it. I asked what he thought made the difference; he said he felt calmer and more attentive since we began the assessment but could not say why. I told him I had not scored his MMPI–2 yet and wanted to do another test that day that would provide information about his relationship difficulties. He agreed and I then administered the Rorschach, using the standard administration from the Comprehensive System (Exner, 1995).

In Therapeutic Assessment, one often follows standardized test administration by engaging clients in targeted, collaborative discussions of their experience of a test or of their responses. After the Rorschach, I asked David about the personal meanings of what he had seen on the cards, much as in Harrower's (1956) projective counseling technique. First, I explained that there were several ways to use the Rorschach to understand someone. I would be carefully scoring David's responses and referring to the wide base of available research to compare his responses to those of other people. However, another way was to look at his responses as possible symbols or metaphors of how he experienced himself and the world. I asked if David would be willing to look over the cards again to see if any of his responses struck him as meaningful in that way. As we reviewed the cards, he immediately brought up his first response to Card I ("Maybe two winged creatures holding onto a middle pole. [Inquiry] The middle core is here. These are the two creatures on either side, the legs, arms holding on, wings, heads").

> *David:* Sometimes I've felt like this. I see them holding on for dear life. If they let go, they're likely to get blown away or fall.
>
> *Steve:* And you relate to that type of situation?
>
> *David:* Yes, that's what I feel if I don't keep busy. Like I'm going to fall into an abyss.
>
> *Steve:* And what's in the abyss?
>
> *David:* [Thoughtfully] I don't know.... Terrible feelings, I guess. I don't know any more than that.
>
> *Steve:* And when you look at these creatures on the card, how do you see them? Are they likely to fall, or will they make it?
>
> *David:* I think right now they're holding on, but if they let down their guard, they could slip and fall.
>
> *Steve:* And does that feel like you also?
>
> *David:* [Long pause] I'm not sure. I mean, I guess I act that way...like I have to hold on hard or something terrible will happen.
>
> *Steve:* And is that why it's so difficult to be alone?

David: Yes, 'cause that's when the abyss feels closer. I don't want to fall.

Steve: And how about right now? Does it feel the same?

David: [Pause] Again, I'm not sure. But it somehow doesn't seem as scary.

Steve: What doesn't?

David: Letting go. Like I can imagine these creatures loosening up a little and nothing awful happening.

Steve: Any sense why it doesn't seem so scary right now?

David: [Laughs] Perhaps because I'm not alone. You're here too.

Steve: Yes, perhaps that's it.

David and I also discussed two responses that were very similar to each other on Cards III and VII. The latter response was:

It also looks like it could be one of those oil derricks. It reminds me of the other one [on Card III]. You can see where they lit it on fire and it's burning, with the large flame coming out of the top. [Inquiry] It's like the other one. It kind of reminds me of those pictures from Kuwait in the Gulf War. Here is the oil derrick coming out of the ground; the white part is the fire. It's being destroyed.

At first David's only thoughts about these responses concerned the TV news of the Gulf War. "It reminds me of the Kuwait oil situation. I saw it on TV. Some friends of mine were firefighters. We were interested in Red Adair, a specialist who puts these kinds of fires out." I then asked for any symbolic interpretations, which led to the following discussion:

David: I know sometimes I feel like that—like a fire that's difficult to put out.

Steve: How so?

David: It's those times I told you about, when I feel agitated. It's like there's something hot and dark boiling in me and I don't know what to do about it. It's so out of my control, just like those fires. No one knew how to handle them.

Steve: Except for Red Adair?

David: [Smiling] Yep. Perhaps I'm looking for an expert like that who knows how to handle me and can tell the other people what to do.

As I smiled in return, I imagined David might be hoping I could play that role.

Standardized Test Results

David's basic MMPI–2 profile is presented in Exhibit 10–1, the Content Scales are presented in Exhibit 10–2, and the Harris–Lingoes subscales are listed in Exhibit 10–3. As I have come to expect in a collaborative assessment in which the client's goals are being addressed, David produced an unguarded MMPI–2 profile (L = 39T, K = 47T). The MMPI–2 code type (7"948') suggested severe anxiety (A = 75T, ANX = 77T) and some cognitive disruption (Scale 8 = 70T, Sc3 = 78T) that David was handling by keeping busy, being very social, and engaging in occasional impulsive, defiant behaviors (Pd2 = 61T). The MMPI–2 also suggested that he was a very sensitive man (Pa2 = 69T; Mf2 = 69T) who was gre-

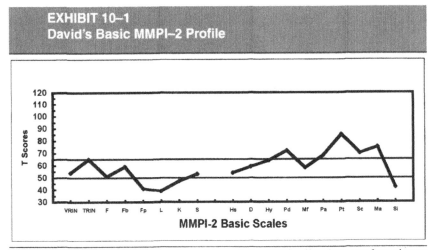

EXHIBIT 10–1
David's Basic MMPI–2 Profile

MMPI-2 Basic Scales

Note. VRIN = Variable Response Inconsistency Scale; TRIN = True-Response Inconsistency Scale; F = Infrequency; Fb = Infrequency Back Page; Fp = Infrequency Psychopathology; S = Superlative Self-Presentation; Hs = Scale 1, Hypochondriasis; D = Scale 2, Depression; Hy = Scale 3, Hysteria; Pd = Scale 4, Psychopathic Deviate; Mf = Scale 5, Masculinity—Femininity; Pa = Scale 6, Paranoia; Pt = Scale 7, Psychasthenia; Sc = Scale 8, Schizophrenia; Ma = Scale 9, Hypomania; Si = Scale 0, Social Introversion.

Source. This and other MMPI–2 profiles are excerpted from the *MMPI–2™* (*Minnesota Multiphasic Personality Inventory–2™*) *Manual for Administration, Scoring, and Interpretation, Revised Edition*, Copyright © 2001 by the Regents of the University of Minnesota Press. All rights reserved. Used by permission of the University of Minnesota Press. "MMPI–2" and "Minnesota Multiphasic Personality–2" are trademarks owned by the Regents of the University of Minnesota.

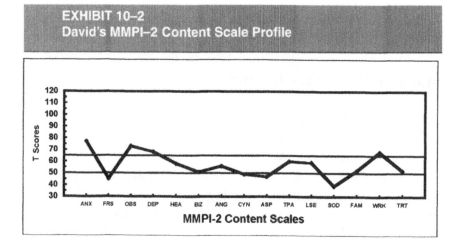

Note.   ANX = Anxiety; FRS = Fears; OBS = Obsessiveness; DEP = Depression; HEA = Health Concerns; BIZ = Bizarre Mentation; ANG = Anger; CYN = Cynicism; ASP = Antisocial Practices; TPA = TypeA; LSE = Low Self-Esteem; SOD = Social Discomfort; FAM = Family Problems; WRK = Work Interference; TRT = Negative Treatment Indicators.

garious and probably had lots of superficial friendships but that he would find it difficult to trust people enough to form intimate, lasting relationships. Several scores suggested that under David's autonomous, energetic exterior (Ma4 = 76T), he might feel discouraged, insecure, and somewhat depressed (D1 = 69T, D5 = 74T). I took special notice of the elevation on Scale 9, given Dr. K's concern about bipolar disorder. A "Caldwellian" (Caldwell, 2001) interpretation of David's profile suggested that David's anxiety, busyness, and defiance were adaptations to a childhood in which adult caretakers were unpredictable, unreliable, and often critical. By keeping busy, failing to meet responsibilities, and worrying, David would distract himself from feelings of emptiness, grief, and terror (Caldwell, 2001). Caldwell also posited that elevations on Scale 7 (and the anxious worrying they depict) are the result of clients' being traumatized by shocking, unpredictable occurrences. I found this interesting given David's report that he was caught quite off guard by his parents' divorce.

[1] I am presenting the fourth edition of the Structural Summary (Exner, 1995), as this is what was available at the time I was working with David.

EXHIBIT 10–3
David's Scores on the MMPI–2 Harris–Lingoes Subscales

Subscales	T Score
Depression	
Subjective Depression (DI)	69
Psychomotor Retardation (D2)	48
Physical Malfunctioning (D3)	43
Mental Dullness (D4)	58
Brooding (D5)	74
Hysteria	
Denial of Social Anxiety (Hy1)	45
Need for Affection (Hy2)	51
Lassitude-Malaise (Hy4)	66
Somatic Complaints (Hy4)	67
Inhibition of Aggression (Hy5)	48
Psychopathic Deviate	
Familial Discord (Pd1)	51
Authority Problems (Pd2)	61
Social Imperturbability (Pd3)	52
Social Alienation (Pd4)	62
Self Alienation (Pd5)	72
Paranoia	
Persecutory Ideas (Pa1)	52
Poignancy (Pa2)	69
Naiveté (Pa3)	60
Schizophrenia	
Social Alienation (Sc1)	59
Emotional Alienation (Sc2)	50
Lack of Ego Mastery, Cognitive (Sc3)	78
Lack of Ego Mastery, Conative (Sc4)	61
Lack of Ego Mastery, Defective Inhibition (Sc5)	51
Hypomania	
Amorality (Ma1)	50
Psychomotor Acceleration (Ma2)	58
Imperturbability (Ma3)	59
Ego Inflation (Ma4)	76

Note. MMPI–2 = Minnesota Multiphasic Personality Inventory–2.

David's Rorschach results are presented in Exhibits 10–4 and 10–5.[1] In contrast to the MMPI–2, the Structural Summary suggested a severe underlying depression (DEPI = 6, S–CON = 9) that most likely was long-standing (CDI = 5) and that was overwhelming David's coping mechanisms at the time of the assessment (Lambda = .13, D = –2). I have previously described this kind of discrepancy between the MMPI–2 and Rorschach, seen so frequently in situations like this in which a client is referred for evaluation by a therapist who is puzzled and concerned about a lack of progress in therapy (Finn, 1996a; see chap. 7).

Unlike some clients I have seen requesting evaluation for ADD, David showed no ideational disturbance (WSum6 = 0) on the Rorschach. However, his mediation scores suggested that he viewed the world quite differently from most people (X + % = .47; X – % = .27; Xu% = .27). Most likely, his emotional difficulties were affecting his ability to accurately perceive the world around him. This hypothesis is strengthened if one examines the Sequence of Scores, as there is an interesting interaction of affect regulation and cognitive interference in David's responses. David gave relatively few responses to the last three cards of the Rorschach, suggesting that he was backing away from the emotionally arousing aspects of those cards (Afr = .36). Nevertheless, his perceptual accuracy on Cards VIII to X was significantly less than on the first seven cards (X + % for Cards I through VII = .64; X + % for Cards VIII through X = .00). Also, David's FQ responses tended to co-occur with S (S – % = .75). All this suggested that although he was most likely a bright man (DQ+ = 8), David's ability to think clearly was compromised when he was emotionally aroused and especially when he was angry. Given this, it was not surprising that one of his main coping mechanisms was to avoid emotions.

Further examination of the interpersonal aspects of the Structural Summary helped explain David's quandary around emotions. In short, it appeared that David had never learned to use others as supports in managing difficult emotions (T = 0; COP = 1; Isolate/R = .40; Pure H = 1). Left to his own resources, David had few options other than to avoid and shut down emotions, for when he let himself experience emotion, it more often overcame his ability to structure it cognitively (FC:CF + C = 1:2). Until he could get better at regulating affect, David desperately needed others to help him contain and process strong feelings. I was reminded of David's telling me after the Rorschach that the "abyss" seemed less close because I was there with him.

EXHIBIT 10–4
The Sequence of Scores for David's Rorschach

Card and Response Number		Loc and DQ	Determinant(s) and Form Quality	(2)	Content(s)	P	Z	Special Scores
I	1	W+	Ma+	2	(H), Hh		4.0	
	2	WSo	FMao		Ad		3.5	AG
II	3	WSo	F–		Ad		4.5	
	4	WS+	ma.CF.C'o		Sc, Fi, Na		4.5	
III	5	D+	Mao	2	H, Hh	P	3.0	
	6	DS+	ma.C'F–		Sc, Fi, Na		4.5	
IV	7	Wo	FDo		(H)	P	2.0	
V	8	Wo	FMao		A	P	1.0	
VI	9	W+	FY.FC'o		Art, Ad	P	2.5	
	10	D+	ma.C'Fu		Sc, Fi		4.0	PER, MOR
VII	11	WS+	ma–		Sc, Fi		4.0	
VIII	12	W+	Mau	2	A, Na, Art	P	2.5	COP
	13	Wo	Fu		Art, Sc		4.5	
IX	14	Wv	CFu		(Ad)			AB
X	15	Wo	FC–	2	A	P	5.5	

In summary, although it was still possible that David's attentional problems were due to ADD, a more parsimonious explanation was that anxiety and a severe underlying depression were affecting his ability to attend and concentrate. David may have been depressed for so long—for example, since early childhood—that he failed to recognize that he was depressed. It was also likely that David had developed a kind of perceptual screening to cope with emotionally arousing situations and that this further interfered with his ability to remember and focus on the world around him.

David's fear of being alone and his tendency to stay with uncaring girlfriends seemed related to this same emotional quandary. Staying busy and highly social and always being in a relationship were ways David worked to hold off his underlying painful emotional states. Probably he knew what it was like to be overwhelmed by such feelings and worked hard to avoid such an experience. Unfortunately, the things he did to help himself contributed further to his already shaky self-esteem ($3r + (2)/R = .27$). In the absence of other evidence, there was no need to invoke repressed sexual trauma to explain David's behavior in relationships; his Rorschach gave ample evidence of why he would let himself be

EXHIBIT 10–5
The Structural Summary for David's Rorschach

LOCATION FEATURES	DETERMINANTS BLENDS	DETERMINANTS SINGLE	CONTENTS	APPROACH Card: Locations:
			H = 1,0	
Zf = 14	m.CF.C'	M = 3	(H) = 2,0	I : W.WS
ZSum = 50.5	m.C'F	FM = 2	Hd = 0,0	II : WS.WS
ZEst = 45,5	FY.FC'	m = 1	(Hd) = 0,0	III : D.DS
	m.C'F	C = 0	Hx = 0,0	IV : W
W = 12		Cn = 0	A = 3,0	V : W
(Wv = 1)		CF = 1	(A) = 0,0	VI : W.D
D = 3		FC = 1	Ad = 2,1	VII : WS
Dd = 0		C' = 0	(Ad) = 1,0	VIII : W.W
S = 5		C'F = 0	An = 0,0	IX : W
		FC' = 0	Art = 2,1	X : W
DQ		T = 0	Ay = 0,0	
.... (FQ-)		TF = 0	Bt = 0,0	SPECIAL SCORES
+ = 8 (2)		FT = 0	Bl = 0,0	Lvl-1 Lvl-2
o = 6 (2)		V = 0	Cg = 0,0	DV = 0 0
v/+ = 0 (0)		VF = 0	Cl = 0,0	INC = 0 0
v = 1 (0)		V = 0	Ex = 0,0	DR = 0 0
		Y = 0	Fd = 0,0	FAB = 0 0
FORM QUALITY		YF = 0	Fi = 0,4	ALOG = 0
		FY = 0	Ge = 0,0	CON = 0
FQx FQf MQual SQx		rF = 0	Hh = 0,2	Raw Sum6 = 0
+ = 0 0 0 0		Fr = 0	Ls = 0,0	Wgtd Sum6 = 0
o = 7 0 2 2		FD = 1	Na = 0,3	
u = 4 1 1 0		F = 2	Sc = 4,1	AB = 1 CP = 0
- = 4 1 0 3			Sx = 0,0	AG = 1 MOR = 1
No = 0 0 0		(2) = 4	Xy = 0,0	CFB = 0 PER = 1
			Id = 0,0	COP = 1 PSV = 0

---------------------RATIOS, PERCENTAGES, AND DERIVATIONS------------------------

R = 15	L = 0.15		FC:CF+C = 1:2		COP = 1		AG = 1
			Pure C = 0		Food = 0		
EB = 3:2.5	EA = 5.5	EBPer = -	SumC':WSumC = 4 : 5.5		Isolate/R		= .40
eb = 6:5	es = 11	D = -2	Afr = 0.36		H:(H)+Hd+(Hd)		= 1 : 2
Adj es = 8	Adj D = 0	S = 5			(H)+(Hd):(A)+(Ad) = 2 : 1		
			Blends:R = 4 : 15		H+A:Hd+Ad		= 6 : 4
FM = 2 SumC' = 4	SumT = 0	CP = 0					
m = 4 SumV = 0	SumY = 1						

				P = 6	Zf = 14	3r+(2)/R = .27
a:p = 9:0	Sum6 = 0	X+% = .47		Zd = +5.0	Fr+rF = 0
Ma:Mp = 3:0	Lv2 = 0	F+% = .00		W:D:Dd = 12:3:0	FD = 1
2AB+Art+Ay = 5	WSum6 = 0	X-% = .27		W:M = 12:3	An+Xy = 0
M- = 0	Mnone = 0	X-% = .75		DQ+ = 8	MOR = 1
		Xu% = .27		DQv = 1	

SCZI = 2	DEPI = 6	CDI = 5	S-CON = 9	HVI = Yes	OBS = No

treated badly by girlfriends. Furthermore, although no test can accurately indicate whether a client has been sexually abused, neither David's MMPI–2 profile nor his Rorschach showed patterns associated with past abuse (e.g., Kamphuis, Kugeares, & Finn, 2000).

Last, regarding the question of a bipolar spectrum disorder, I viewed David's test results as equivocal. He did have an elevation on Scale 9 of the MMPI–2, and his Structural Summary showed some features common to individuals with bipolar disorder (H. K. Singer & Brabender, 1993). However, the Rorschach showed no signs of severe bipolar disorder (e.g., WSUM6 = 0). As was clear from my interview with him, David did have some hypomanic periods, but the testing suggested no psychotic process was present at the time that I tested him.

Assessment Intervention Session

In Therapeutic Assessment, *assessment intervention sessions* are special testing sessions sometimes conducted after standardized testing is completed to explore working hypotheses about clients' problems in living and give them a chance to collaboratively reach new understandings (see chap. 8). When David and I met next, I set out to explore my hunch that emotional flooding was largely responsible for his attentional problems. I also hypothesized that quite often, David was close to painful feelings of grief connected to his childhood experiences. With these thoughts in mind, I prepared four or five alternate number recall tasks, similar to the Digit Span subtest on the Wechsler Adult Intelligence Scale–III (Wechsler, 1997). I also reviewed and selected several Thematic Apperception Test (TAT; Murray, 1943) cards for us to do.

David arrived looking very upset; he confided that he had just had a fight over the phone with his ex-girlfriend and was still very angry. I listened while he vented for a short time then interrupted and said I wanted to use this opportunity to check out some things I thought I understood about his problems with attention and memory. Was that OK? He said it was, so I first asked him to rate how agitated he felt at that moment on a scale ranging from 0 to 10, with 0 being *not agitated at all* and 10 being *the most agitated he'd ever felt.* He rated his agitation at 10. I then administered the first number recall task. David did quite poorly, being able to remember only four digits forward and three digits backward. He agreed this was no surprise, as he had said previously that he could not remember things at times he felt agitated. We then worked to find out what would decrease his agitation. First, we tried simply talking more about the situation with his girlfriend, with me listening carefully and mirroring back what he said. This brought his agitation down to a 7. I then led him in a short relaxation and breathing exercise, after which he rated his agitation as 5. We then did another digit recall task; this time he did better and remembered seven digits forward and five backward. After we finished, we talked:

> *Steve:* Well, what did you notice?
> *David:* I could remember more that time. I wasn't so distracted. How well did I do?
> *Steve:* That was a normal average score.
> *David:* Really? That's good to know.
> *Steve:* And perhaps we've also learned something about what's going on when you're agitated, and what helps to calm you down.
> *David:* You mean like when I feel agitated, I might be angry, and I need to talk and get over it and maybe slow down and breathe?
> *Steve:* That seems like one possibility. Does that fit for you?
> *David:* Yes ... [Tentatively]. Although I'm not sure I'm angry all that much.
> *Steve:* I believe you, let's try one other thing.

I then pulled out the TAT cards I had selected and asked David to tell a story to card 3BM (using the standard instructions). His story was as follows:

> This looks like a woman who is so confused that she's dropped to the ground where she was standing and had a mental shutdown. She looks very distraught and grief stricken. Before she was getting ready to go somewhere. She was all dressed up. But then she got some news of some kind—a phone call or a letter—horrible news. She dropped everything, fell to the ground, and her mind stopped. [Steve: After?] She came back to reality and the reality of it hit her again. But then she cried for an hour until she fell asleep.

Following the story, David rated his level of agitation at 7 and we did yet another digit recall test. This time he could only remember six digits forward and five backward. We noted this and he took a moment to tell me, "This picture is what happens to me when I get a big shock. My brain has a meltdown." I asked for times when he might have felt like this, and he told of a childhood incident after his parents divorced. His father and he were going out to dinner and David got angry over something. His father said he could not go because he was mad and then left him. He eventually came back and got David, but David had been near hysterical with fear in the meantime. I then selected another TAT card (13B) and asked David to tell me a story to fit that picture:

> It looks like a little boy who's got more on his mind than a boy his age should have on his mind....He's thinking hard and emotions are flying around his head. He almost looks adultlike, but he's a child. It looks like maybe his parents are children as well as him. The adults in the family are acting like children and the children are being forced to act like adults without wanting to. He's being forced to be alone. The family doesn't know what's going on. Feelings are washing over him. [Steve: What does he need?] He needs parents that are actually adults and that have wisdom. He needs someone to treat him like he's a child, so he doesn't have to be so self-reliant.

At that point David began to cry. We talked quietly together as he explained that this picture reminded him of himself as a child. He said that he and Ms. S had talked about this period of his life, but that he never let himself really feel what it was like. We agreed that he had been a tough kid who had tried hard to act like a grownup and that this pattern was hard to break. David slowly calmed, then sat up, turned to me, and changed topics:

> *David:* I don't think I have ADD after all.
> *Steve:* Tell me more.
> *David:* I think this is all about feelings. I can't concentrate when I have too many feelings. My brain melts down and I can't think. And there are so many things I have stored up inside—that I've never gotten to—and it's bad for me. I've been holding all this in for too long and I've got to stop running.
> *Steve:* I think you might be right. And it's like you said last time—you can loosen up a bit and you don't die.
> *David:* You're right. I actually feel good getting into this. This is what I need to do with Elizabeth. Can you tell her?

I told David I would be glad to help and I reminded him that our next meeting was a joint one with Ms. S to review the results of the assessment. I also said I would be talking with her before that meeting and would certainly pass on what we had discovered.

Consultation With Ms. S

Shortly after this session with David, I arranged to meet with Ms. S another time at her office. I had explained that I wanted her thoughts about the results and her help thinking about how to discuss them with David. I began by telling Ms. S that I could see why she had been puzzled about David. His testing suggested he was quite a complicated young man and that it was not easy to figure out the best way to approach his therapy. Immediately Ms. S seemed relieved. I also told her it was clear to me that she and David had formed quite an attachment and that I thought she should be proud of this, as his testing suggested this was not easy for him to do. Again, Ms. S seemed pleased to have me validate her experience.

Then I slowly went through each of the tests, showing Ms. S the results, explaining how I interpreted them, and describing in detail my interactions with David during our sessions. Ms. S was particularly interested in the projective testing, never having seen how it actually worked, and she gave additional associations to David's Rorschach responses based on her therapy with him. Finally, I summarized my tentative answers to some of Ms. S's questions: David did not appear to have a dissociative disorder, might have hypomanic tendencies, and, as she suspected, his attention problems did not appear to be due to ADD per se. I was carefully broaching Ms. S's theory about David's having been sexually abused when she broke in:

> *Ms. S:* Oh, I see now that I was way off in that.
> *Steve:* You've changed your mind?
> *Ms. S:* Yes. I think I was just grasping for something to explain David's lack of progress. But you've already explained what was going on, don't you think?

I concurred, and then Ms. S and I discussed ways she and David could work differently in therapy to slowly and gently access more of his underlying painful affect. I explained that while doing this, Ms. S would need to teach David how to lean on her more as an emotional support. Without learning this in tandem, he could easily become overwhelmed, which would only reinforce the need for him to continue avoiding his feelings. Ms. S asked me specifically how she could support him and asked me to discuss this directly with David in our next session.

Summary/Discussion Session

In Therapeutic Assessment, we no longer call the sessions at the end of an assessment "feedback sessions," as this name implies a unidirectional flow of information from assessor to client. In fact, when I arrived at Ms. S's office for our meeting with David, he was already there and he quickly took the lead in explaining his new insights about how "old feelings" were causing his "brain to melt down." I filled in how these same feelings made it difficult for him to be alone and kept him stuck in bad relationships. David then told Ms. S that the two of them needed to "get at these feelings" and how good he had felt after crying during the TAT with me. Ms. S said she was committed to doing this kind of work with David and asked me to describe how to make it safe. I then talked with them both about the relationship between affective management and object relations:

> *Steve:* Imagine that when we're born, we have a little container inside to hold emotions. At first this is the size of a thimble. When it gets "full" it overflows, and the baby will feel distressed and cry....If all goes well, an adult caregiver, usually the mother, then comes and acts like a "saucer" under the infant's "cup." She holds and soothes the baby, "catching the overflow" of emotion. When this happens consistently, the cup grows, say from a thimble size to the espresso-sized cup of a 1-year-old, the coffee cup size of a 2-year-old, and so forth. If we've had enough good emotional saucers, when we get to be adults we have big "bucket-sized" containers inside that let us hold lots of emotion without being anxious, losing our ability to think clearly, acting out in self-destructive ways, or getting depressed....Of course, we still need emotional saucers, and will our whole lives. But...we can handle those situations where support isn't immediately available. David, from your testing it looks like you didn't have reliable saucers growing up and were faced with emotions no kid could handle on his own....Now, your job is to learn to use Elizabeth as a saucer, or you'll just repeat your childhood experience of being flooded by feelings you can't handle and feeling all alone with them.

> *David:* So what does that look like to use someone as a saucer?
>
> *Steve:* It means staying in contact with them and letting then "hold you" with their eyes and their heart. I bet, if you think about that, you've already had some experiences like that with Elizabeth.
>
> *David:* [Tentatively] I guess I have. But the whole idea is really pretty strange.

David then asked me directly if I thought the Luvox might help him; I said it might, explaining it was another way to help manage overwhelming emotions. He confessed that actually he had not been forgetting to take it, but that it was incompatible with his "tough guy" aspirations to be on an antidepressant. I said this was understandable; growing up he had been treated as if he should be able to handle difficult emotions on his own. This expectation was unreasonable, and he must have developed shame about wanting or needing help with his feelings. I then mentioned that David might even consider some other medications that could help reduce his agitation and that Dr. K would be the real authority on these. We all agreed that I would call Dr. K to discuss the assessment and that David and Ms. S would follow up with him shortly.

Toward the end of the session, David asked about the advisability of discussing his childhood experiences with his parents. Ms. S and I concurred in suggesting he go slowly with that also. I explained that such interactions might also stir up a lot of emotion for David and that he and Ms. S would want to prepare for that eventuality. In addition, I recommended that he think carefully about what he hoped to get out of such discussions. Shortly after this, I left, giving David and Ms. S time to discuss the assessment alone together. They both thanked me and said my work with them had been extremely valuable. I offered to be available to either of them in the future, and David and I talked about the possibility of our having a follow-up session in about a month. I left feeling quite optimistic that the assessment had helped the two of them get "unstuck" in the therapy and that I could be a resource if they ran into further problems.

Written Feedback and Immediate Follow-Up

Approximately 2 weeks after our final session, I sent David a letter summarizing what we had learned in the assessment (see Appendix). I asked

Ms. S to review a draft of this letter before I mailed it, and I made several changes based on her suggestions. I also asked David to complete two forms used in our practice for clients to give feedback after an assessment: a questionnaire consisting of a series of open-ended inquiries and the Assessment Questionnaire–2 (AQ–2; Finn, Schroeder, & Tonsager, 1994), a standardized instrument of clients' satisfaction with different aspects of a psychological assessment. I also asked Ms. S to fill out an open-ended questionnaire concerning her impressions of the assessment.

On the AQ–2, David rated himself as highly satisfied with the assessment (Total Satisfaction = 60T) relative to a sample of clients who had been evaluated previously at the Center for Therapeutic Assessment.[2] His AQ–2 component scores showed that his high satisfaction was based fairly equally on (a) feeling he had learned new things about himself, (b) feeling more secure about who he was after the assessment, (c) liking me and feeling liked by me, and (d) having few negative emotions during the assessment sessions. In the open-ended feedback questionnaire, David explained his feelings in his own words (responses are in italics):

How well did the assessment meet your expectations?
It was far better. I did this mainly because Elizabeth thought it would be helpful. I had no idea it would help so much.

What part(s) of the assessment did you find most valuable?
The whole thing, but especially crying during the stories. I saw how much I've been avoiding my past and how it affects my memory and ability to think.

What suggestions do you have for improving the way we do assessments?
Can't think of any.

What would you tell a friend who was considering getting an assessment from us?
Do it! Dr. Finn is a really nice man and you'll learn a lot about yourself.

Please give any other comments.
I really appreciated the way you included me from the beginning. I didn't realize you would listen so much to my ideas and this helped a lot.

---

[2]The standardization sample for the AQ–2 tended to be quite satisfied with their assessments; thus, the T scores exhibit a ceiling effect.

Interestingly, Ms. S reported similar feelings in some of her written feedback:

> How well did the assessment meet your expectations?
> *Far exceeded. I had heard good things about your work but frankly had no idea the assessment would be so useful.*
>
> What part(s) of the assessment did you find most valuable?
> *Having the testing validate some of my ideas, while showing others to be red herrings. I now feel much more secure about how to proceed in the treatment.*
>
> What suggestions do you have for improving the way we do assessments?
> *None, just publicize more what you do!!*
>
> Please give any other comments.
> *Thank you for the respect you showed me during the assessment. I was afraid a psychologist would come in as the "big expert" and look down on me, but you never made me feel that way.*

Long-Term Follow-Ups

Approximately 6 months after the assessment, I got a call from Ms. S asking if she could consult with me again about David. I said I would be happy to talk with her and noted the worried tone in her voice. When we met, Ms. S reported that right after the assessment her therapy with David had seemed to have new purpose and clarity. The two of them had begun to talk in more detail about David's early experiences in his family and how these related to his adult relationships. As predicted, David had begun to experience strong feelings of sadness and anger, and Ms. S had reminded him to use her as a support. During this time, David had increased his therapy sessions to twice a week and was taking the Luvox Dr. K had prescribed. About 4 weeks prior to Ms. S's calling me, however, David had a particularly emotional session with her right before she left on a brief vacation. Then, while Ms. S was away, David had rather impulsively and angrily confronted his mother about his "terrible" childhood, and she had reacted defensively, blaming him for being such a difficult child. By the time Ms. S returned, David was severely depressed, had been drinking heavily, and was furious at her for being away. He talked alternately about quitting therapy and leaving town or about committing suicide. Ms. S had reacted by insisting that David make a suicide contract with her; he refused and they had spent two very difficult sessions in a power struggle about this. Finally, the two of them had agreed that Ms. S would consult with me about what to do.

I sympathized with Ms. S about how scary it was to hear a client talking about suicide and how frustrating it must have been to have David "jump the gun" in talking to his mother about his childhood. I asked Ms. S if she felt guilty at all about taking her vacation and she confessed that she did. In retrospect, she wished she had reminded David in that last session she was leaving so they could have slowed down their work before she went away. We agreed that might have been good, and that possibly David's "plunging in" was his way of acting out his various feelings about her going. Last, I asked if Ms. S felt she could be a good saucer for David's feelings of wanting to hurt himself or flee. She seemed startled when I asked this, then quickly saw that she had been so intent on preventing his acting out, she had not mirrored at all his desperation, fury, and fears of being hurt all over again. She told me that at times she was scared by the intensity of some of David's emotions. I said I could see why, given what had showed up on his Rorschach, and I asked if she had enough saucers to hold her while she was busy holding David. Ms. S laughed and mentioned he was not the only one who tried to manage difficulties all alone. I said I related to this and commended her on calling me when she needed help. Two weeks later, Ms. S called to say that she and David were out of their power struggle and back on track. In fact, the crisis had led to several breakthroughs: David had acknowledged how much he needed her and how terrified he was of getting abandoned. Also, his mother had called him, contrite, and asked for a joint session with him and his therapist. Ms. S and David were carefully planning how to approach that meeting.

These events all took place over 6 years ago. Ms. S and I talked briefly during this period, but in preparing this article, I got quite curious about what had happened to David. Thus, I called Ms. S to ask for an update. She related that she and David continued to work hard in twice-a-week therapy for about 5 years after the assessment. David periodically experienced bouts of serious depression; however, each time these came up, the two of them had worked together to help him manage the feelings. Also, after the crisis I had heard about, David joined a weekly therapy group to get additional support when Ms. S was sick or out of town. Gradually, David's moods stabilized and his romantic relationships improved. In fact, Ms. S told me that about 1 year ago, David got married to a lovely woman and relocated because of his wife's job. They had a touching and good termination, with David's being able to feel sad and acknowledge how important the therapy had been to him. Recently Ms. S had a card from him saying that he and his wife were expecting their first child and that if it was a girl, he wanted to call her "Elizabeth." Ms. S and I laughed together and talked about our therapy "children" and "grandchildren."

Summary and Conclusions

Admittedly, not every instance of Therapeutic Assessment has such an unequivocally positive outcome as the one I have presented here. However, I chose this case not only to demonstrate the effectiveness of Therapeutic Assessment, but because it illustrates several important points.

Collaborative Assessment Helps Clients Change Their Life Stories

How can such a relatively brief procedure as a Therapeutic Assessment help foster such important and long-lasting outcomes for a client? Psychologists know that normally, people do not change that easily! As my work with David shows, collaborative assessment techniques are powerful because they focus on helping clients "rewrite" the stories they tell themselves about themselves (which psychologists usually call *identity*) when those stories have become problematic or incomplete in important ways. My purpose with David was to discover his existing stories, use psychological tests as "empathy magnifiers" to come up with new possibilities (Finn & Tonsager, 1997), and then provide David with a set of memorable events (such as my TAT intervention), that would help him revise his self-concept. In this instance, David's old story ("I have ADD") shifted to a new story ("I have too many emotions I've never dealt with that are overwhelming my thinking"), which led to a new set of actions that gradually changed his experience of the world. I also had the advantage in this assessment that a significant figure in David's life (Ms. S) was able to support his new views and ways of being and follow up with him as he integrated his new story into his life.

Compared to other forms of therapeutic intervention, psychological assessment has the advantage of quickly gathering detailed specific information about clients' self-schemas and interpersonal schemas. Furthermore, when Therapeutic Assessment techniques are applied, clients are enlisted as active participants—in everything from specifying the goals of the assessment, to collecting collateral information, to helping interpret test results. I believe traditional assessment approaches—in which results are either never shared with clients or are shared as a *fait accompli* at the end of the assessment—do not work as well for changing a client's life story. This is because to all of us as humans, our identities are like precious works of art, which we have constructed on the basis of innumerable life experiences and in which we have a great deal of ownership, investment, and pride. Research has demonstrated that in most cases people will distort or discount perceptions and information that challenges their existing self-schemas to verify and maintain those schemas (Swann, 1997).

It is mainly by presenting clients with significant experiences during an assessment, which we as assessors then help to reframe or label in new ways, that we can assist them in authoring new identities. This type of collaboration challenges us as psychologists to contain our hypotheses and insights longer and to give more thought about how to assist our clients in developing new insights. Psychologists may feel less important and more like midwives than parents. However, I am convinced that what is lost in grandiose self-esteem through this process is gained in effectiveness with clients.

Collaborative Psychological Assessment Is a Powerful, Nonthreatening Way to Consult to Colleagues

This case also illustrates the potential utility of psychological assessment in consulting to treating professionals. Others have recognized that assessment is useful in this way, especially in clarifying diagnostic uncertainties about a client (e.g., Allen, 1981). However, with the exception of Fischer (1985/1994), few people have noted how often diagnostic referral questions actually reflect more complex treatment quandaries based on the relationship between client and treating clinician. In my experience, this is no less true with highly experienced treaters than with therapists like Ms. S, who are early in their careers. When this fact is fully appreciated, a different view of assessment as consultation emerges: It is a systemic intervention affecting a client, therapist, and their relationship (see chap. 9). Thus, assessors must be highly skilled in managing complex systems to avoid splitting or becoming triangulated in an unhealthy way with the therapist–client pair.

In Therapeutic Assessment, such pitfalls are avoided by treating both client and referring therapist as essential collaborators in the assessment. As already noted, clients are enlisted as co-participant observers throughout the assessment. This case also demonstrates how the same end is achieved with referring professionals. I involved Ms. S in each step of the assessment: (a) explaining the purpose of the assessment to David, (b) supporting him as the assessment unfolded, (c) interpreting his test responses, (d) discussing the assessment results with him, and (e) constructing the written summary at the end of the assessment. At each stage, I endeavored to take neither a one-up nor a one-down stance towards Ms. S, to respect her vulnerability in seeking my assistance, and to openly join her in acknowledging the difficulties of becoming intimately involved with clients like David. As sometimes happens, this led to her feeling free to consult me again when she and David reached another crisis later in their treatment relationship. I suspect that if more assessors approached referring professionals in this collaborative manner, there would soon be even more call for assessment as consultation to client–therapist pairs in difficulty.

APPENDIX
Excerpts From Feedback Letter to David

Dear David:

As promised, I'm writing to summarize the information we went over in your assessment feedback session with Elizabeth Smith on June 27, 19– –. My hope is that you and Elizabeth will then have a written document to refer to as you proceed in your therapy.

I'll structure this letter by addressing the questions we came up with for the assessment. Before doing this, however, let me say again how much I respect the way you put yourself into the assessment, David. I am well aware that psychological testing is a vulnerable and difficult thing for anyone to do, and I know from your test results that it is not always easy for you to trust others. I saw the real effort you made to let me see who you are, David, even when that was a bit uncomfortable. I appreciate the courage and trust you showed. Also, thank you again for allowing me to videotape our sessions to use in training other psychologists.

Now to your questions:

—*Why can't I break up with girlfriends when they're treating me badly?*
—*What in me is too weak to do this?*
—*Why is it so hard for me to be alone?*

David, your personality test results showed that you are trying to manage a lot of overwhelming emotions, which have been around for a long time. Underneath your energetic and optimistic exterior, you are struggling with a great deal of depression and sadness, anger (especially at authority figures), feelings of worthlessness, and a sense of powerlessness. Although you are an extremely intelligent guy with a lot of varied coping mechanisms, this inner pain has currently exceeded your ability to manage it, with the result that you are experiencing severe anxiety and periodic bouts of depression. As you told me, at times it feels that if you let down your guard, you will fall into an abyss. When you reach this type of situation, you always have the option of making a large geographic move—as you have in the past—which distracts you and provides you new and exciting people to interact with. Another past option has been to become immersed in a romantic relationship where you can lose yourself and gain some temporary relief from your inner pain.

In short, it is your unresolved inner pain that makes it difficult for you to be alone and that sets you up for getting caught in bad relationships. Until you can explore and resolve some of the depression and anger you are carrying, it will be difficult for you to (a) choose good partners for romantic relationships, (b) set appropriate limits so you don't get abused by your partners, (c) feel secure that others are telling you the truth, and (d) stop from re-creating relationships where you get emotionally abandoned.

As I mentioned in our last session, your longing to be connected to someone is a good sign—and shows that you haven't totally given up on other people. However, until you have resolved more of the issues from your past, it may be wisest to avoid getting involved romantically and to use therapy and nonromantic friends for your social and emotional support.

—*Do I really have ADD and if not, why do I have trouble concentrating and remembering things?*

As we discussed in our last session, this is a difficult question that we cannot answer with total certainty at this time. It is clear that you are distractible and highly active, David, and you have many of the symptoms of Attention Deficit Disorder. However, as you yourself decided in our next-to-last session, it is quite possible that your attentional problems are caused mainly by your anxiety and depression and by your attempts to cope by staying highly active, "up," and distracted from your negative moods.

I am fairly certain from the testing and from the stories you told that the events of your childhood had a detrimental impact on you. Your parents' divorce and their inability to help you process your anger and sadness about their separation probably left you with a lot of confusing and overwhelming feelings. One of the stories you told to the picture cards seems a good description of what you probably experienced at the time:

> It's a little boy who's got more on his mind than a boy his age should have on his mind. He's thinking hard about a turn of events. It looks like he's not looking at anything. He's thinking hard—with lots of emotions flying around in his head. He almost looks adultlike, but he's a child. It looks maybe like his parents are children as well as him. The adults in the family are acting like children, and the children are being forced to act like adults without wanting to. He's being forced to be alone. The family doesn't know what's going on. Feelings are washing over him. He needs parents that are actually adults...that have wisdom. He needs someone to treat him like he's a child, so he doesn't have to be so self-reliant. (TAT 13B)

If this story is an accurate description of a period in your childhood, David, it helps to explain a lot of the problems you are having now. The divorce and separation were probably quite traumatic for you, in part because you didn't have adequate "saucers" to help hold and process the painful emotions you were experiencing. Thus, you had to "cut off" whole parts of your emotional experience and develop ways to manage on your own. Those protected emotions still exist, as you said, "in deep storage," and you add to them still because you continue to manage difficult feelings by avoiding them if you can.

For now, I recommend that you seek treatment for your anxiety, depression, and anger—with psychotherapy and medication—and see if this makes an impact on your attentional problems. If you make significant progress in addressing these underlying issues and still find yourself highly distractible, further testing could help identify other neurologically based causes to your attentional problems.

David, these are the recommendations we discussed in the last session:

(1) Think seriously about your impulse to leave town, as it may represent an old way of coping with your anxiety and depression. I know you are unhappy with your current job, but a move will only temporarily postpone the inner pain you are feeling. It might be best to stay put and work hard in therapy to resolve your emotional issues.

(2) Keep resisting the urge to get into a romantic relationship, and learn to rely on Elizabeth and on friends more. I know that you don't really know how to do this, as you don't have much experience letting others support you. But keep asking Elizabeth what it would look like to use her as a "saucer."

(3) It might be wise to increase your individual sessions with Elizabeth right now, or to add other supports (such as a therapy group). In either case, your work in therapy right now is to access your inner pain—little by little—while getting support from others so it doesn't overwhelm you. As we discussed, you may find yourself distrusting whether Elizabeth (or others) can handle your emotions; if so, such feelings also should be discussed. By alternately exploring your distrust and your inner pain, you should find yourself less anxious and depressed and more able to tolerate aloneness.

(4) Your idea of discussing your childhood with your parents is a good one. But take time to work with Elizabeth about how to handle the feelings that could result and to clarify your goals for such discussions.

(5) Work with Dr. K to find an antidepressant that works for you. The Luvox may or may not be a good drug for you; he and you may also want to discuss adding a mood stabilizer (such as Depakote™) to help with your overactivity and agitation.

Thank you again, David, for letting me get to know you. I admire your many strengths and was impressed by how well you manage some very difficult emotions. If you have any questions or comments about this letter—or if you would like to schedule the follow-up session we discussed—feel free to contact me.

One last request: Would you be willing to complete the enclosed forms about your experience of the assessment and return them to me? Your feedback will help me work in the future with people in situations similar to yours.

Best wishes,

Steve Finn

11

Collaborative Sequence Analysis of the Rorschach

In this chapter, I describe how it proved helpful—and perhaps essential—during an assessment to involve a client in jointly interpreting the sequence of his responses to one Rorschach card. *Collaborative sequence analysis* is one of many extended inquiry techniques used in collaborative and Therapeutic Assessment (see chap.1).

Case Study

Background Information

The client was a middle-aged man, Jeff, who came with his wife, Ann, for a couples' assessment several years ago. The couple had been in marital therapy for over 3 years, attempting to deal with Ann's long history of severe depression and Jeff's increasing exasperation that she wasn't getting well. Ann had been hospitalized several times, but each time she wasn't good at following through with the aftercare that was prescribed when she was released (taking medication, exercising, etc.). Recently, the couple had been increasingly distant from one another—with Ann feeling Jeff was less and less sympathetic about her depression, and Jeff being frustrated when he came home from work to find that Ann had slept

---

This chapter is based on a paper presented at the XVIII International Congress of the Rorschach and Projective Methods (Finn, 2005a).

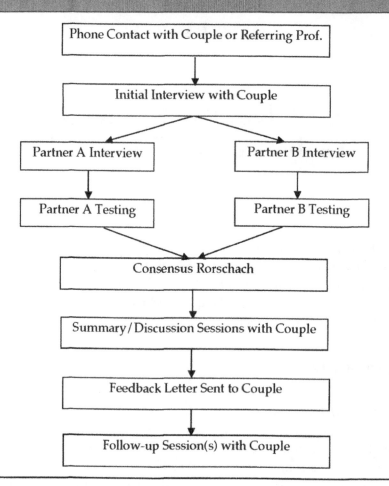

EXHIBIT 11–1
Flow Chart of a Therapeutic Couples Assessment

Phone Contact with Couple or Referring Prof.

Initial Interview with Couple

Partner A Interview

Partner B Interview

Partner A Testing

Partner B Testing

Consensus Rorschach

Summary / Discussion Sessions with Couple

Feedback Letter Sent to Couple

Follow-up Session(s) with Couple

all day, hadn't cooked or cleaned, or paid much attention to the children. The couple and their therapist felt "stuck" in the marital treatment, and hoped that a psychological assessment might shed some light on next steps to take.

Procedures

Exhibit 11–1 shows the general flow chart for Therapeutic Assessment of a couple. As you can see, I meet with the couple first to gather questions they hope to have answered, then perform individual assessments

---

EXHIBIT 11-2
Sample Questions Posed by Jeff and Ann to Guide
the Assessment

From Both

- We feel stuck in not being close to each other, not communicating, just coexisting under the same roof. Why hasn't therapy helped more and how can we get back on course in our relationship?

From Ann

- How could I be so strong at the beginning of the marriage and yet be so unable to function now?
- What do I need to do to get out of this depression?

From Jeff

- How should I deal with the feelings I get when she tells me that she slept all day?
- Is there anything I can do to help her with her depression?

---

on each partner (including the Rorschach and a variety of other tests.) I then typically follow the individual testing with a Consensus Rorschach (see chap.12), which I discuss with the couple, and with 4 to 5 hours of feedback, where I discuss the individual test results and how these fit together to make sense of the couple's problems.

Assessment Questions

Exhibit 11-2 shows some of the questions Ann and Jeff came up with at the beginning of the assessment. As you can see, Ann was puzzled about her depression, Jeff was trying to manage his frustration and find out how to be helpful, and both were struggling to know how to relate to one another other in a more intimate way. Incidentally, in gathering questions from members of a couple, I discourage those of the form "Why does my partner do X?"—which are primarily about the other person. Instead I ask the individuals to frame questions about themselves or that "include themselves," for example, "When my partner does X, why do I

EXHIBIT 11–3
Sequence of Responses and Scoring from Jeff's
Individual Rorschach

Card	Free Association	Scoring
II	2 clowns playing patty cake	W+ Ma.FCo 2 H, Cg 4.5 COP
	A smashed bug	Wo FC.V— A, Bl 4.5 MOR
	A butterfly hovering above a creek with trees on the side	WS+ FMp.CFu A, Bt 4.5
III	A ripped tuxedo	DdS99+ FC'.FCu Cg 5.5 MOR
	A picture from *National Geographic*—2 native women doing laundry	W+ Mp.mpo 2 Art, H, Cg P 5.5
IV	An upside down bat, hanging by its feet	Wo FMp.FC'o A 2.0
	One of those pictures from the 60s, a "Keep on Trucking" guy leaning against a mirror	W+ Mp.Fru (H),Art 2.5 PER

feel Y?" My intent here is to disrupt the projections the two partners put on each other, which I believe sets the stage for therapeutic change.

Standardized Testing

The events I describe took place during Jeff's individual Rorschach in the early part of the assessment. I should mention that at this point in the process, Jeff had produced an MMPI–2 profile that fit his presentation as a person with no emotional problems, as there were no significant elevations on any clinical scale. There was, however, a very low score on Scale 9 (Hypomania), suggesting that Jeff was tired and had very low energy.

While I was giving the Rorschach, I noticed early on a pattern in Jeff's responses that continued throughout the Rorschach: He repeatedly gave what I saw as "depressive" responses (e.g., including MOR, C', or V) that were immediately followed by various "defensive" responses, typically involving intellectualization (i.e., scored AB, Art, Ay, or Sc), schizoid withdrawal (scored Bt or Ls or Na), or narcissistic defense (Fr). Exhibit 11–3 shows the sequence of Jeff's responses and scores to Cards II, III, and IV. I've omitted the inquiry to simplify the table.

As you can see, on Card II, Jeff saw: (a) two clowns playing patty cake (a somewhat manic response); (b) a smashed bug (a depressive response that included both MOR and V); and (c) a butterfly hovering above a creek (a more schizoid response involving botanical content). On Card III he saw: (a) a ripped tuxedo (a depressive response emphasizing the

EXHIBIT 11–4
Lower Portion of the Structural Summary for Jeff's Rorschach

```
-----------------------------RATIOS, PERCENTAGES, AND DERIVATIONS-----------------------------
R    = 32    L    = .14            FC:CF+C  = 3 : 3          COP = 2    AG= 1
                                   Pure C   = 0              GHR:PHR  = 4 : 4
EB   = 10: 4.5  EA   = 14.5  EBPer = 2.2   SmC':WsmC = 4 : 4.5        a:p      = 11 :12
eb   = 13: 13   es   = 26    D    = -4     Afr      = 0.6            Food     = 0
              Adj es = 18    Adj D = -1    S        = 6              SumT     = 2
                                           Blends/R = 13 : 32        Human Cont = 12
FM   = 8     SumC'= 4     SumT = 2         CP       = 0              PureH    = 6
m    = 5     SumV = 2     SumY = 5                                   PER      = 6
                                                                    Isol Indx  = 0.25
a:p        = 11 : 12  Sum6  = 1    XA%    = 0.87   Zf    = 25   3r+(2)/R   = .50
Ma:Mp      = 6 : 4    Lv2   = 0    WDA%   = 0.94   W:D:Dd = 26: 3: 3  Fr+rF    = 2
2AB+Art+Ay = 19       WSum6 = 2    X-%    = 0.13   W:M   = 26: 10  SumV     = 2
MOR        = 4        M-    = 0    S-     = 0      Zd    = +1.0   FD       = 5
                      Mnone = 0    P      = 8      PSV   = 0      An+Xy    = 0
                                   X+%    = 0.56   DQ+   = 17     MOR      = 4
                                   Xu%    = 0.31   DQv   = 2      H:(H)+Hd+(Hd) = 6:6

PTI  = 0    DEPI = 5      CDI  = 1    S-CON = 7    HVI  = No      OBS  = No
```

achromatic coloring); and (b) a picture from *National Geographic* showing two native women doing laundry (an intellectualized response). His responses to Card IV were: (a) an upside-down bat, hanging by its feet (that I saw as rather passive); and (b) one of those pictures from the 1960s, a "Keep on Trucking" guy, leaning against a mirror (another intellectualized picture with significant metaphorical content). I began to develop a hypothesis that Ann wasn't the only member of the couple who was depressed, but that Jeff warded off his depression with a variety of coping mechanisms and "kept on trucking." As you can see in Exhibit 11–4, Jeff's Structural Summary confirmed my impression that he was depressed, although I didn't know that for sure at the time.

By the way, at the time I had never seen the Robert Crumb "Keep on Trucking" poster Jeff alluded to, but after looking it up on the internet, I scored that response to Card IV as unusual form quality because it was rare, but fit the contours of the blot.

Extended Inquiry

Following my standardized administration and inquiry of the Rorschach, my next goal was to discuss my hunches with Jeff. I pulled my chair around and asked him, "What was that test like for you?" and "Did you notice anything in particular about your responses?" He didn't. I then asked if he would listen to me read some of his responses and give me his impression. I chose and read together all the responses that would receive a depressive score. I asked Jeff what he thought of them. He said they seemed "upsetting and gloomy." I agreed and told him that all of them would be scored in a way that indicated depression. He said he wasn't surprised, and that if he let himself, he could feel really depressed about the situation at home. I then asked Jeff how he kept from feeling depressed. He said in his German family, people didn't get depressed. One just put one foot in front the other and went to work each day. "Oh," I said, pulling out Card IV, "That explains the order of your responses on this card." Jeff asked me to explain. "Your first response—the bat hanging upside down—gets a score for depression," I said. He could see that. "Do you remember your next response?" "The 'Keep on Trucking' guy," said Jeff, with dawning recognition. "That's what I do! When I'm depressed, I just keep on trucking. And I don't understand why Ann can't do that too." We then talked about how different people have different coping defenses, and that Ann might not be able to push her depression to the side the way he could. Jeff said he could imagine this, and that he had always appreciated her emotional sensitivity, as contrasted with his family's denial of emotions. I asked Jeff if Ann knew that he struggled not to be depressed too. He said he had never told her because he didn't want to burden her. "You mean the way you are burdened by her depression?" I asked. Jeff smiled and said he could see what I meant.

It's difficult to describe the wonder and relief that showed on Jeff's face at that point, as he recognized his own depression, found a framework for his frustration with Ann, saw that he was being unfair to himself by not talking to Ann about his depression, and realized that his own mind had given the key for understanding all this through what he saw on the Rorschach. I felt excited and good about the session as we said good-bye and Jeff went home.

Ripple Effect in the Couple

What I was not prepared for was the almost immediate systemic shift that began to take place in the couple. At our next joint session, Ann said that Jeff had told her that he was depressed too, but just wasn't letting it show. She asked if this was true. I had scored Jeff's Rorschach at that point, and was able to confirm that fact, and Jeff asked that we show her the sequence of his responses on Card IV. We reviewed those responses and also looked at Cards II and III. (Ann had already completed her individual Rorschach.) Ann quickly saw the pattern Jeff and I had seen and agreed with our interpretation. She said she hadn't realized that Jeff was depressed too, and that it made her sad that she hadn't been trying harder to help around the house. Jeff said he hadn't realized that Ann couldn't just "keep on trucking" the way that he could, and he was sorry that he had been so frustrated with her lately. These understandings continued to deepen and be incorporated as we finished the assessment over the next several weeks, and as Ann and Jeff returned to their couples therapist, who attended the final assessment summary/discussion session.

Follow-Up

When I saw the couple for follow-up a month after the assessment, I was amazed at the changes that had taken place. Ann was much less depressed and was keeping the household together, and Jeff was pushing himself less and asking Ann for help with various things. I'm still not sure what happened, but I believe that Ann's learning about Jeff's depression helped her access a nurturing, caretaking side of herself that pulled her out of her depression. As Ann gave Jeff more attention, he felt less frustrated and was able to be more empathic to her. Also, we might hypothesize that Ann was "holding" depression for both of them, and that as Jeff acknowledged his own depression, Ann no longer had to be depressed for him. I saw the couple one more time, 18 months after the assessment, and they were doing fairly well. Ann was back at work and had had no more hospitalizations, and Jeff reported that he "had [his] wife back."

Conclusion

There were several memorable moments in this couples assessment, but one of the most important, I think, was the collaborative sequence analysis of Jeff's individual Rorschach. This case shows the usefulness of the extended inquiry procedure following standardized testing, and how both the actual test scores and collaborative discussion come together to illuminate important patterns in clients' behavior. This case also shows how in couples' assessments, one partner's testing can help the other partner become empathic to that person's dilemmas of change. This by itself can produce far-reaching systemic changes.

In the following chapter I discuss another potentially powerful tool in Therapeutic Assessment of couples: the use of the Consensus Rorschach as a couples' assessment intervention.

12

Using the Consensus Rorschach as an Assessment Intervention With Couples

As mentioned in chapter 11, my colleagues and I often use the Consensus Rorschach—in which multiple individuals are asked to view the cards and come up with joint responses—as an assessment intervention in couple and family assessments. This procedure is extremely useful in exploring systemic patterns in couples and families, including roles or power struggles, and in seeing how family members respond to each other's emotions and conflicts—conscious and unconscious—in ways that produce vicious behavioral cycles. Also, the clinician can assess the flexibility of the family system and its individual members by attempting to intervene in problematic behaviors. When such interventions succeed, the couple or family may be able to generalize what they have learned to the world outside the assessment office. As such, the Consensus Rorschach can serve as a kind of brief couples' or family therapy.

The Consensus Rorschach has a venerable history as a group interaction assessment technique. As reported by Aranow, Reznikoff, and Moreland (1994) and Handler (1997), over the years such eminent individuals as Blanchard (1959, 1968), Roman and Bauman (1960), M. Singer and

This chapter is based on a paper presented to the Society for Personality Assessment (Finn, 1996c). I am grateful to Carol V. Middelberg for her comments on an earlier draft.

Wynne (1963), Loveland (1967), Klopfer (1969), Dorr (1981), and Nakamura and Nakamura (1987) described the use of the Consensus Rorschach with couples, families, groups of school children, incarcerated youth, and groups of co-workers. More recently, Aranow et al. (1994), Handler (1997), and Noy-Sharav (2006) detailed their own variations on the technique and provided useful case examples.

As an assessment intervention with couples, the Consensus Rorschach is used primarily to help a couple become aware of assessment findings that would be difficult to grasp in a summary/discussion session. I find that the most difficult Level 3 information for many couples involves systemic or intersubjective aspects of their "dance" together, that is, how "the behavior of one partner maintains and provokes the behavior of the other" (H. G. Lerner, 1985, p. 56). Because most of us develop our "stories" about the world and ourselves primarily from our subjective experience, we lack the data necessary to fully understand interactional phenomena. For example, we know that (a) we have trouble communicating about sex with our current partner, (b) we never had this trouble with previous partners, and understandably conclude that (c) our partner has a hang-up about sex! We are unable to see that we may be part of the problem, it's just that none of our previous partners have elicited this difficulty from us before in talking about sex. The Consensus Rorschach as described in this chapter can help illuminate such relational phenomena and help couples move beyond blaming each other for problematic interactions.

If you refer back to the flow chart of a couples assessment in the previous chapter (see Exhibit 11–1), you see that I typically administer the Consensus Rorschach towards the end of a couple's assessment, after each partner has completed standardized individual testing and individual assessment intervention sessions and just before the summary/discussion sessions.[1] As you may remember from chapter 8, this is the typical placement of assessment intervention sessions. Very often, each member of the couple has taken the Rorschach alone at this point, but this is not always the case and it is not necessary. For example, to keep the costs of

---

[1] I have on occasion administered the Consensus Rorschach as a stand-alone assessment technique, for example in consulting to a marital therapy that is at an impasse. It has seemed to be quite useful in that context also.

an assessment down, I have sometimes met for an initial session where I gathered assessment questions, gave each person the MMPI–2, then proceeded at a subsequent meeting with the Consensus Rorschach, and followed up later with a conjoint summary/discussion session. I encourage you to adapt this method to your practice and the needs of your clients.

I now go through the steps for using the Consensus Rorschach as an assessment intervention, and then present several brief case examples.

Procedure

Preparation

Before the couple arrives for the session, review their questions for the assessment and any individual test results. Think about hypotheses you have for how these two people "come together," that is, how do their individual strengths and struggles contribute to their interactions as a couple? What do you already know about the type of couple "dance" they tend to do? Does one person pursue and the other avoid? Is one overresponsible and the other underresponsible? How would you expect these patterns to be reflected in the joint Rorschach task? Also, ponder what would be difficult to say to the couple if you did a summary/discussion session at this point.

Then choose one or more of the couple's assessment questions as useful foci for the assessment intervention. When the couple arrives, check in with them so you know any important context. (They may have had a fight on the way to the session!) Then explain to them that you will be doing a task you hope will help illuminate the assessment questions you have chosen.

Seating

Sit across from the couple—with them next to one another so they can view each card at the same time. If possible, videotape the couple as they perform the first part of the assessment intervention. It is not necessary to have yourself on camera.

Part 1

Step 1

Let the couple know that you will be asking them to do the "inkblot
test." (If individual Rorschachs have been administered previously, tell
them you will be doing the test again but in a different way.) Give the di-
rections for the Consensus Rorschach:

> I have a series of cards here that have inkblots on them. As I show you
> each card, I want you to talk out loud together about what you see.
> Your task is to come up with responses that both of you can see and
> both of you agree upon reporting. When you agree, let me know and
> I will write down your response and ask you some questions about it.
> Any questions before we begin?

Answer most questions (e.g., Can we take turns? Do we have to say
what we saw before? Can we give more than one response per card?) with
the usual phrase: "It's up to you." If the couple tries to report separate responses, remind them, "Look for things you both can see and both agree
upon reporting."

Administer—in Order—Cards I, II, IV, VII, and X. This card
set was investigated by Nakamura and Nakamura (1987) and found to be
productive and evocative when used with families. It is possible to use the
entire set of 10 cards, and there are some advantages to this, but such a procedure results in a lengthy (3 to 4) hour session, unless you limit the number of responses to each card. For the purposes of the assessment intervention, we have found this subset of cards to be sufficient and quite useful.[2]

Step 2

Observe the couple as they interact, making notes about significant
events and patterns that you see. Intervene in the interactions only if one

---

[2]One advantage to using the full set of cards is that the assessor can score the consensus protocol and compare the scores to those obtained by each partner on their individual Rorschachs.

Noy-Sharav (2006) wrote about this option and about other innovative ways to score consensus protocols.

person attempts to report a percept that the other has not agreed to. Then gently remind the couple of the instructions: "Did both of you agree on this one?" or "Do both of you agree on this part of the response?"

Record the responses as they are given and inquire after each response about location, determinants, and so forth. Be alert for pseudo-agreements, where the partners appear to agree, but in fact are using different areas of the blot or different determinants. Highlight such discrepancies if necessary by asking, for example, "Are you sure you're using the same area of the blot?" or "Mary, are you seeing it the same way as John?"

Step 3

After Card X is completed, let the couple know that you will be giving them a short break (15 to 20 min). Ask them not to talk with one another about the Rorschach during this break.

While the couple is on break, review your notes and observations. What characteristic patterns or significant events did you witness during the administration? How might these behaviors be connected to the couple's presenting problems and goals for the assessment? See if you can think of another way that the couple could have approached the Consensus Rorschach so as to avoid or mitigate the problems you observed. What did the couple do well on in the interaction? Choose which of these patterns and events you wish to discuss with the couple and cue up the videotape to illustrative points in the administration. It is particularly helpful if the excerpts you show clearly relate to one or more of the couples' assessment questions.

Part 2

Step 4

Have the couple come back in the testing room and begin by asking them about their experiences during the Consensus Rorschach. Be cautious about sharing your observations at this point; instead inquire about their feelings, thoughts, and observations—listening for any experiences that seem to fit with your previous hypotheses or any that seem highly discrepant. Remember, in collaborative assessment, we prefer to build on clients' observations and insights if at all possible before we introduce our own.

Step 5 (Eliminate this step if you have not videotaped the administration.)

Show the couple the section(s) of the videotape you previously selected as being illustrative. Then ask them to comment on what they experienced or observed watching the tape. I typically start with an open-ended question like, "What did you notice?"

Step 6

After the partners have shared their thoughts, you may decide to share yours and help the couple draw connections between what happened during the Rorschach and what happens at other times (e.g., "Is this what happens when you have to cooperate on a task at home?" "Now I see what you meant by your communication difficulties!" "John, is this an example on Card V of what you meant about Mary's indecisiveness?"). Continue these discussions until you and the couple understand more about the interactional patterns you witnessed. You may want to slowly watch portions of the videotape again, stopping frequently to discuss and share observations. Try to highlight especially systemic aspects of the interactions, for example, "Do you see how you both play a part in the pattern we saw?" "John, what did you notice about your response when Mary did X?" "Mary, did you notice what you did right after that?"

Step 7

Ask the couple to think of another approach to the Rorschach task that would eliminate or alter the problem sequences. Adopt the couple's proposed solution or suggest a modification or alternative. Then—using any of Cards III, V, VI, VIII, or IX (which were not administered initially)—have the couple try out the new approach and observe and/or comment on their experience. Keep shaping the interaction until the couple feels some success modifying the problematic pattern.

Step 8

If the new approach is successful, explicitly draw a parallel to outside problem situations, for example, "Do you think you can do the same thing when you find yourselves arguing at home?" "Mary, what would it take for you to express your anger like that when you are alone with Joe?" If there is to be a next session, ask the couple to try out what they learned during the week, and to report back at that time.

Alternate Procedures

Sometimes couples who typically have extremely problematic and conflictual interactions in their daily lives surprise themselves and the assessor by working together extremely well during the Consensus Rorschach. In such instances in Part 2, you may cue up videotape excerpts of especially nice interactions, and initiate a discussion of what allowed those interactions to take place and what it would take to "export" them to the couple's life outside the testing room. If you can, identify specific factors that made a positive difference and helped "set up" the couple for success.

Another option I have used is to intervene when handing Card X to the couple in the first part of the administration. I have given the following instructions: "Now I want the two of you to think about an instance when you were at your worst together. Can you think of a time together?" I wait until the couple agrees on a particularly difficult situation they had, then continue: "Now I want you to do this last card together as if you were in that situation again. Try to treat each other the same way and get the same feelings, but this time while doing the Rorschach task." Most couples I have tried this approach with have been able to reenact their problematic patterns when given these instructions. Then I have proceeded with Part 2 of the Consensus Rorschach, contrasting the partners' experience before and after Card X.

Case Examples

Case 1—Kathy and John

Background.   Kathy and John were in their mid–40s and had been married 7 years when they were referred by their couples therapist for an assessment. It was a second marriage for each. Their major question for the assessment was "How can we avoid the terrible scenes we get into?" and they explained that they periodically found themselves in violent physical fights, often when they had been drinking, and often beginning (they said) with some irrational outburst on Kathy's part. The implication at the beginning of the assessment was that Kathy was more of the problem, and the referring couples therapist confessed to me that she thought Kathy had borderline personality disorder. Kathy, for her part, was struggling with shame and regret over her outbursts, but persisted in trying to understand why she acted this way. One of her assessment questions was "Why am I acting like such a nut in this marriage when I've never acted this way before?" John seemed quite happy with the idea that Kathy was "the crazy one," although he admitted that he was quite reactive and cruel once things started to deteriorate between them.

Individual Test Results.   The MMPI–2 profiles I obtained fit with the idea that Kathy was more emotionally disturbed than was John. Her basic profile was quite unguarded and had multiple elevations on Scales 2 (79T), 3 (70T), 4 (81T), 6 (74T), 7 (77T), and 8 (72T). To me, the MMPI–2 suggested significant problems with emotional regulation in a sensitive woman who felt anxious, depressed, and alienated. I knew from the couples' therapist that Kathy came from a family that was quite neglectful and chaotic, and I saw this profile as fitting with that background. I did remember, however, that Kathy's work and relationship history had been extremely stable (before John) and that she was responsible and well liked at her job. These facts puzzled me, as such characteristics generally do not accompany the kind of MMPI–2 profile Kathy produced.

John's MMPI–2 was somewhat guarded and suggested that he, by nature, tended to keep his "cards close to his chest" and "put his best foot forward" (K = 68T, F = 42T, S = 70T). As might be expected, John had no significant elevations on the MMPI–2 Clinical scales. He did, however, have a low score (38T) on Scale 9, which made me wonder about an underlying depression.

Given these findings, John's and Kathy's Rorschachs surprised me, and I must confess that when I first saw the Structural Summaries, I thought that I had inadvertently mixed them up. Kathy's protocol did show significant indications of problems with emotion management (Afr. = .78; FC/CF+C = 2/5; Pure C = 2) and a great amount of painful longing (T = 3). Also, her mediation scores suggested that she sometimes had significant difficulties making sense of the world and of relationships (XA% = .68, M- = 3), especially when she was caught up in emotionally arousing situations (almost all her FQ- responses occurred on Cards VIII, IX, and X). However, Kathy showed less depression, anxiety, and emotional distress on the Rorschach than would have been expected from her MMPI–2 (DEPI = 3, Y = 1, D = +1, AdjD = +2). Her protocol was not "coarctated" (see chap. 7; R = 31, Lambda = .39), and I saw no reason why she would feign or exaggerate psychopathology on the MMPI–2. I could only wonder if she had somehow come to see herself as more disturbed than she actually was.

John's testing fit the pattern of "good MMPI, bad Rorschach" described in chapter 7. His Structural Summary suggested he had a significant underlying depression, low self-esteem, and emotional distress (DEPI = 6; 3r+(2)/R = .26, V = 4; D = −3), that he managed primarily through emotional constriction and withdrawal (FC/CF+C = 2/0; Afr. = .32; SumC'/SumC = 6/1), and intellectualization (2AB + Art + Ay = 8). And his mediation and ideation scores suggested that if anyone in the couple was crazy, it might be him (XA% = .35, WSUM6 = 34)!

From the integration of the couple's MMPI–2s and Rorschachs, I developed the hypothesis that the terrible scenes the couple fell into were actually an example of projective identification in action. John was carrying a level of pain and disintegration that he kept tightly under wraps; but it was pushing for expression. I wondered if somehow, he got Kathy to "act this out" for him, and that she was vulnerable to this dynamic because of her sensitivity, difficulties with emotion management, and longing to be accepted. To the extent that the projective identification succeeded, Kathy ended up feeling ashamed, and John "exported" his shame and "craziness" and got to feel superior. Kathy, for her part, longed to be taken care of, and unconsciously benefited from John's appearing stable and strong much of the time. She had grown up in a chaotic family and wanted someone who could protect her. By accepting the role of the "nut" in the marriage, she helped John appear saner than herself and thereby felt safer. I hoped if my hypotheses were useful, that the Consensus Rorschach would help me illuminate these patterns.

Consensus Rorschach, Part 1.   Kathy and John said they were a little nervous when I checked in, but could not say more about that. When I told them that we would be using the "couples Rorschach" to explore their question of why they got into bad scenes together, John rolled his eyes and groaned. He had greatly disliked the experience of his individual Rorschach, and he and I had talked extensively about that fact. I got their permission to videotape, gave them the instructions I laid out earlier, and held out Card I, which John took. The following is a transcript of the first part of the administration:

(The couple looks at Card I and then at each other.)

> *John:* What did you see?
> *Kathy:* One thing I saw was a butterfly.
> *John:* Hmmm...what else?
> *Kathy:* I also saw a bat with its wings spread.
> *John:* Anything else?
> *Kathy:* Uh huh. A woman...right here in the middle. She's held prisoner by these two creatures on the side. I don't know what they are, griffins or something. She's struggling to get away from them but they have a tight hold on her.
> *John:* Griffins? (skeptically)
> *Kathy:* Yes! (defensively) It's a mythical creature that's half eagle and half lion. Haven't you ever heard of them? You can see the wings here, but they also have the tail and fur of a lion on their legs.
> *John:* That one's too weird for me. (Looks at me and rolls his eyes.) But I can see the other ones.
> *Kathy:* (looks deflated) OK, let's use those...unless you saw something else entirely.

From this interaction, I felt confirmed in my hypothesis about how this couple functioned intrapsychically. John, as predicted by his MMPI–2, "held his cards close to his chest" and seemed noncommittal about Kathy's first two highly conventional responses. By not agreeing or disagreeing with these, he played to Kathy's desire to be accepted, then got her to "climb out on a limb" and reveal a much more vulnerable response. At that point, he rejected the response, implied that Kathy was crazy, and left her feeling ashamed and one-down. By accepting this frame and going one-down, rather than standing up for herself, Kathy helped John stay stable, which helped fulfill her fantasy of a calm, reasonable partner. This same type of pattern was repeated on Cards II, IV, and VII, with Kathy looking more and more frustrated and demoralized as the task went on, but seeming unable to figure out a way to change the pattern.

On Card X, things seemed to come to a head. Kathy started off appearing to try something different, by asking John to go first, but he easily got her off track by using humor and appealing to her care-taking impulses:

> *Kathy:* You go first on this one. What did you see?
> *John:* I don't remember. I hated these colored ones especially. I can't remember what I said. I guess I've just blotted it all out. (He smiles cutely and we all laugh at his pun.) Honey, you know I'm not good at these things. What did you see?
> *Kathy:* I thought this was a bunch of bugs at a party. See here's two ants, and a couple of beetles waving party favors. And these are two crabs...
> *John:* Crabs aren't bugs.
> *Kathy:* I know, but they're at the party too.
> *John:* If you say so.
> *Kathy:* What the hell is that supposed to mean! (angrily)
> *John:* Nothing! (innocently) I was just trying see what you saw, but it doesn't make sense to me.
> *Kathy:* No you weren't. You were putting me down.
> *John:* Honey, don't be so sensitive. See (turns to me)...this is the kind of thing that happens at home all the time.
> *Steve:* Yes, I know. Kathy, how are you feeling right now?
> *Kathy:* Like I just want to throw the cards at him.
> *Steve:* And can you say why?
> *Kathy:* No I can't. And even if I could it wouldn't help.

Steve: Well, I think this is a good time to take a break. I'm going to ask the two of you to leave me alone for 15 to 20 minutes. I'll cue up some portions of the videotape, and when you come back we'll see if we can make sense of what just happened.

Consensus Rorschach, Part 2.   When Kathy and John came back in the office after the break, Kathy apologized for losing her temper and John looked a bit smug. I asked them their impressions of what had happened, and at first, the "old story" came out, with which I was familiar:

Kathy: I guess I'm just too sensitive and emotional some times. I don't know what comes over me, but I lose my temper. And then, quite understandably, John gets angry in return, and we get in those big scenes.

John: I'm glad you got to see this, because this is what happens at home. And then when we've been drinking, it just snowballs until we're at each other's throats.

I nodded and said I was sure the drinking made it worse. But I thought we could understand better what set Kathy off. Would the couple be willing to watch the videotape with me and see if we could figure that out? Kathy eagerly said yes. John agreed also, but looked less than thrilled. I showed them their interactions over Card I, then stopped the videotape and asked, "What did y'all see?"

Both seemed confused at this point. Kathy commented that John seemed to be "deferring to her," which she said he often did on matters relating to "art or emotions or relationships." John repeated again that he could see two of the things Kathy saw, but not the third one, explaining that he didn't even know what a griffin was. I asked Kathy what she had been feeling when John rejected her third response, and she admitted, "Rejected. It was one of my favorite responses." I asked if either had noticed that John never put forward one of his own responses (they hadn't) and I showed them Card II to illustrate what I meant. Kathy looked excited at this point and we all had the following interchange:

Kathy: I see what's going on. He never has to face rejection. He lures me out, then shoots me down, and he never runs the same risk.

John: But I didn't remember what I said, I already told you. And you're better at this kind of thing than I am. You always have been.

Steve: Kathy, do you buy that?

Kathy: No, not really.

Steve: And John, I don't think you're doing this intentionally, but I think something else is going on. You saw some pretty gory things on the Rorschach when you took it yourself, and it was hard...it was a pretty unpleasant experience, as we talked about. You told me that it was maddening not knowing what a good response was and that you worried that I would think you were crazy. Remember?

John: Yeah.

Steve: So I wonder if this pattern I'm seeing is a way you unconsciously protect yourself from feeling insecure and vulnerable. And Kathy, do you know why you play into it?

Kathy: Because I'm so much hoping that he'll be able to see what I see.

Steve: Exactly! And also, I wonder if you don't want John to get off balance, because that would be scary for you. If that seems right, let's see if what we're seeing here is at all similar to what happens when you get into those big scenes at home.

They both agreed that my interpretations might be true, and we went over a recent fight and tried to apply what we had learned. I then asked them to think of a different way to do the Rorschach task.

Kathy: Well, I guess I should ask him to go first.

Steve: Good idea. Or at least take turns.

John: But what if I can't remember what I said?

Steve: Well, you could just look and see what the card looks like today. Or if you want, you could ask me and I'll remind you of your other responses.

John: OK. (I hand him Card III.) I remember this one. I saw two people whose hearts are being ripped out of their bodies. They're in love, but are involved in a real painful interaction. It's a painting and the red symbolizes the broken hearts.

Kathy: That must be how you feel about us.

John: I never thought of it that way.

Steve: And Kathy, can you see what John saw?

Kathy: Yes, clearly, and I feel really sad for John.

Steve: John, what is that like for you?

John: Uncomfortable. I don't like feeling those things and I don't like other people seeing me feel them.

Steve: And can you feel the support in what Kathy's saying?

John: I guess so.

Steve: And what is that like?

John: I'd really prefer it if I could just leave the room. I feel like you both have the goods on me now.

John and I then had a long discussion about how sadness and other "tender" feelings were not considered manly when he was growing up in his German family. I then was able to make a more compassionate interpretation, based on Middelberg's (2001) guidelines, of the dance between him and Kathy. I hoped this would address his shame:

Steve: And John, I want to say explicitly that I don't think you got Kathy to go first with the Rorschach and then rejected her responses in order to be mean. I don't think you were even conscious of what you were doing. As I'll talk about more next week when we go over your test results, I think you have a lot of painful feelings inside—like shame and rejection—that you don't know what to do with and that are really overwhelming. You just found a way to have Kathy hold some of those feelings for you until you could find another option. And Kathy, you were all too willing to do so, so that you could have a partner who didn't appear to struggle with difficult emotions. Does this make sense?

They both agreed that it did, and I felt I had prepared them well for the summary/discussion the next week. In this instance, the assessment intervention had worked beautifully to help the couple see an interactional dance that would have been very difficult to explain otherwise. It had also confirmed a hypothesis I had derived from the standardized testing, and gave a potent memorable example that all of us could refer to in the work ahead.

Case 2—Tom and Kirk

Background.   Tom and Kirk were a gay male couple in their late 30s who sought me out for counseling after reading a book I co-wrote about gay relationships (Driggs & Finn, 1990). They had met 2 years earlier at an Alcoholics Anonymous (AA) meeting, and had been living together for about 9 months at the time I saw them. Although they hadn't requested any psychological testing, both men seemed to have difficulties putting their feelings into words, and I suggested a brief couples assessment very early in our work to "get more information that would help with therapy." They were amenable and had generated questions and each completed an MMPI–2 by the time we met for the Consensus Rorschach. Their major presenting issue was how to manage a pronounced pursuer–avoider dance (Middelberg, 2001) that recurred every time they had a significant disagreement. At such times, Kirk would push to "talk the issue through" and Tom, after a few moments, would grow silent and/or retreat physically. This had resulted in several scenes where Tom had locked himself in the bathroom and Kirk had pounded on the door and entreated him to come out for over 30 min.

At the time we did the assessment, I knew just a little about each man's background. Both had had serious problems with drug and alcohol abuse, but were sober at the time, Tom for 4 years and Kirk for 2 years. Both had histories of trauma and neglect. Kirk had been sexually abused as a child by an uncle, and Tom told me that he spent ages 10 to 12 living with his mother in an abandoned car. So far, I hadn't collected a lot of information about such topics, as both men seemed reluctant to talk about their pasts. Neither had been in individual or couples therapy before coming to see me, but both were working hard in their 12-step recovery programs. I really admired both men for the strides they had made and for the support and caring they showed towards each other in my office.

Individual Test Results.   Tom's basic MMPI–2 profile is shown in Exhibit 12–1 and Kirk's in Exhibit 12–2. As you can see, the profiles were remarkably similar to one another.

EXHIBIT 12–1
Tom's Basic MMPI–2 Profile

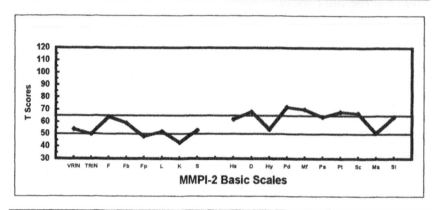

MMPI-2 Basic Scales

Note. VRIN = Variable Response Inconsistency Scale; TRIN = True-Response Inconsistency Scale; F = Infrequency; Fb = Infrequency Back Page; Fp = Infrequency Psychopathology; S = Superlative Self-Presentation; Hs = Scale 1, Hypochondriasis; D = Scale 2, Depression; Hy = Scale 3, Hysteria; Pd = Scale 4, Psychopathic Deviate; Mf = Scale 5, Masculinity—Femininity; Pa = Scale 6, Paranoia; Pt = Scale 7, Psychasthenia; Sc = Scale 8, Schizophrenia; Ma = Scale 9, Hypomania; Si = Scale 0, Social Introversion.

Source: This and other MMPI–2 profiles are excerpted from the *MMPI–2™* (*Minnesota Multiphasic Personality Inventory–2™) Manual for Administration, Scoring, and Interpretation, Revised Edition*, Copyright © 2001 by the Regents of the University of Minnesota Press. All rights reserved. Used by permission of the University of Minnesota Press. "MMPI–2" and "Minnesota Multiphasic Personality–2" are trademarks owned by the Regents of the University of Minnesota.

Both were essentially 2–4–7–8 profiles, consistent with the trauma and neglect in each man's background. Kirk appeared to be more emotionally expressive and gregarious than Tom, as indicated by his elevation on Scale 3 (66T) and his low score on Scale 0 (42T). Tom was a bit more guarded (Scale 6 = 64T) and reserved (Scale 0 = 64T) as a person. But apart from these differences, both profiles suggested that the men struggled with mild to moderate depression, anxiety, and impulse control. I hypothesized that each could get emotionally overwhelmed rather quickly, but that Kirk was more likely to move forward in such a state, while Tom was more likely to withdraw. Neither was likely to be able to step aside at such times to find a more adaptive solution.

Consensus Rorschach, Part 1. On the day we met for the Consensus Rorschach, Tom and Kirk said they were doing well together and had just gotten back from a science fiction convention, an interest they shared. I had explained that we would be doing a task that might shine more light

EXHIBIT 12–2
Kirk's Basic MMPI–2 Profile

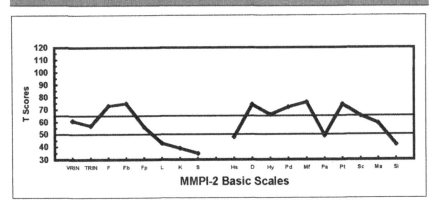

Note. VRIN = Variable Response Inconsistency Scale; TRIN = True-Response Inconsistency Scale; F = Infrequency; Fb = Infrequency Back Page; Fp = Infrequency Psychopathology; S = Superlative Self-Presentation; Hs = Scale 1, Hypochondriasis; D = Scale 2, Depression; Hy = Scale 3, Hysteria; Pd = Scale 4, Psychopathic Deviate; Mf = Scale 5, Masculinity—Femininity; Pa = Scale 6, Paranoia; Pt = Scale 7, Psychasthenia; Sc = Scale 8, Schizophrenia; Ma = Scale 9, Hypomania; Si = Scale 0, Social Introversion.

on their strengths and struggles as a couple, and as neither had taken the Rorschach before, I asked if they had heard about the Rorschach inkblots. Both had, and were excited about getting to take the test. I got their permission to turn on the video camera, gave them the instructions for the Consensus Rorschach, and handed them Card I. Without a pause, Kirk jumped right in:

> *Kirk:* Ooo, this is cool. I see a person being tortured. Here he is strapped to the table, and these figures on the side are some sort of torture masters. They have on big robes and are standing over him supervising the procedure.
>
> *Tom:* Neat! And maybe they've cut of his head already, or no, let's say it's bent way back, so you can't see it. That's part of how they're tormenting him. And he's either crying…or he's passed out. What do you think?
>
> *Kirk:* Passed out. And would that be the kind of shift they have him in that you can see through? It's really flimsy so that he shivers down there in the dungeon.
>
> *Tom:* I hadn't noticed that before. That's a nice detail.

Kirk: (Pause) Do you see anything else?

Tom: It could also be a damaged bat—the whole thing. These are holes in his wings where he's been shot or something. And these are little pieces falling off. Do you see that?

Kirk: Yeah, I like that. And the fact that it's black really helps with the "bat-ness" or should I say "battiness" too. (Both laugh.) Shall we tell him those two now since we both agree?

Tom: Sure. Good idea. Do you want to or shall I?

Kirk: Why don't you do one and I'll do other, and we can help each other.

I must say I was fascinated and somewhat astonished as we proceeded with Cards II, IV, and VII in a very similar manner. The interaction between the two men could not have been nicer. They collaborated beautifully, taking turns, modifying each other's responses, and showing openness and curiosity about what the other saw. And almost every response they came up with had morbid, aggressive, or traumatic content. Many had FQ-scoring, but both men could see every one, and they seemed to get great pleasure from sharing their percepts with each other.

I felt somewhat guilty as I modified the instructions for the last card, Card X:

Steve: Good job. Now I want to give you different instructions for this one. I want you to do the same task, but this time I want you to do it as if you were in your very worst place together. Let's think back to a recent bad time that you had. Can you think of one?

Kirk: You mean like that last fight we had? When Tom locked himself in the bathroom?

Steve: Yes. That's a good one. Tom, do you remember that scene? (Tom nods tentatively.) I want the two of you to do this card together with the same feelings you had that day that you fought. OK? Are you willing? (Both nod; I hand them Card X.)

Tom: (Looking scared.) I saw two spiders, here and here.

Kirk: (Sounding angry.) Well that's the sorriest, dumb-ass thing I ever heard! Can't you come up with something better than that, you moron?

At that point, Tom fell silent, his face went white, and he seemed to sink into the couch. I stopped what we were doing and asked what he was feeling. He couldn't talk at first, then said he felt paralyzed and that he couldn't think clearly. Kirk was immediately concerned, put his hand on Tom's knee, and said that he had only been "play-acting." Tom said he knew that, but that it had still affected him. I asked Tom to stand up and walk around a bit, and I got him a glass of water. Gradually, he got more color in his face, and I suggested we take a 15-min break. Both men agreed and went out to walk around the park near my office. I had some water myself and considered what to do.

Consensus Rorschach, Part 2.   When Tom and Kirk returned from the break, they both seemed fine, and Tom said he was glad "we did that last part" so I could see what happens between them. I agreed that it was useful and asked him if he had any words for the state he had been in. "Frozen shock," he said, and I agreed that it seemed to be a kind of "shock" state associated with being "flooded with emotions." Tom said that made sense, and I asked Kirk if he ever got like that when he was emotionally overwhelmed. He said that he used to, but now he was more likely to lose his temper and "go on the warpath." I asked if Kirk went on the warpath when Tom went into "frozen shock" and Kirk admitted that he did because he felt Tom was "ignoring" him. Tom jumped in to say that he wasn't trying to reject Kirk, and Kirk said he saw that, but that it was hard to keep in mind. Kirk started to tear up, and Tom looked guilty, so I decided to talk to them both about what I thought had happened.

> *Steve:* Guys, none of this is anybody's fault, and I think what we're seeing here is the flip side of a strength you have in your relationship. (They look interested.) Did you notice how each of you were able to see anything the other one saw on the Rorschach? (They did.) That is very unusual in itself and what was even more remarkable was that each of you saw some pretty difficult things. (They asked how.) Well a lot of those responses you gave were fairly gory and painful in their content. Do you see that? (They did.) Those are the kinds of things people see who have had pretty hard things happen to them in the past, like sexual abuse, or living in a car. (That made sense to them.) Well, I think a strength of your relationship is that the two of

you can relate to the pain each other has been through, which means you understand things that other people don't get and can keep each other company in some very difficult places. Does that seem right? In a way, you're very compatible with one another. (They agreed.) But the fact that you both had such painful childhoods also means that sometimes you get triggered by one another, and go into what we call a *retraumatized place*. When any of us is traumatized, we're biologically wired to do one of three things—fight, flee, or freeze. Unfortunately, when you freeze, Tom, you Kirk are likely to attack. And when you fight, Kirk, you're likely to freeze, Tom. At the moment, neither of you can stop this pattern when it gets going, in spite of how much you care about one another. It's just not possible until you know how to keep from going into a retraumatized place.

I then let both men respond and ask questions. Both seemed to get the major concepts involved in what I had said and to agree with the gist of my interpretation. Given that I knew I would be working with them in ongoing psychotherapy, I felt it was wise to stop the session where we were, rather than try to practice some kind of method of interrupting their downward spiral. I knew we would have plenty more opportunities to discuss ways to interrupt the pursuer–avoider dance, and frankly I was exhausted and I sensed they were too.

This case demonstrates how the Consensus Rorschach can be used in ongoing psychotherapy and how it is useful even if the partners in a couple haven't taken individual Rorschachs beforehand. It also shows an example of the modified instructions I gave earlier.

Conclusion

There are several different methods that can be used as assessment interventions in couples assessments: family sculpting, projective drawings, explicit role enactments, and so forth. In this chapter, I presented one technique, the Consensus Rorschach, and illustrated its usefulness with two different types of couples. The goal of the Consensus Rorschach, like other assessment interventions, is to get a couple to bring their problematic "dance" into the office where they and the assessor can begin to observe the roles each play and imagine and begin to practice other responses. If a couple feels some success in breaking their typical pattern of interaction with the assessor's support and guidance, it can give them hope and provide practical strategies for modifying such patterns in their daily lives.

As with other assessment intervention techniques, many assessors are initially intimidated by the Consensus Rorschach. Admittedly, it can be difficult at first to manage the complex, multileveled interactions that take place in the Consensus Rorschach. Also, if you are just learning the technique, you may doubt whether you'll actually be able to see any useful patterns. I encourage you to simply start giving the Consensus Rorschach to couples (and families) and see what happens. I predict that over time, you'll come to recognize common ways that couples approach this task, and also be able to see unique and meaningful aspects of each couple's interactions.

13

"But I Was Only Trying to Help!": Failure of a Therapeutic Assessment

Finn and Tonsager (1997) defined one instance of failure in Therapeutic Assessment as when the client feels "less capable, demoralized, and even abused after the assessment" (p. 380). Because I have devoted much of my professional career to studying how psychological assessments can be therapeutic for clients, I was very concerned several years ago when a couples' assessment I conducted resulted in one member of the couple feeling highly traumatized. Since that time, I have reflected a great deal on that particular assessment. In this chapter I share what I have learned so far.

Summary of the Assessment

The flow chart for a therapeutic couples' assessment was presented in an earlier chapter. (See Exhibit 11–1).

Referral. Ted and Nancy, as I'll call them, had been married 13 years when they were jointly referred to me by their family/couples therapist, Sara, and by Nancy's individual therapist, Louis, both of whom were long-time friends of mine. Both clinicians said that they felt stuck in their work

This chapter is drawn from a paper I presented to the Society for Personality Assessment (Finn, 2004). I am grateful to Gregory J. Meyer for his comments on an earlier draft.

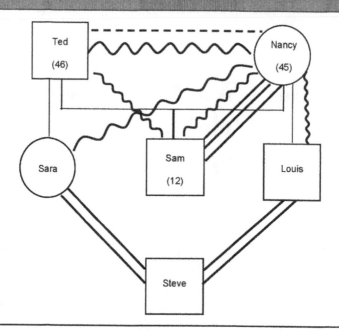

EXHIBIT 13–1
Sociogram of Relationships at the Beginning of Assessment

with these clients, but this was especially true of my friend, Sara. When making the referral, Sara explained how upset she was that Nancy and Ted set few limits on their 12-year-old son, Sam, who in turn was becoming increasingly aggressive at home and at school (see Exhibit 13–1). Sara thought that Ted wanted to be firmer with Sam, but that Nancy had convinced him that firm limits were unreasonable. Sara also believed that Nancy was setting Sam up to be abusive and physically violent, and that this was part of Nancy's desire to play the "victim," while getting Sam to act out her anger. Sara was clearly frustrated with Ted's passivity and inactivity, but less so, in retrospect, than with Nancy's subtle control over the family. Sara believed that individual and marital issues were getting routed through Sam, and had tried to get the couple to work on their own relationship, but she reported that conjoint sessions almost always got waylaid to talking about Sam. When the couple's issues did get discussed, Nancy would characterize Ted as "harsh" and "uncaring," a picture that Sara said did not fit with her experience of him. In fact, Sara saw Nancy as being quite "mean" towards Ted, who "just took it." Sara hoped the assessment would help highlight the couple's issues for Ted and Nancy and help correct what she saw as Nancy's "distortions" of Ted.

Nancy's individual therapist, my friend Louis, was in contact with Sara and was aware of her experience of the couple. Louis complained that he had to "walk on eggshells" in his work with Nancy. If Louis didn't mirror her exactly in their sessions, Nancy would get quite defensive or "crater" into deep sobbing. Louis believed Nancy hadn't really worked through a number of issues from her family of origin, but Louis hadn't been able to say this to her directly as Nancy strongly believed she had "been there and done that." Louis hoped the assessment would help Nancy come closer to facing her unresolved issues and to understanding her own part in the problems with Sam and with Ted.

Initial Contacts.   Nancy called me to initiate the assessment; unfortunately, due to my schedule, I was not able to see the couple for about 4 months. At our initial meeting, Nancy opened the session by thanking me for seeing them and saying that she was excited about the assessment. It soon became clear that Ted did not exactly share this sentiment. He claimed not to have seen the information sheet I had mailed them months earlier, clearly was quite skeptical about the process after I explained it, and said bluntly that he was not sure the assessment would be worth the money it cost. I was a bit taken aback at his flat-footedness. Nancy also caught me completely off guard by saying she had arranged for their insurance company to mail me an application to be a preferred provider; as soon as I filled that out, everything would be finalized for them to proceed. When I made it clear I had no intention of completing the 50-page application, Nancy said she was sure that I had agreed to this over the phone. I knew I had not and said so. At this point, Ted got even more upset and said he would have to think the whole idea over more. I thought this was an excellent idea. We talked more about what the assessment would be like if they proceeded, and I asked them to call me when they had made up their minds. To my surprise, a month later Ted called to say they would go ahead and I set up the individual meetings that form the first part of the couples' assessment.

Early Assessment Sessions.   The initial assessment meetings seemed to go quite well. Nancy—who had once trained to be a mental health professional—approached her assessment sessions with eagerness and dedication, asking a number of sophisticated questions about herself and the couple relationship (see Exhibit 13–2).

I was impressed by Nancy's systemic thinking and the willingness to "own her part" that seemed to be reflected in her questions. Early on,

---

EXHIBIT 13–2
Ted and Nancy's Questions for the Assessment

Nancy's Questions

1. Why doesn't Ted care enough to see me? Why doesn't he care enough to address my needs too?
2. I really wonder about Ted's level of depression. He doesn't seem curious about that. What can I do in that situation?
3. Am I carrying depression for more than myself and if so, how can I not?
4. I see Ted as very angry. He doesn't see himself that way. What can I do about that?
5. Where are my blind spots? Where is my "bad stuff" and what I don't want to see about myself?
6. How am I participating in projective identification in this relationship?
7. What can I do if Ted chooses not to grow and change?
8. What are all my tears about? I understand the grieving process is necessary, but how much more do I have to do?

Ted's Questions

1. Why—when we have differences of opinion—can we only come up with decisions that are win-lose, not win-win?
2. Why is Nancy more unhappy than I am? What can I do that would help her be happier?
3. What would it take for me to be more in touch with my feelings?

Questions from Both

1. What's keeping us stuck? We rarely can reconcile differences.
2. What gets in the way of our showing our love for each other?
3. Why hasn't couples therapy helped us more? Should we find a new couples therapist?

Nancy also brought me in numerous pages of material she hoped would help me understand her—including a genogram of her family with detailed notes about how family relationships had affected her, as well as journals and other writings from significant periods of her life. Ted—a computer designer—was somewhat harder to engage and posed many fewer questions to be addressed by the assessment. He clearly was less comfortable with the language of emotions and admitted he was skeptical about many of Sara's ideas about Sam's problems. But, he seemed genuinely puzzled by why Nancy was so unhappy in the relationship and what he could do to make things better. He warmed up and showed real passion when he talked about his work and how competent and comfortable he felt in that venue. I came to admire his willingness to keep working in therapy and to do the assessment with Nancy, although it clearly was very unfamiliar territory.

The early testing sessions—where I administer standardized tests to each member of the couple—seemed to go quite well. Again, Nancy was quite forthcoming. She quickly completed the MMPI–2, journaled long entries to the Early Memory Procedure (EMP; Bruhn, 1992) and produced a 31-response Rorschach protocol. She also broke down crying at numerous points when we discussed the painful humiliation she had received from her parents, a difficult first marriage, and how lonely she felt in her relationship with Ted. And although she seemed ashamed of her emotionality, saying that she had been sure she had resolved all the pain from her childhood, I thought I was able to support her in accepting her feelings by saying that I too was often caught off guard by finding unresolved feelings I had previously worked on in therapy.

Ted worked quite hard on all the tests, but was more taciturn and less psychologically minded when we discussed them. He admitted there were some similarities between his deferential approach to his controlling mother and his stance towards Nancy, but otherwise he had little reactions to the EMP. He had trouble remembering any incidents before age 10. His Rorschach was shorter than Nancy's (R = 22), but had much more color and a lower Lambda than did hers. (His Lambda was .16 and hers was 1.38.) Overall, I felt good about the assessment at that point, and both referring therapists reported that the couple had said they were enjoying the process. Thus, I took a week off from meeting with Ted and Nancy to analyze the test results and plan the assessment intervention and the eventual feedback to the couple.

Reviewing the Standardized Testing. In retrospect, I think it was at this point that I made my first significant mistake. Typically, when conducting complex assessments, my colleagues and I at the Center for Therapeutic Assessment present our work in a group meeting and assist each other in understanding the clients and planning the later stages of those assessments. Unfortunately, I was unable to do this with my assessment of

Ted and Nancy, as several members of our group had a previous relationship with Nancy. I have a second group of experienced colleagues where I regularly get consultation; but members of this group also knew Nancy from another setting, so I decided, with some regret to "go it on my own," rather than look farther for someone with whom to talk things over.

I especially regretted the lack of collegial support in this case because as I looked at the results of the testing, it appeared to me that Nancy's protocols suggested many more character difficulties and much more underlying distress than did Ted's. Her MMPI–2 was fairly guarded (L = 62T, K = 78T, and S = 75T), but nonetheless revealed a spike of 71T on Scale 4. I realized that this elevation reflected in part the spunk and determination Nancy had used to survive a difficult childhood (Caldwell, 2001); but to me it also fit my experience of Nancy as being somewhat of a bully. Her Rorschach scores gave further evidence of an externalizing and somewhat obsessional character adaptation (HVI and OBS were both positive). However, the Rorschach also suggested that this character armor protected a great deal of unresolved pain and anger, as indicated by DEPI = 5, S = 5, Fd = 1, and a Trauma Content Index (Armstrong & Lowenstein, 1990) of .16. Apparently, Nancy's self-view—that she had worked through all her major issues—did not appear to be accurate, and the evidence suggested she was prone to project her unresolved issues onto others.

Ted's MMPI–2 was just slightly guarded (K = 60T, S = 70T) and had only one minor elevation, on Scale 0 (60T). Taken together, these scores seemed to reflect his reserved and somewhat constrained character. I also noted with some interest his score of 62T on the MMPI–2 Overcontrolled Hostility scale, which did not surprise me as I suspected he was full of resentment towards Nancy and other people whom he "let get their way." I was surprised, however, by the amount of chromatic color on his Rorschach. His Weighted SumC was 4.5. (He had 9 M, so was solidly introversive as I had expected.) And his FC/CF+C ratio was 3/3—suggesting to me that he was much more emotionally responsive than he appeared. Ted's protocol also had a number of shading responses, including two Texture responses and a Vista response, although his EA was so large that he had a D of 0 and an Adjusted D of 0, which fit his report that he was not experiencing much distress. The Rorschach also suggested that Ted leaned towards withdrawal and self-involvement in his character defenses, for he had two reflection responses and his Isolation Index was .27.

In sum, I could see how Ted's emotional awkwardness, withdrawal, and narcissistic self-involvement could rub salt in Nancy's wounds. I could even see him as being passive–aggressive at times. But I found no evidence in the testing or in my interactions with him that he was severely depressed, full of anger, or incapable of feeling for others as Nancy suggested and as was reflected in her questions. In fact, Nancy—who believed her years of therapy had resolved her emotional issues satisfactorily—appeared to be projecting some of her own characteristics on Ted. In turn, Ted, who wasn't confident or skilled enough to counter such projections—instead was withdrawing, pulling inward, and overcontrolling his anger, thereby acting in ways that appeared to confirm Nancy's attributions.

As I pondered these thoughts, I felt anxious. By that point in the assessment, I knew Nancy was not ready to entertain such hypotheses from me, and I suspected Ted wasn't either. Most of what I wanted to say seemed like Level 3 (or Level 7!) information. Thus, I put a great deal of hope on the assessment intervention session, believing that we could begin talking about some of these issues at that time.

Consensus Rorschach. As described in chapter 12, in couples' assessments I often employ a modified form of the Consensus Rorschach as an assessment intervention. I hoped this task would give Ted, Nancy, and me an *in vivo* example of their problematic interactions, so that we could observe them, discuss them, and collaborate in reaching new understandings. As sometimes happens with this procedure, however, Ted and Nancy worked together beautifully in reaching conjoint Rorschach responses to the five cards I gave them. There was almost no tension as they discussed their individual responses, negotiated "win–win" compromises, and reported their joint decisions to me to write down. At the midpoint of the procedure, I asked them to take a 15-min break, while I cued up portions of the videotape for us to watch and discuss (see chap. 12). I planned to show these excerpts and to ask them about the contextual factors that made this joint task so easy for them, compared to their attempts to work together at home. I urged them not to talk to one another about the task until we could do so together after the break.

However, when I went out to the waiting room, I found Nancy in tears, and Ted looking shut down and sitting across the room from her. I invited them back into my office and gently asked what had happened. Apparently, they had started off the break reading magazines, until

Nancy asked if Ted wanted to talk. He (thinking of my admonition not to discuss the Consensus Rorschach) had quipped, "What shall we talk about, the abject misery of our lives?" Nancy had felt very hurt by this comment, and had crumpled. Ted explained to me that he had been trying to make a joke and had told Nancy so. Nancy did not believe this, however, and said this was the kind of "sadistic" remark Ted always made, and that he had intended to humiliate her about being unhappy with their relationship. Ted tried to defend himself, at which point Nancy accused him of not caring about her feelings. He had then retreated, which is when I had found them in the waiting room.

As I listened, I thought I might understand what had happened and I asked Ted if he had been feeling unsure of himself when Nancy asked if they might talk together. He said that he had, and agreed that his "joke" had been an attempt to deal with his awkwardness about not knowing what to say. I asked Nancy if she could believe that Ted hadn't intended to hurt her, and she said no, she was sure he had meant to "stab her in the heart." I then backed up and asked Ted if he could "feel for Nancy's pain," even if he hadn't intentionally caused it. He said he did. I asked if he knew from previous experience that Nancy didn't react well to jokes with any hint of sarcasm in them. He agreed he should have remembered this, and said again that he hadn't meant to hurt her. I then wondered aloud if it had been at all scary for them to get along so beautifully during the Consensus Rorschach. They both said they had been very surprised at how well it went. At this point, Nancy stopped crying. I said that sometimes, when things go really well for a couple, when previously there has been a lot of disappointment, the partners find it hard to tolerate the good period, and unconsciously find ways to create more distance so as to not get their hopes up and get hurt again.

Ted said he could see how that would work and perhaps his comment had been his way of "getting back to familiar territory." Nancy countered that these things happened all the time, even when they were getting along terribly, and that she wasn't afraid of being close to Ted; it was what she most longed for. I asked her what would happen if she let herself entertain the possibility that Ted hadn't been malicious when he made his comment. She said she would have to completely change her conception of things, that she didn't trust him to know what he was feeling, and that she was really good at telling what was going on with people.

I think at that point I was frustrated myself and also felt protective of Ted. My intent was to help Nancy see the systemic aspects of her and Ted's difficulties, but in retrospect, I went "one-up" and proceeded to give Nancy a little lecture. I told her I thought both she and Ted had had parents who were controlling and critical, but that the two of them had reacted to this in very different ways. I said she had learned to scan the environment carefully and to be very distrustful of other people's motives. Ted, in contrast, had learned to withdraw and put up a thick barrier. The result, I explained, was kind of like the marriage between a "bull in a china shop" (i.e., a seemingly insensitive person) and the "princess and the pea" (an overly sensitive person). This was at times a disastrous pairing, but I believed neither person consciously intended to hurt the other.

Summary/Discussion Sessions. Again, in retrospect, I now see that I "lost" Nancy at that point in the assessment. I remember her somewhat dazed look as she and Ted left that evening. They did return several weeks later for two long summary/discussion sessions (which Sara and Louis were unable to attend), where I tried my best to present a balanced systemic picture of the difficulties in their relationship. Nancy cried through most of the feedback about her individual test results, but insisted that we continue even when I expressed my strong reservations that the information clearly was overwhelming her. I asked her at numerous points what she thought of my hunches—that her childhood had been even more neglectful and abusive than she had previously realized and that she still had more "unprocessed" feelings from those events than she had recognized. She said that she guessed this was in fact true. When I reviewed Ted's test results and asked her reactions to these, she meekly said that she guessed she had been distorting him. When we discussed their questions about the couple relationship, she again appeared to agree with my formulations, but there was very little energy in her statements.

Postassessment Feedback. Still, it wasn't until after I sent my summary letter that I learned how traumatic the assessment was for Nancy. I heard from my friend Louis, Nancy's individual therapist, that Nancy had taken to bed for a week after receiving the letter. Nancy complained to Louis that I was much "harder" on her than on Ted in the letter and had blamed her for all the couple's problems and the difficulties with Sam. Incidentally, at first I didn't think this was at all true, and Louis and Sara reassured me that it was not. However, recently I reviewed the letter again with a different colleague, who pointed out several places where the letter came across as imbalanced.

Around this time, Nancy told Louis that she was considering filing a formal complaint about me with the Texas psychology licensing board. She never did this, but she did—according to Louis—spend months in her individual therapy energetically refuting the various statements I had made about her in the letter. Ted reportedly had initially felt fine about the assessment, but then backed Nancy up in her huge disappointment, saying that he never had believed the assessment would be worth the money it cost. The couple did follow my recommendation to find a new couples therapist, who would work with them separately from the family therapy with Sara, and Ted even contacted me at several points to get referrals. I sent word through Louis that I would be willing to meet with Nancy or with the couple, free of charge, to discuss their experience of the assessment, but they never took me up on this. Recently, I learned that Ted, Nancy, and Sam left town due to a change in Ted's job, so I imagine I will never get the chance to meet directly with Nancy.

Lessons Learned

In the months since this assessment, I have spent considerable time rehashing it with Louis and Sara, and various outside consultants, including Dr. Paul Lerner. Here are a few of the things I've learned so far:

Beware of "Oracular" Transferences

In his classic book, Shafer (1954) elegantly described the various transferences pulled for by the assessment situation and cautioned against clients' tendency to see the assessor as an "oracle." I now believe that Nancy's hurt at the end of the assessment was magnified by her idealization of me at the beginning (which was fed, in part, by Louis and Sara), and that Nancy genuinely hoped and expected me to help her by "getting the goods" on Ted in the assessment and then scolding him resoundingly for being callous towards her. Nancy's putting me on such a high pedestal not only left more room for me to fall,

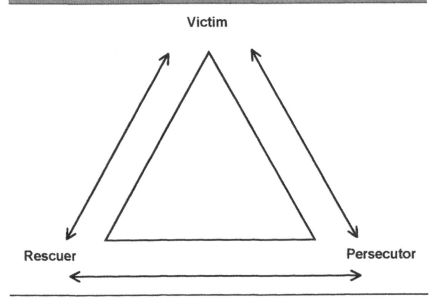

EXHIBIT 13–3
Karpman's (1968) "Drama Triangle"

Victim

Rescuer   Persecutor

but it also meant that hypotheses I put forward were harder for her to reject and therefore more painful.

In retrospect, I didn't do as much as I could have to dispel Nancy's (as well as Sara's and Louis's) idealized view of me and of the assessment situation. I could have said plainly at the beginning that I didn't know if the assessment would be helpful, although I hoped it would. In the summary/discussion sessions, I could have made it clear that I don't view test scores as "Truth" about an individual, which might have made it easier for Nancy to reject statements I made that were not useful for her to hear at that point in time.

Karpman's Triangle Is Hard to Avoid

Some of you may be familiar with Karpman's (1968) "drama triangle," describing the reciprocal roles of victim, persecutor, and rescuer (see Exhibit 13–3). Karpman describes the power that these internalized "scripts" of relationships have over us, and how difficult it is for most of us to avoid these roles as they become activated. In retrospect, both Nancy and Ted came into the assessment presenting themselves as victims, and to some extent so did the therapists, Sara and Louis, although both professionals also admitted to struggling with impulses to act out as persecutors. I was initially invited in as an idealized rescuer, and willingly took on this role, thinking I could maintain an equidistant stance. However, as Karpman predicts, all our roles were unstable and by the end of the assessment, I had fallen, subtly, into the persecutor role by attempting to "set Nancy straight" about her part in things—which in retrospect was the hidden agenda of Ted, Sara, Nancy, and perhaps even Louis. I don't mean to deny my own responsibility here; I had my own reasons stemming from my own psychology for having fallen into the persecutor role. Still, at the point that I acted out as a persecutor, Nancy was confirmed in her victim role, she and Ted pulled together more closely together, and when she threatened to report me, I got a chance to feel like a victim, just like Nancy. It was at that point, when I found myself protesting, "But I was only trying to help!" (a direct quote from Karpman's account of the rescuer-turned-persecutor-turned-victim) that I realized I was in the drama triangle script, and I was able to take another step back and analyze what happened.

The Payoff of Masochism

Before this assessment, I thought I understood from my work with traumatized clients the kind of sadism that can be expressed through the victim role. But it was Paul Lerner who helped me realize that I hadn't fully appreciated another payoff of masochism—the sense of omnipotent control over others. When I discussed this case with Lerner, he pointed out that Nancy's many questions about herself—for example, "Where are my blind spots?" "How am I participating in projective identification?"—although sophisticated, were most likely not questions that she wanted me to help her answer through the assessment. As Lerner explained, these were in fact, invitations for me to "beat her up" by presenting her with conclusions she was in no way ready to consider. Depending on your theory, you can believe that Nancy unconsciously (a) wanted me to accept her invitation to traumatize her, as object relations theory might posit; or (b) secretly hoped I would pass the test by turning down her invitation, as control mastery theory would suggest (Weiss, 1993). In either case, if I fell into confirming Nancy's beliefs that others were out to harm her, she would have the decidedly bittersweet relief of knowing that her "story" still seemed to fit the relational terrain she found herself in, and that she, as she said, "was really good at knowing what was going on with people."

The Multiple Motives Behind Assessment Questions

This leads to another conclusion that in retrospect seems really obvious. In Therapeutic Assessment, when we invite clients to pose questions to be addressed by the assessment, we should not assume that they are open to all possible answers to such questions. In retrospect, I should have known this, as I have written before about the need to carefully adapt assessment feedback to people's existing conceptions of themselves. But I don't believe I have ever understood so clearly before this assessment how difficult it can be for us assessors to "contain" certain ideas we have when a larger system is pushing for us to express them. I have started a new practice of asking—early in an assessment—not only about people's "best guesses" to the answers to their assessment questions, but what would be "the worst possible thing" they could be told about themselves through the assessment. If I had done this with Nancy, I fantasize that I would have been even more prepared for the possible trauma that could result from the assessment (assuming, of course, that she would have been able to honestly answer this question).

Be Careful of Taking on the Agendas of Referring Therapists

As I mentioned earlier, I now suspect that the two referring therapists— Sara and Louis—secretly hoped the assessment would confront Nancy with information about herself that they were finding it difficult to manage—that is, how she could come across as fragile and controlling at the same time, and how difficult it was to relate to her because of her tendency to feel wounded by anything but absolute agreement with her point of view. I have long been aware of the complexity of managing referring professionals' hidden agendas in an assessment (see chap. 9). However, I now suspect that I was even more at risk to "take on" Sara's and Louis's frustrations because they were dear and trusted friends of mine. And I probably was more anxious than I was aware of because I wanted to impress my friends and help them in a touchy situation. This awareness will make me more cautious in the future when assessing clients for referring professionals who are also friends.

Therapeutic Assessment Is Often Too Difficult to Do Alone

Finally, I am humbled to be reminded of something I have written about before: Therapeutic Assessment, because of the brief and powerful connections formed between assessors and clients, is often too difficult to do without the assessor having the backing and collaboration of a community of skilled and savvy colleagues (Finn, 2002a). The transferences, countertransferences, and attachments formed in these encounters are extremely intense; it is partly due to this fact that Therapeutic Assessment can be so powerfully beneficial. But for these same reasons, the techniques of Therapeutic Assessment are also potentially harmful, and should be practiced in certain instances only with the support and assistance of others. I fantasize that if I had pushed myself to obtain consultation before the final stages of the assessment—perhaps by calling Dr. Lerner or someone else—that I might have avoided this assessment failure and helped Ted and Nancy achieve a new point of view. I often struggle to recognize that I need help and to ask for it when I do. This experience was a powerful reminder of the potential costs of that kind of hubris.

14

Collaborative Child Assessment as a Family Systems Intervention

In schools and inpatient hospitals, it is still fairly common that young children undergo psychological assessments with minimal involvement of parents or other family members. In outpatient clinical practice, parental involvement is more feasible and also typically necessary to promote parents' cooperating with a child's assessment (e.g., their giving consent, bringing the child to appointments, and paying the bill). Thus, most assessors involve parents in outpatient child evaluations in certain basic ways, for example by: (a) interviewing them at the beginning of the assessment about a child's problems; (b) asking them to complete rating scales, such as the Child Behavior Check List (Achenbach, 1991) or the Parenting Stress Inventory (Abidin, 1995); and (c) giving parents some feedback at the end of the assessment about the child's test results.

In this chapter, I argue that whenever possible, it is extremely useful to involve parents and other custodial guardians (e.g., stepparents, grandparents) as full collaborators in a child's assessment. Such involvement can take many forms; however, the basic principle is that parents are treated as essential participant–observers, who work with the assessor to jointly construct an understanding of the child's problems in living. I have come to believe that the best way to help children through as-

This chapter is based on a paper presented to the Society for Personality Assessment (Finn, 1997a).

sessment is by assisting their parents and caregivers in developing more accurate, empathic, and useful "stories" about why those children have problems. When parents are involved as active collaborators in an assessment, the assessor has more of a chance to influence the current story. Also, the assessor gains rich information about a child's interpersonal network and the contribution of family dynamics to the child's problems in living. Last, the assessor is presented with numerous opportunities to make systemic interventions that address the child's or family's presenting issues. As such this approach fits with the idea that psychological assessment of a child is potentially a potent family systems intervention (Fulmer, Cohen, & Monaco, 1985; Ziffer, 1985).

I now discuss ten instances of parent–assessor collaboration and illustrate their usefulness as systemic interventions (see Exhibit 14–1).

1.   Work with Parents to Define the Goals of the Psychological Assessment

As explained in chapter 1, in Therapeutic Assessment, we begin an evaluation by asking clients to pose questions that they wish to address with psychological assessment. When I assess young children, I typically invite parents alone to an initial meeting, where I work with them to define their questions and goals.[1] I listen carefully and compassionately to their concerns and gather information about the presenting issues. This practice serves many systemic purposes. First, by acknowledging the parents' right to specify the parameters of the assessment, I support them as heads of the family and as the people who can have the most impact on a child. Even if a school, therapist, or other professional have requested the assessment, I reinforce the idea that parents are the most important people in a child's life. Second, by asking parents to leave the child at home for the initial session, I reinforce an appropriate generational boundary that is not always kept in some families. I remember one mother who insisted that it would be fine for her 6-year-old son to attend

---

[1] I use the word "parents" throughout the chapter, but recognize that many children are raised by grandparents, aunts and uncles, foster parents, and other caregivers.

EXHIBIT 14–1
Ten Ways to Make Child Assessment Collaborative

1. Work with parents to define the goals of the psychological assessment.
2. Negotiate with parents to allow an adolescent to have private questions for the assessment.
3. Ask parents to prepare a child for the first meeting with the assessor.
4. Ask parents to observe a child's testing sessions and discuss their observations afterwards with the assessor.
5. Enlist parents in collecting historical information or systematic data about a problem behavior.
6. Ask parents if they are willing to be tested as part of their child's evaluation.
7. Schedule one or more family or parent-child sessions as part of a child's assessment.
8. Ask parents to corroborate and modify assessment findings presented in the summary/discussion session.
9. Ask parents to review reports for schools, therapists, or other referral sources and to help present assessment findings.
10. Involve parents in giving oral or written feedback to the child about the assessment results.

---

the initial session with her and her husband.[2] "Oh, we talk with him about anything," she told me. "He already knows everything we think." I requested that we meet alone, and was pleased at the end of the initial meeting when she spontaneously commented that it was "probably good" to have left the boy at home, so we all could talk more freely.

Whom one invites to the initial session can also impact a family system. It is not unusual that a mother sets the appointment and asks if her husband "really needs to be there" as "he has to work." I do everything I can to get both parents to attend significant portions of the psychological assessment and have found that this alone seems to have an impact, for example, by getting an emotionally distant parent reinvolved, or setting the stage to discover that the parents disagree about the best way to

---

[2] I had already verified that this was not a matter of the family not having child care and therefore needing to bring the child along.

handle the child's problems. In the case of divorced parents, even if only
one has initiated the assessment, I inquire whether they would be comfortable meeting together for the initial session. And I almost never undertake a child assessment without the consent and full cooperation of
both parents. This stance sends the message that I consider both parents
important to understanding the child and also that it will be best for the
child if the parents have a cordial enough postdivorce relationship that
they can cooperate on matters involving the child's mental health care.

The questions parents generate are themselves rich sources of information about the family system. Contrast these two sets of questions: (a)
"Why does Johnny lie and fail to take responsibility for things?" and
"Would a boy's ranch be the best place for him?" versus (b) "How can we
bring out the best in Aaron?" and "Is there anything we are doing that is
contributing to Aaron's problems?" As you see, such questions not only
provide information about a child, but also about the parents, and potentially, important family dynamics that might relate to the child's problems. When the grandparents who posed the first set of questions told
me that Johnny had always been difficult and was "just like his father"
(their son), I wondered if they were scapegoating Johnny to avoid personal or marital difficulties, or grief about their shortcomings as parents.
In the second instance, I suspected that Aaron's parents were open to
feedback about their overprotective style and I was able to gear the assessment to help them coddle him less.

Of course, it is not only the content of parents' questions but the process through which they are generated that is informative and potentially therapeutic. I have had parents who never could agree on a single
assessment question, and had to give separate lists of questions. As you
might suspect, the parents' inability to "get on the same page" was part
of the child's problems, and I made it a goal of the assessment to help the
parents reach a common understanding of the child that would be ac-
ceptable to each. I'm also very interested when one parent dominates the
initial session, posing lots of questions, while the other sits passively by.
Again, this makes me wonder if the child's issues pertain in part to one
overinvolved and one underinvolved parent.

Last, I believe that the process of gathering assessment questions from
parents can promote their curiosity, lessen their anxiety, enlist their observing egos, and help disrupt projections they may have on a child.
More than one couple has commented to me that they felt better about

their child just from having put their concerns into words and knowing that those concerns would be explored and addressed in an assessment.

2.   Negotiate with Parents to Allow an Adolescent Child to Have Private Questions for the Assessment

Typically, when a child is older (e.g., age 13 and above), I ask parents beforehand if they will allow the child to pose his or her own questions for the assessment, which I answer to the child, and that will remain private from the parents unless the child opts to share them after feedback. Quite frankly, I started this practice as a way to get adolescents to cooperate with psychological assessment, and then discovered that it was a potential family systems intervention in itself. Obviously, this approach promotes differentiation and separation–individuation in a family, and I have had several instances where enmeshed parents initially objected to the idea of their child's having any privacy. By talking with them about adolescent development and the need for teenagers to have some autonomy, I eventually got these parents to agree to my plan. Interestingly, in all the families, the children immediately became more cooperative and less rebellious, which by itself made quite an impression on the family.[3]

3.   Ask Parents to Prepare a Child for the First Meeting With the Assessor

With young children, my second session is with the parents and child together. In preparation, at the prior meeting, I ask parents to talk to their

---

[3]In adolescent assessments, my initial meeting involves both parents and child. Following this, I have separate meetings with the adolescent and the parents. Typically, I share parents' assessment questions with the adolescent, but not vice versa. This is my way of acknowledging that the adolescent is in the more vulnerable position, especially if the parents are not being tested.

child about the purpose of the assessment before we all meet. I also ask if they know what they will say, or if they would like guidance from me. If appropriate, I then coach parents on how to handle this discussion with their child.

Clearly, this practice gives additional information about the family system and about potential targets of intervention. I have had several families who didn't want to say anything to their child about the real purpose of the assessment for fear the child would feel badly, and one family who asked if I would come to their house and pretend to be a family friend so the child "wouldn't have to feel ashamed" about seeing a psychologist. (As you might imagine, I concluded it was the parents who were struggling with intense shame about their child's difficulties.) In other families, this discussion highlighted unhealthy triangulations within the family system, for example, the father who said he would tell his son, "Your mother thinks you have a learning disability. I don't, but we're going to have you tested anyway." In one other case, my coaching led to our seeing that an assessment was not really necessary. The parents told their daughter they wanted to have her assessed because they were afraid she was using drugs, something they had been afraid to say before. Through their discussions with her, the parents discovered that they had been misinterpreting a lot of her normal adolescent behaviors, in part because of their own drug use as teenagers. Trust was restored once they all started talking.

In general, by asking parents to discuss the assessment with their child, I am sending the message that "nothing is too bad to talk about." Also, I am modeling respect and empathy for the child, as if to say, "It may be scary and confusing for your child to come for an assessment without being given some explanation first. Your child has a right to be told something about why she is being asked to do the testing." Last, if I do coach parents on what to say, I generally suggest that they frame the intent of the assessment systemically, for example, "We're hoping the psychologist can help us all figure out why you're depressed and how the family can help with this," rather than, "We want to know why you're depressed all the time." Clearly, a single communication will not change a family system, but such statements reflect a whole philosophy that I attempt to impart to families throughout an assessment.

4.   Ask Parents to Observe a Child's Testing Sessions and Discuss Their Observations Afterwards With the Assessor

This is a tactic I borrowed from Fischer (1985/1994). Although not always feasible or advisable (e.g., with adolescents, or with overinvolved parents), it sometimes can be extremely useful to have parents observe assessment sessions. When possible, it seems best to have parents observe unobtrusively, through a two-way mirror, over a video hook-up, or with the parent(s) behind the child's back, off to the side of the room. If the parent is out of room, I always let the child know he or she is being observed. Afterwards, the parents and I compare notes and ask each other questions about what we observed. If the child is not old enough to be alone while the parents and I talk, I usually call after the session and talk with the parent(s) over the phone.[4]

I find that having parents observe testing sessions empowers them and demystifies the psychological assessment process, as well as giving parents a chance to discover answers to their own questions about their child. (Remember, in collaborative assessment, we consider it more useful for clients to reach their own insights with our guidance than for us to offer interpretations they have not yet considered.) When parents observe assessment sessions, it also provides a chance for the assessor to intervene on a "perceptual level" with parents who are projecting on their children. I remember one parent who watched me give the Bender Visual Motor Gestalt Test (Bender, 1938) to her depressed 12-year-old son. The boy was very self-critical and kept saying that he didn't think he could do the task. After the session, the mother and I had the following exchange:

---

[4]A not unreasonable concern is that if a child knows parents are observing, it will inhibit the child so much that the assessment is hampered. If I believed this was happening in a particular case, I would discontinue the parental observation. However, my experience with young children is that they either seem unphased by their parents' watching, or they use the opportunity to send the parents "messages" they want the parents to hear and that I can help make sure the parents grasp.

Mother: Did you see how manipulative he was? That's the way he is at home all the time!

Steve: I'm not sure. What did he do that looked manipulative to you?

Mother: Why, when he kept saying he couldn't draw those designs. He was just being lazy! It's like at home when I ask him to do chores and he doesn't want to do them. He just expects to be waited on!

Steve: Oh, is that how you saw it? I had a different idea at the time: that he felt insecure and afraid that he would fail, so he kept trying to get out of performing. He seemed like he doubted his own abilities.

Mother: Really? I never thought of it that way!

Steve: Well, I'm not sure that I'm right. But I also wondered if he might be depressed. Does he always look so sad and tired?

Mother: I'm not sure. That just seems normal to me.

As you can see, in such interactions I'm careful not to insist on being right, because I may not be. But just comparing different interpretations of events often helps parents start to see their child differently and more compassionately.

Another marvelous possibility is that parents will feel less inadequate when they see the assessor struggling with the same problems they encounter with their child. Some years ago, a mother watched me try to handle her 5-year-old daughter as she threw a major temper tantrum when I wouldn't let her do whatever she wanted in our assessment session. Afterwards, the mother told me she was so relieved to see that it "wasn't just her," and she and I compared notes about what did and did not work when her daughter was in such a state. Much later, the mother told me that event was "worth all the money" paid for the assessment, because her relatives and the girl's teachers had been implying that the girl's tantrums were entirely the mother's fault. Eventually, with the mother's input, I found a way of handling the 5-year-old's meltdowns by stating firm limits beforehand, sticking to them, and ignoring her when she had a tantrum. Even better, the mother was able to successfully adopt this approach at home.

Finally, when parents observe assessment sessions, it provides an opportunity to help them think contextually and to disrupt global attributions they have of their child. For example, after several sessions with a child who was well-behaved with me but rebellious at home, the parents admitted, "We can't believe he's so good with you. They've told us he's an angel at school, but we haven't believed them. I wonder if we're doing something wrong at home?" I was able to lead them in thinking about what was different about the assessment and school context, and to see if we could export any of those elements to the home.

5. Enlist Parents in Collecting Historical Information or Systematic Data About a Problem Behavior, Either by Themselves or With the Help of Other Family Members

When there is a problem behavior that occurs within the family context and is not likely to be so visible in sessions with the assessor, it can be very useful to train parents and other family members to be objective observers of the behavior and to contribute data to the assessment. For example, parents might be asked to track a child's temper tantrums, what happens right before they occur, how the parents respond, and what happens afterwards. Alternatively, parents may be asked to contact collateral sources and other informants to collect information that is relevant to their assessment questions. When parents are enlisted as "co-investigators" in such ways, I find they have increased curiosity, are less reactive to their child's behavior, and often have insights that they can readily put to use in addressing their own presenting concerns.

This approach also provides an indirect way of assessing a family's readiness to change. For example, I kept asking a set of parents to contact their pediatrician for records pertaining to their child's early history. They kept "forgetting" to do so. Eventually, it became clear that the parents were so overwhelmed with various responsibilities that they found even this simple task impossible. We then were able to discuss how little energy they had to make substantial changes in their lives. It became clear that any suggestions I came up with would have to take account of this reality. Yet another family made it clear that they didn't want to "do any work" to understand what was going on with their son; they preferred to just "drop him off" and let me deal with the problem. When I questioned this approach, I found that both parents came from wealthy families and had been raised by hired caregivers. Although they were trying to be more involved with their son than their parents had been with them, clearly they hadn't yet shed all the attitudes their parents had modeled for them.

By enlisting parents as data gatherers, one can sometimes "alter proximity" (i.e., shift interpersonal closeness) within a family. For example, some years ago I assessed a 10-year-old girl with inconsistent enuresis. I asked her parents to chart the child's fluid intake during and after dinner and to keep track of her bedwetting. To do this, the parents had to pay more attention to their daughter in the evenings. To our surprise, the enuresis decreased. It later came out through the testing that the girl felt neglected by how tired and uninvolved the parents were at night after working all day. Her enuresis seemed to be one way of drawing their attention.

In another instance, I was asked to see a 6-year-old boy with severe temper outbursts and his mother. Due to the mother's drug abuse, the boy been raised by his maternal grandparents during the first 4 years of his life. At the time of the assessment, child and mother had little contact with his grandparents. I asked the mother if she would be willing contact her parents to get information about the boy's early developmental milestones. Her phone call brought them all back into contact and eventually provided the mother and child with greatly needed support. I don't think this would have happened if I had been the one to call and talk with the grandparents.

6. Ask Parents if They Are Willing to Be Tested as Part of Their Child's Evaluation

Some assessors routinely do this whenever parents will cooperate. I don't always test parents, but try to judge whether they are likely to feel threatened by such a request. One way to gauge this is to look at parents' questions for the assessment. If the questions are totally child focused and/or scapegoating, it probably is too big a jump to suggest that the parents' personalities have any import for addressing the child's problems. Some parents, however, ask a question like, "Are there any things we can do for Amy that we are not doing?" Such questions show the parents are open to looking at their role in the child's problems. With such families, I suggest that it might be helpful to get a formal measure of the parents' personalities, strengths, and struggles. I remind parents of their relevant assessment questions and then present my rationale in more or less systemic terms: "In thinking about what else you can do, it will be useful to see how your personalities interact with that of your child" or "I'd like to see how your child's problems have been impacting you." I might also help the parents take my request less personally by saying that parental testing is a routine part of many child assessments.

Obviously, how parents react to a request to be tested provides excellent information about whether they are ready to accept systemic formulations of their child's problems. If a parent asks, "How the heck would my MMPI–2 tell us anything about Johnny's frequent headaches?" I try to explain my request in as nonthreatening terms as possible, or I may simply back down and realize that the new "story" I offer that parent about their son cannot be centered on a systemic view of the child's headaches. As you might guess, it is good to know such things before a summary/discussion session!

If parents will participate in testing, it shifts the focus of the assessment off of the child to some degree, which some children find relieving. I have seen several children become less symptomatic after learning that "Mommy and Daddy are doing testing too." Obviously, parental test results also allow an assessor to think about interface issues, or ways that parents are engaged in projection or projective identification with the child. For example, several years ago I assessed a mild-mannered single father and his 8-year-old acting-out son. The father had four percepts of exploding volcanoes on his Rorschach, and I developed the hypothesis that the son was acting out anger for the father. In another instance, a mother was very concerned that her low-achieving son was depressed; the testing indicated that he wasn't, but her MMPI–2 showed that she was struggling with severe depression. When confronted with her MMPI–2 profile, the mother realized that she needed help herself. When she started to see a psychotherapist, her son immediately started doing better in school.

7.   Schedule One or More Family Sessions or Parent–Child Sessions as Part of a Child's Assessment

This is something I do in almost all child assessments, except again in those instances where parents need to see a child as the sole source of problems. Such family sessions are in addition to the conjoint session that typically takes place at the beginning of the assessment. Typically, I try to involve all family members living in the home—including siblings, grandparents, and other relatives. I may give the family a task to do together such as the Consensus Rorschach (see chap. 12), planning a family vacation, or a family art project. Or I may ask them to play together or simply talk about the presenting issues. In some instances, I simply want to "see what happens" when I get the family together. At other times, I have a more focused assessment intervention in mind.

Whatever the structure, family sessions provide a very useful opportunity to observe family dynamics and sometimes lead to major breakthroughs in assessments. For example, not long ago I assessed a child who was having frequent nightmares, and whose Trauma Content Index (Armstrong & Lowenstein, 1990; Kamphuis et al., 2000) on the Rorschach was quite high, which made me wonder if he had experienced some emotionally overwhelming events. The parents were at a loss as to what could have happened. It wasn't until I observed some disturbing interactions in the waiting room and asked more questions that it came out that he was being severely tormented at home by his older siblings when the parents were away. The parents were clueless to this dynamic, and horrified once they found out what was happening.

Family sessions also provide an opportunity to identify and explore those child problems that are limited to the family context and to help parents see family influences. Here I remember an assessment where parents complained that their son was sleepy all the time. Their physician had assured them that there was no medical reason for the boy's problem. The boy's teachers said he was alert at school, and I found him lively and focused with me in the testing sessions (which the parents observed). However, the boy fell asleep during the family session. Eventually it came out that there was tremendous tension in the parents' marital relationship, which I believe the boy was clued into. He "slept through" most family interactions to keep himself from becoming aware of what he unconsciously knew.

Last, as mentioned earlier, family sessions can be used in the later stages of a child assessment to explore and highlight systemic issues in an assessment intervention session. One useful technique is simply to ask family members to reenact problematic scenes from home, and then get them to switch roles and play each other. When doing this, I typically ask parents to role-play the child, in hopes it will give them more empathy for the child's perspective. Then, one can get the family to think of and try out possible solutions to problematic behaviors. Like other assessment interventions, this works best if the assessor and family keep revising the new strategy until the clients feel some success.

In one memorable assessment, a 10-year-old boy, James, got into terrible "spells" at home when he was angry, in which he would rage and destroy furniture and other family members' cherished property (e.g., an heirloom clock from his mother's family). The father often got so overwhelmed during such scenes that he would barricade himself in the bedroom, leaving it to the mother to try to cope. I asked the family to role-play the scene for me, and then asked the father and son to play each other's parts. When the boy (playing his father) was in the bedroom with a pillow over his head, I asked him "What are you thinking?" The boy replied, "That I wish James had never been born. Then I wouldn't have had to get married. I hate my life!" I knew this in fact to be true of the father, but when it came out of the boy's mouth, everyone was stunned into silence. I then asked the father (playing James) what he needed from his father. Without thinking he said, "To know that my father really loves me." James and his father then started crying and hugged each other. This was the beginning of substantial positive changes in the family system.

8.   Ask Parents to Corroborate and Modify Assessment Findings Presented in the Summary/Discussion Session

I give assessment feedback to all parents and children. Typically, I meet with the parents first, then with the child and parents together. The exception is with adolescents; I discuss the findings with them alone first and answer their own assessment questions. Then I meet with their parents and give the adolescent the option of attending this session. As with all summary/discussion sessions in Therapeutic Assessment (see chap.1), I present my thoughts as hypotheses, order them according to how much they agree with the parents' existing story about their child, and I ask parents to corroborate, modify, or reject what I am saying. The parents and I refer back to things they observed during the assessment and to real-world events that support the new story. We then talk about what this new story suggests about the family's next steps.

Here is an excerpt from the summary/discussion session with James's parents, the boy who raged and destroyed personal property.

> *Steve:* [reviewing the Rorschach] So as we talked about before, James scores suggest that he is severely depressed, and that he feels pretty terrible about himself. You might remember that we talked about all the dead and damaged things he saw on the inkblots.
>
> *Father:* So what does that have to do with his rages?
>
> *Steve:* Do you remember that article I gave you several weeks ago, which explained that depression in children often comes out as angry behavior?
>
> *Father:* Oh yes, I remember now. That's confusing because he doesn't look depressed, he looks angry.
>
> *Steve:* I know what you mean.
>
> *Mother:* And if I understand what we learned last week, he feels terrible because he knows we didn't really want him at first. I almost had an abortion, but then we decided to get married.
>
> *Father:* I don't think he knows all that, do you?
>
> *Steve:* He may not know about the abortion, but I think the family play we did showed that he knows you [father] sometimes wish you never had him, and that makes him think that you don't love him.
>
> *Father:* I know I haven't been very good about showing that lately.
>
> *Mother:* But you've been trying hard this week.
>
> *Steve:* And how has it been working?
>
> *Mother:* It's been the best week we've had with James in months.
>
> *Steve:* I wonder if he's been blaming himself for your [father's] unhappiness?

As Fischer (1985/1994) wrote, this is essentially a hermeneutic approach to assessment feedback. Hypotheses are considered, revised, and tied to examples. All participants offer information from their own perspectives, resulting in a new understanding of the child that is more complete, accurate, and useful. As parents "get on the same page" and develop a coherent and similar story about the child's problems, the chances of their being able to implement next steps increases.

Also, this approach is respectful of parents and of any cultural differences that exist between them and the assessor. Parents are able to explain how they—from their own backgrounds—view different aspects of the family and child system, while the assessor is able to listen, ask questions, and suggest different points of view. I'm reminded of a boy I assessed with strong cross-gender interests whose parents were divorced. The Caucasian mother was quite concerned about the boy's desire to dress in girl's clothes and about the vicious taunting he got from other boys at school. The Native American father was less concerned about the boy's behavior and explained that in his tribe, boys and men with feminine interests are considered "special" because they are "in between" and therefore closer to the spirit world. Gradually, with much discussion among the three of us, both parents agreed that the bullying at school was the boy's major problem. This led us to strategize an intervention with the teachers and principal and helped the parents work together in implementing this intervention.

9. Ask Parents to Review Reports for Schools, Therapists, or Other Referral Sources and to Help Present Assessment Findings

This brings up another collaborative, potentially therapeutic technique. I always ask parents to review and comment on any report I write for a school, physician, or other referral source. Normally, I keep revising the report until the parents and I are comfortable with the way things are worded. I then ask parents to work with me in presenting the assessment results to the school or other party.

This tactic can be a way of unobtrusively coaching parents to be seasoned advocates for their child in other systems. For example, I might ask, "How do you think we should word this recommendation so your child's teacher is most likely to accept it?" or "Since we've agreed that these would be good goals for your child's therapy, should we think of a way to know if these goals are being met?"

This kind of collaboration can also facilitate (sometimes strained) relationships between parents and other members of the child's system. For example, after one meeting where parents and I shared assessment findings with school personnel, the principal told me, "I've never liked them before, but today I really did." Also, parents can watch how I interact with teachers, therapists, and other important people and learn to adopt a similar approach.

10.   Involve Parents in Giving Oral or Written Feedback to the Child About the Assessment Results

As stated earlier, I always offer feedback to children about their assessment results. For very young children, I often write a story that captures the assessment feedback in metaphor and then invite the children to modify, and illustrate the story. (See Fischer, 1985/1994, and Becker, Gohara, Marizilda, & Santiago, 2002, for examples of this approach.) Often I ask parents to collaborate in writing the story or to make comments and changes on my draft before it is presented to child. Alternatively, they may attend the session where the story is read to the child or even be the ones to read the story aloud.

Again, by involving parents in this way, I acknowledge that they are the most important people in their child's life and can have more impact on the child than a therapist ever can. Also, when parents assist in writing the child's feedback story, it provides an opportunity for them and me to help each other "get in the child's shoes." For example, a mother might say, "I think we should make the leopard in the story a cheetah. She has a favorite book about cheetahs." Or I might explain—in response to a parent's suggestion—why I don't think we should put a happy ending on a story: "I think Johnny will see that ending as ignoring his reasonable anxiety about how things are going to turn out. Can we think of a way to give him hope while also recognizing that there are some big unknowns ahead?" Last, when the child senses that the feedback story is a joint product and that the parents endorse it, he or she is more likely to accept the therapeutic messages contained in the story.

Conclusion

As discussed in chapter 4, there are many reasons to engage in collaborative assessment practices. One may do so for humanistic or philosophic reasons or because it facilitates clients' cooperation with assessment. But in child assessment, I believe there is one overarching reason to involve parents as active collaborators: Only by doing so can we understand the full context of a child's problems in living, and only by working with the child's family system can we produce substantial, lasting therapeutic change. The techniques outlined in this chapter are basic steps in practicing Therapeutic Assessment with children and families. In the near future, I hope to write more about the complexities and challenges of this type of assessment.

15

Teaching Therapeutic Assessment in a Required Graduate Course

As a member of the psychology faculty at the University of Texas at Austin from 1984 to 1992, I routinely taught the theory and techniques of Therapeutic Assessment to first-year clinical psychology graduate students in their required course on personality assessment. This course involved a theoretical and/or factual component as well as a practical and/or hands-on component. Students read research and theory about the major personality tests, learned the administration and scoring of each test, and conducted a number of practice assessments while being closely supervised. Early on it became clear to me that students in this course were not only learning how to assess clients; they themselves were also going through an important assessment—of their knowledge of psychological testing and their suitability to be clinical psychologists. Furthermore, the assessment to which my students were subjected was analogous to the most difficult of clinical assessment situations—in which clients are tested in part against their will, are ambivalent about self-disclosure, and are aware that assessment results will be used by others to make major decisions affecting their lives.

This chapter is excerpted from one (Finn, 1998) previously published in the book, *Teaching and Learning Personality Assessment* (Handler & Hilsenroth, 1998).

I am grateful to Jim Durkel for his comments on an earlier draft and to the many students who instructed me in how to teach psychological assessment.

To be more specific, my observations about students' personality traits, clinical skills, and knowledge of assessment were often weighed heavily by the clinical psychology faculty in deciding whether to retain a student at the end of the first year. Students were well aware of this and felt great pressure to do well in my course. This pressure, in turn, had the potential to inhibit greatly students' comments in class and their willingness to take risks while practicing assessment. In effect, the evaluation component of the course tended to set up a transference situation where I was seen as a feared, omnipotent authority rather than as a benevolent, human instructor. I soon realized that I might best address this stressful assessment situation by applying the same principles and techniques to my teaching that I was educating my students to use in their clinical interactions with clients. In this way I would be "practicing what I preached," and students would have the benefit of experiencing Therapeutic Assessment at the same time that they were learning to do it themselves. I describe the course in its final form, even though different elements were changed and added over the years.

Principles of Therapeutic Assessment as Applied to the Graduate Course in Personality Assessment

The underlying principles of Therapeutic Assessment in clinical assessment situations are articulated elsewhere (Finn, 1996b; Finn & Tonsager, 1997). A modified set of these principles as applied to a required graduate course in personality assessment guided my teaching:

(1) A required graduate course in personality assessment is an unsettling and personally challenging experience for students. It demands interpersonal and emotional skills and ways of thinking that have not typically been required in other academic courses; also the instructor's ratings of students are used by others to make major decisions regarding the students' lives. These factors can cause considerable anxiety for students.

(2) A graduate course in personality assessment is also an interpersonally challenging situation for an instructor. It involves (a) providing factual information, (b) giving feedback to students about clinically relevant personality characteristics, (c) modeling inter-

actions with clients, and (d) supporting students through their first interactions with clients. This multifaceted role has the potential to generate considerable anxiety in the instructor.

(3) When students and instructors are anxious, they are prone to enact highly stereotyped roles in which instructors play all-knowing experts and students act the part of deferential, passive novices. Such roles interfere with active learning on the part of both students and instructors.

(4) Students have the right to know, at the beginning of the course, what aspects of their performance will be evaluated, the procedures used to assess their performance, and how the results may affect them when the course is completed. Providing such information may decrease students' feelings of powerlessness and lower their anxiety.

(5) The instructor has the responsibility of clarifying with the students the goals, purpose, and requirements of the course.

(6) Students become most engaged in and benefit most from a course when they are treated as collaborators whose ideas and cooperation are essential to the learning process.

(7) Students become most invested in a course when it addresses, in part, their own personal and professional goals.

(8) When a course addresses students' goals and students are treated as collaborators, their anxiety is lower and their motivation is higher; thus, their course performance is more likely to reflect accurately their abilities and personal potential.

(9) Giving students feedback about their course performance in a collaborative manner can help them understand and address any performance deficits.

(10) When instructors discuss course ratings with students in an emotionally supportive manner, students often feel affirmed, less distressed, and more hopeful, even if the feedback is initially difficult for them to hear.

(11) A course on personality assessment can have a lasting impact—both personally and professionally—on students' lives.

(12) A collaborative approach to teaching personality assessment also creates opportunities for instructors to learn, hone clinical skills, and be challenged by their teaching.

Flow Chart of a Course in Therapeutic Assessment

Exhibit 15–1 represents a flow chart of my course in Therapeutic Assessment. Let me explain the steps in detail here.

Step 1: Assessment Questions Are Specified and Gathered

In Therapeutic Assessment, the assessor engages clients as collaborators at the beginning of the assessment by helping them identify personal goals and form questions to be addressed during the assessment (Finn, 1996; Finn & Tonsager, 1997). In involuntary assessments (such as court-ordered assessments, disability evaluations, and personnel-screening evaluations), clients typically are reluctant to frame personal goals for an assessment; they may even feel that posing assessment questions is dangerous in that such information may be used against them. In such situations, assessors can often gain clients' cooperation by first sharing the referring persons' assessment questions with clients, and negotiating beforehand with the referring person for permission to keep the client's own questions confidential (Finn & Tonsager, 1997).

In my graduate course, I followed the protocol for involuntary assessments by reviewing at the first class meeting the questions the clinical psychology faculty members would ask me to answer about each student at the end of the course. These questions were:

(1) Does the student have an adequate knowledge of the theory and research related to personality assessment?
(2) How well was the student able to conceptualize clinical case material?
(3) Has the student adequately mastered the administration and scoring of major personality tests?
(4) How well did the student write assessment reports?
(5) At what level are the student's basic clinical skills—for example, empathy, active listening, and ability to maintain appropriate boundaries?
(6) How did the student respond to supervisory feedback?
(7) Did the student demonstrate any behavior that raises concern about her or his suitability to be a clinical psychologist?

EXHIBIT 15–1
Flow Chart of a Course in Therapeutic Assessment

Step 1—	Assessment Questions Are Specified and Gathered
Step 2—	The Course Contract Is Finalized
Step 3—	The Assessment Task Is Explained and Conceptualized
Step 4—	The Assessment Task Is Demonstrated by the Instructor
Step 5—	Students Rate and Give Feedback to the Instructor
Step 6—	Students Role-Play Each Assessment Task
Step 7—	Students Perform Each Assessment Task With a Client
Step 8—	Students Are Given Feedback on Each Task
Step 9—	Students Try Out Modifications of Each Task
Step 10—	Students Repeat the Assessment Task With Another Client
Step 11—	End of Course Summary/Discussion Session With Student
Step 12—	Written Report on Student Is Prepared and Student Comments Invited
Step 13—	Students Anonymously Give Feedback to the Instructor
Step 14—	Report and Student Comments Are Presented to Faculty

Note. Steps 3–10 are repeated throughout the course for each assessment task (e.g., initial interview, Rorschach administration, summary/discussion session).

(8) Is the student ready to participate in a clinical practicum?

I promised students that I would discuss my answers to these questions with each of them at the end of the semester before I gave my report to the clinical psychology faculty. I also stated that I would be very interested in their ideas and reactions to my answers and would incorporate their ideas in my report. I then invited students to pose additional individual questions that might be useful to them for me to address during and at the end of the semester. I assured them that these questions (and my answers) would not be shared with the clinical-training committee without their permission and that their course evaluation would not be influenced by whether they came up with additional questions, or by the content of these questions. I gave examples of questions students had posed in previous years (e.g., "Why do I find it hard to talk about sex with clients?" "Am I too shy to be a good therapist?" "I've been told I need to be warmer with clients. How can I do this?"). Last, I let students know that they could offer these questions at any point during the semester by discussing them with me or jotting them down and putting them in my mailbox.

Step 2: Course Contract Is Finalized

During the first class meeting, I also handed out a detailed syllabus of the course requirements, including information about how each assignment would be graded. For example, as part of the course, students were required to learn the administration of the Rorschach according to the Comprehensive System (Exner, 1995). The course information specified when students would be tested on administration and included a rating sheet I used to grade the observed administration. Last, I answered any questions students had about the course structure and requirements until they and I were satisfied that we had a mutual understanding of the course contract.

The majority of the syllabus was structured to follow the flow of a standard Therapeutic Assessment of a client, that is, initial interview, standardized testing, assessment intervention session, summary/discussion session, and written report (Finn & Tonsager, 1997). For each of these tasks, I would repeat the following steps (3 through 10) during the course.

Step 3: The Assessment Task Is Explained and Conceptualized

First, I provided readings about each task, and students and I discussed the techniques and underlying principles involved. For example, we thoroughly explored the purpose of the initial interview of a Therapeutic Assessment, the types of problems that can arise, and how to handle these various complications.

Step 4: The Assessment Task Is Demonstrated by the Instructor

Before the course began, I invited colleagues in the community to refer clients to be assessed by the students and me as part of the course. (It was not difficult to find clients who would agree to such an arrangement in return for a free assessment.) I would select one of these clients for me to assess myself. Then, I demonstrated each assessment task in front of the class, before the students performed the task on their own. For example, after the students and I had discussed the initial session of a Therapeutic Assessment, I interviewed a volunteer client while students observed during a class meeting. Later, I worked with this same client to demonstrate other parts of the assessment. I videotaped some lengthy tasks, for example, the Rorschach administration, outside of class sessions. I then showed portions of the videotape during class periods and/or asked students to watch the tape on their own before we met. I openly discussed any anxiety I felt about such demonstrations, in order to normalize the students' anxiety about being observed. I also modeled steps I took to deal with my anxiety.

Step 5: Students Rate and Give Feedback to the Instructor

While I demonstrated each assessment task, students rated me on the same form the teaching assistants (TAs) and I would later use to rate them. After I completed each task, I would also rate myself. Then the students and I would discuss our observations and ratings of my performance. I would try to model a nondefensive receptivity to their feedback and to be open to learning from the students' observations. This was rarely difficult, as students generally made sensitive, accurate, and insightful comments.

Repeatedly my students told me that my willingness to demonstrate each assessment task was extremely valuable and greatly appreciated. It was also an important way to embody the collaborative principles underlying Therapeutic Assessment. By making myself vulnerable and openly acknowledging my anxiety, mistakes, and learning, I reduced the power imbalance between students and myself and helped to alleviate their anxiety. One can never completely eliminate this power imbalance, nor is it the goal of Therapeutic Assessment to do so. The instructor and/or assessor is still seen as an expert on assessment, but one who recognizes that no one person has the entire truth about any interpersonal situation and who is willing to learn from the student and/or client. By demonstrating my work, I also managed to engage the students as co-assessors and collaborators in the course and in the observed assessment and thereby increased their excitement and motivation to learn. Last, my actions communicated my respect for students as individuals and as a group, and seemed to empower them to believe that they too could become skilled assessors.

Step 6: Students Role-Play Each Assessment Task

Following the observed demonstration, students would practice each task (e.g., the initial interview) in pairs or small groups—with myself, the TAs, or other students role-playing clients. I tried to encourage students to give each other feedback, based on their subjective experience of playing assessors or clients. By letting students supervise each other, I again tried to resist being viewed as the only expert.

Step 7: Students Perform Each Assessment Task With a Client

Next, students were individually observed while performing each assessment task (initial interview, Rorschach administration, summary/discussion session, etc.) with a volunteer client. The TAs or I would observe these sessions and rate students on the appropriate rating form. Students would rate themselves on the same form after completing the task.

Step 8: Students Are Given Feedback on Each Task

The TAs and I compared our ratings and observations of the students' performance on each task with the students' own ratings. Both strengths and weaknesses were brought up for discussion, and we asked students to respond to our comments, rather than passively accept them as "ultimate truths." We paid special attention to issues students had identified in their individualized assessment questions (posed at the beginning of the course). This approach parallels the feedback process in Therapeutic Assessment, in which clinicians tie assessment findings to clients' individual goals and engage clients in discussing the accuracy and meaning of test findings, rather than acting as if such results represent absolute reality.

Step 9: Students Try Out Modifications of Each Task

In the assessment intervention stage of Therapeutic Assessment, clients and assessors use test behaviors as analogs of extra-test problems in living. Then they search for new solutions to external problems by identifying new ways for the client to approach test materials (see chap. 8). For example, a client who has posed the question, "Why do I have trouble completing my assignments at work?" may copy the Bender-Gestalt figures in an obsessive, painstakingly slow manner. After discussing with the client the similarities between his behavior in the two situations, the assessor might ask the client to draw the figures again, but more rapidly. By trying different ways to speed up the Bender-Gestalt copy, the client and assessor may identify ways that the client can complete more assignments at work.

In the assessment course, after students and I noticed problems in their performance of any assessment task, we would role-play the task again and again, identifying possible solutions and/or blocks to behavior change. For example, a student and I might discover that she failed to do an adequate Rorschach inquiry because she was afraid of annoying the irritable, easily offended client she had been assigned. The student and I would discuss ways to deal with such clients' annoyance, and would try out these strategies together until we were both reasonably confident that she could handle such situations in the future. In class, I would explicitly state my belief that such problems arise for all beginning assessors and that the purpose of the practice assessments was to identify such difficulties and address them before students went on to practicum placements. In rare instances, students and I found that they were unable to modify easily problem behaviors that showed up during their assessments. In such cases, if the problems were significant, I sometimes suggested to students that they consider getting psychotherapy.

Step 10: Students Repeat the Assessment Task With Another Client

By the end of the course, students observed me many times, and they, too, were observed many times, as they honed or modified their assessment skills, and repeated each assessment task with another client. Students generally completed two to three full personality assessments as part of the course requirements. Although I had no illusions that this amount of experience would identify and address all potential problems students might encounter, I felt fairly confident that students would have the chance to address most major clinical and characterological issues.

Step 11: End of Course Feedback Session Is Given to Student

When all course requirements were completed, I offered an individual summary/discussion session to each student, which I conducted according to the techniques of Therapeutic Assessment, for example, addressing students' individualized goals, offering balanced (both positive and negative) feedback, beginning with feedback that was likely to fit students' self-concepts, allowing students to challenge my comments (see chap.1). As with earlier supervisory sessions, I tried to engage each student in a dialogue about my observations and I carefully listened to any disagreements or modifications of my feedback. Before the session ended, I told each student her or his grade and I invited feedback about the course and/or about me as an instructor. I let students know they would have another opportunity to give me feedback anonymously.

Step 12: Written Report Is Prepared and Student Has Option of Commenting

In Therapeutic Assessment, reports are written in language that clients can understand and are virtually always shared with clients. In addition, clients are given the chance to respond in writing to their reports (Finn & Tonsager, 1997). In my course, I followed this approach with students. Shortly after the summary/discussion session, I prepared my written report about each student for the clinical psychology faculty, including modifications that came out of my discussions with students. I gave students copies of their reports and I invited them to put any reactions or disagreements in writing and give them to me. I promised to present such comments to the clinical psychology faculty at the same time I gave my own report. I believe that my commitment to showing students my reports helped keep my assessments precise and balanced. I avoided impressions and comments that I could not adequately support. Also, as in a clinical assessment, students' comments on my reports were often illustrative of my impressions, and were thereby useful to the other faculty.

Step 13: Students Anonymously Give Feedback to the Instructor

In my practice, all clients are invited to rate their assessment experiences on a standardized form (the Assessment Questionnaire–2; Finn, Schroeder, & Tonsager, 1994) at the end of an assessment. My department routinely required students to anonymously complete course evaluations at the end of the semester. I always let students know that I paid careful attention to their ratings and comments in designing the course for the following year. I sometimes found that students were more forthcoming in their feedback on the anonymous course ratings than they were when discussing the course with me in their feedback sessions. I see this as an inevitable result of the distrust inherent in involuntary assessment situations.

Step 14: Report and Student Comments Are Presented to Faculty

Finally, I shared my report about each student, along with any comments she or he had written, with the clinical psychology faculty. My observations were integrated with those of other faculty members to make recommendations about commendation, remediation, or dismissal of students from the department.

Case Example—Elizabeth

Let me now illustrate the approach I have described with the case of one student, a 23-year-old woman whom I name Elizabeth.

First Impressions

In the initial class session, Elizabeth impressed me as a bright, nervous woman. She asked several excellent clarifying questions about the course syllabus, but spoke in a rapid, breathless voice, sometimes stumbling over words. She repeatedly twisted a bead necklace that she wore throughout the class meeting, and several times I had a vision of its breaking and spilling all over the floor. I vaguely remembered meeting Elizabeth 4 months earlier, at the departmental party at the beginning of the first semester, where we chatted about our mutual interest in horseback riding. I also recalled Dr. Smith, the first-semester assessment instructor, telling me that Elizabeth seemed quite "anxious." In keeping with these experiences, I received the following note in my department mailbox the day after the class session:

> Dr. Finn,
> I have one additional question for us to consider during the course. Dr. Smith told me that I talk too much with clients and I haven't been able to stop this. I hope you and I can figure out why I do this and how to help me stop.
> Elizabeth

I was impressed by Elizabeth's awareness of a problem and her willingness to disclose it to me. I was also encouraged by the "you and I" phrasing in her note, which seemed to indicate her acceptance of the collaborative frame of the course.

Initial Session

I briefly acknowledged Elizabeth's note at the beginning of the next class session, and she appeared calmer in this and the next several class meetings. She continued to ask excellent questions in class and made insightful comments about the readings I had assigned. I began to see her as a bright and very dedicated student who worked hard and prepared carefully for class sessions. She and I had a short meeting before her first client session, after I interviewed the client I was assessing in class. I took the opportunity to ask Elizabeth more about her "talking too much" with clients. I found out that Dr. Smith's observation reminded her of comments several friends had recently made—that she seemed "wound up." She confessed that this feedback had surprised her at first because she had often been told she was "too quiet" in college. When I asked Elizabeth what she thought about this discrepancy, she said it might be because she "tried too hard" with new things, but then calmed down after a while. I sympathized with the anxiety of doing new things and of overdoing as a result, and we agreed that Elizabeth should "do her best" but not "try too hard" in her first client interview. She also agreed to role-play an initial interview with one of the TA supervisors prior to meeting with her client. At the end of our meeting, Elizabeth also asked me how I felt when the client I had interviewed in class began to cry.

Early Assessment Sessions

Elizabeth's first assessment client was a subdued, apparently chronically depressed young man who sought psychological testing to explore why he had so much trouble keeping friends. As I watched her initial interview I was struck by Elizabeth's calm, firm demeanor with the client, and I wondered if Dr. Smith or Elizabeth's friends had misperceived her, or if she had simply corrected her tendency to "talk too much" and "try too hard." After the interview, we both agreed that the session had gone quite well and that Elizabeth had done a good job of both directing the client and letting him talk. I commended her for her poise; she said that she had felt in the interview as she did when riding a "good horse": "comfortable and not at all afraid." We sketched out the next steps in the assessment and scheduled a time for me to watch Elizabeth administer the Rorschach to her client several days hence. She had already watched me administer the Rorschach and had passed a trial administration during which one of the TAs played a client.

Partway into the observed Rorschach session, I noticed a marked change in Elizabeth's comportment, compared to the beginning of the Rorschach or the initial interview. She began to fidget in her seat, several times cut-off the client in midsentence with questions, and her speech became rapid and breathy, as I had noted in the first class session. As I watched, I remembered that Elizabeth asked me about my experience of the client I had interviewed, and I developed a hypothesis about her apparent rise in anxiety. The young man Elizabeth was testing had become noticeably distressed on Card V of the Rorschach, after seeing "a bat flying home over a battlefield. His wings are burned and torn. He's been through something terrible and is just trying to make it through—to make it back to his cave." This response was followed by numerous morbid percepts, and the client's general flat affect became more and more depressed until, on Card IX, he began to cry.

Elizabeth reacted by becoming more and more directive and by speaking very rapidly, especially during the Inquiry. This seemed to confuse the client, and there was a rather tense ending to the Rorschach administration. After the session, Elizabeth herself was upset, and she commented that she was aware she had "talked too much." When I asked if she knew why, she said she had been anxious because this was her first Rorschach, and she felt she had once again "tried too hard." When I shared my hypothesis that she had gotten more active as her client got more distressed, Elizabeth paused to consider and then quickly agreed that this was so. She said she had been afraid the client was going to "fall apart" and she had no idea "how to put him back together again." This led to a fruitful dialogue, where I noticed that Elizabeth had seemed calmer in the initial interview, where the client was somewhat withdrawn and depressed, but not overtly upset. Elizabeth agreed and spontaneously noted that both of the clients she had tested in the previous semester (under Dr. Smith's supervision) had been highly emotional and very distressed. We hypothesized that Elizabeth got uncomfortable when clients showed painful emotions, and she tended to react by talking too much and becoming controlling. I reminded her of her question about how I felt when the client I interviewed began to cry, and we spent some time discussing my reactions and ways to handle such situations.

Assessment Intervention

The next day, Elizabeth and I met to role-play ways to handle distressed clients. I modeled simply acknowledging clients' pain, without trying to fix or control it. Elizabeth confessed that this was a novel idea for her; she tended to feel responsible for others' distress. At first, as I role-played a weeping client she reacted by trying to cheer me up. I drew an analogy to horseback riding, and we discussed how a rider must stay calm and unruffled if a horse is frightened by a sudden noise or event. At this point, Elizabeth seemed to catch on and she successfully handled several other situations that I presented to her. Last, we reviewed how she could have responded to her client when he began to cry during the Rorschach. Later that week, Elizabeth met with her client again to conduct the assessment intervention session for his assessment.

I had asked Elizabeth to begin by asking the client about his experience of the Rorschach administration. Not surprisingly, the client seemed even more subdued and withdrawn at the beginning of the session. However, he was able, with Elizabeth's help, to say that he felt upset after their previous meeting. I was pleased as Elizabeth calmly asked questions about his perception of her. Then, to my surprise, the client spontaneously offered, "You know, what happened with us happens with me and my friends all the time. That's part of the problem I've been having." The client went on to relate how his friends couldn't handle his depression, and how misunderstood he felt when they offered suggestions, told him to "stop moping," or suggested he "just go out and have fun." Elizabeth participated in this discussion beautifully, and was able to incorporate the client's observations later in the TAT testing we had planned. After the session, she and I joyfully discussed the client's learning and her ability to react well to his distress.

Later Assessment Sessions

For Elizabeth's second assessment, we both agreed that she would work with a middle-aged woman who was described by the referring therapist as "prone to fits of hysterical crying." I did not personally supervise this assessment, but the TA reported that Elizabeth handled the initial interview and early testing sessions quite well, even though the client became markedly distressed at several points. Then, during the summary/discussion session, Elizabeth again became rather anxious and strident, and insisted on the rightness of several of her interpretations. Afterward, both she and the TA were puzzled about her [Elizabeth's] behavior, because the client had not been markedly distressed during the feedback, and in fact, had seemed pleased and appreciative of the assessment.

I was concerned when Elizabeth came to see me during my office hours the next day, for she looked disheartened and a bit haggard. Once again, she was rather breathless as she talked about the summary/discussion session with her client, speaking rapidly and stumbling over words. I gently probed about what might have made her anxious during that session, until Elizabeth broke down and began to cry. I remembered my advice to her and stayed calm and inquisitive, as Elizabeth finally disclosed another piece of the puzzle: Her mother had been diagnosed recently with ovarian cancer. In fact, Elizabeth had found out about her mother's illness only the morning before the first assessment class meeting. (No wonder she had been so anxious that day!) The day of the summary/discussion session with her second client, Elizabeth had learned that her mother's cancer was not responding to chemotherapy. Furthermore, it came out that Elizabeth was extremely close to her mother, who was a highly emotional woman who had always looked to Elizabeth to help contain her depressed feelings.

I sympathized with Elizabeth's situation, recommended that she seek support during such a difficult time, and gave her the name of several good psychotherapists in the community. This event demonstrates the fine line that often exists between supervision and therapy. I do not inquire about students' personal issues during supervision unless there is an impasse in their ability to work with clients. Once personal issues are identified, I generally refer students to an outside therapist to explore the personal issues further.

Elizabeth calmed down considerably and appeared to leave my office with renewed hope and determination. I was left musing about how I too tend to avoid seeking help when I need it, and I realized that I had never discussed with students the impact that personal emergencies can have on an assessor's ability to be with clients. I resolved to add such a discussion to my course in the future.

In the following weeks, Elizabeth appeared calmer and happier in class sessions. She did an excellent third assessment on a difficult client, and showed no disabling anxiety or controlling behavior during that assessment. Her reports were well crafted and insightful. She also achieved the highest grade in the class on the written final exam.

Summary/Discussion Session

My summary/discussion session with Elizabeth, held jointly with the TA supervisor, was smooth and productive. We reviewed Elizabeth's considerable strengths as an assessor and again discussed the difficulties she had shown earlier in the semester. I commended Elizabeth for her ability to improve her clinical skills, and Elizabeth thanked me for my support and responded briefly to my inquiries about her mother's health. She also shared, in an appropriate way, some additional insights she had discovered in therapy about her reactions to others' distress. The TA and I said a few words about our own learning process in this area and we all parted with warm feelings.

Written Report

My written report on Elizabeth's course performance (Exhibit 15–2) was given to the clinical psychology faculty. I shared this report with Elizabeth several days before the faculty met to discuss her performance.

EXHIBIT 15–2
Written Report Concerning Elizabeth's Course Performance

PSY389L—Theory and Technique of Assessment II—
Spring Semester 20XX
Course Evaluation

Student: Elizabeth J. *Course Grade:* A
TA Supervisor: Mary Jones

Elizabeth impressed me as an intelligent, caring, responsible student who worked very hard on the course assignments and on improving her clinical skills. Both the TA supervisor and I feel Elizabeth has adequately addressed certain difficulties that Dr. Smith noted in her interactions with clients the first semester:

1. Does this student have an adequate knowledge of the theory and research related to personality assessment?

Yes. Elizabeth obviously prepared each of the course readings with great care and made insightful and useful comments in class discussions. She received the highest grade in the class on the final exam, and her answers demonstrated a sophisticated knowledge of the theory and research regarding personality assessment.

2. How well was the student able to conceptualize clinical case material?

Elizabeth showed a good ability in supervision sessions to think psychologically about cases and to integrate theory and case material. She was more able than most first-year students to analyze clients' interactions with her during assessment sessions and to connect these with clients' problems in their outside lives.

3. Has the student adequately mastered the administration and scoring of or personality tests?

Yes. Elizabeth is able to adequately administer and score the tests covered in the course. She was precise and careful in her test scoring. However, like almost all students at her level of training, she will need ongoing assistance with the scoring of difficult Rorschach protocols.

EXHIBIT 15–2
(Continued)

4. *How well did the student write assessment reports?*

Elizabeth's reports were finely reasoned and elegantly worded. She always met deadlines for revisions, even when a quick turn-around was needed.

5. *At what level are this student's basic clinical skills—e.g., empathy, active listening ability to maintain appropriate boundaries?*

At several points early in the semester, Elizabeth's clinical interactions were influenced by her anxiety and her attempts to manage it. At such points, Elizabeth tended to be overactive and controlling with clients-not listening well and imposing too much of her own agenda on sessions. Elizabeth was aware of this tendency from feedback she received last semester and she worked hard to overcome it during this course. I now feel that Elizabeth has adequately addressed the underlying issues contributing to her anxiety, and she now shows good empathy, listening skills, and appropriate flexibility with clients.

6. *How did the student respond to supervisory feedback?*

Elizabeth was receptive to supervisory feedback and was able to use it to improve her skills with clients. She also appropriately reached out for support from her supervisors when she was troubled by family issues that were influencing her course performance.

7. *Did the student demonstrate any behavior that raises concern about her suitability to be a clinical psychologist?*

8. *Is this student ready to participate in a clinical practicum?*

Elizabeth performed in an ethical and responsible way throughout the course. I have no concerns about her taking part in the second-year practicum. I believe that Elizabeth has the abilities, temperament, and dedication necessary to become an excellent clinical psychologist.

Stephen E. Finn
Course Instructor

Elizabeth's Comments on the Report

Elizabeth wrote a brief response to my report, which I also shared with the clinical faculty:

> I agree with Dr. Finn's report and feel that I learned a lot about myself and about assessment through his course. Dr. Finn discreetly mentioned "family issues" that were troubling me during the semester. I want to clarify this. My mother was diagnosed with cancer earlier this year and her health is going downhill quickly. This has been quite upsetting for me and my family, but I think that I am handling it as well as can be expected and I have lots of support. I will be spending the summer with my mother and I plan to return to my studies in the fall.

Summary and Conclusions

In this chapter, I highlighted the similarities between a required graduate course in personality assessment and the clinical assessment of clients who are involuntarily referred for psychological testing. I attempted to demonstrate how the same principles underlying clinical Therapeutic Assessment may also be applied to the educational setting. By (a) minimizing any unnecessary power differential between themselves and students; (b) addressing students' personal goals in course evaluations; (c) modeling vulnerability and openness to feedback; and (d) treating students as collaborators in the learning process, instructors of personality assessment may increase the professional and personal impact of their courses on students. Such an approach is challenging to instructors in that it requires them to be aware of their own anxiety and to minimize defensive reactions to it. However, the rewards of this method are great. Over the years, I have had the pleasure of receiving feedback from former students that my course in personality assessment was one of the most important in their graduate training. I am also very aware of how much I have learned about myself, about teaching, and about personality assessment from instructing others in Therapeutic Assessment.

Part III

Theoretical Developments

16

Please Tell Me That I'm Not Who I Fear I Am: Control-Mastery Theory and Therapeutic Assessment

I am always searching for new "lenses" to use in looking at the complex process of psychological assessment. Thus, it was with some excitement that I joined a study group in Austin several years ago run by Dr. Elayne Lansford, an expert on Control-Mastery theory. I already knew a bit about this theory and suspected that some of its insights into human nature and psychotherapy would be useful in my practice of Therapeutic Assessment. I was right, and in this chapter I review the major concepts in Control Mastery theory and illustrate their applicability to Therapeutic Assessment through several case examples. I then discuss how Control Mastery theory helps us understand the phenomenon of "failed" assessments, in which clients feel less capable or even traumatized following a psychological assessment. Finally, I offer some general thoughts on the role of theory in psychological assessment.

This chapter is drawn from a paper I presented to the Society for Personality Assessment (Finn, 2005c).

A Brief Introduction to Control-Mastery Theory

Control-Mastery theory is a relatively new psychodynamic theory, first articulated by Joseph Weiss, M.D. in the 1960s. In 1972, Weiss and his colleague Harold Sampson, PhD, co-founded the San Francisco (formerly Mt. Zion) Psychotherapy Research Group, and although Weiss died in 2004, this group continues to theorize, teach, and conduct research about psychotherapy. In fact, Control-Mastery theory is the only psychodynamic theory that I know of supported by a wide body of quantitative research.

The basic tenets of Control-Mastery theory are relatively simple at first glance, although they have far-reaching implications. First, it is assumed that clients' problems in living derive from unconscious pathogenic beliefs they developed from early traumatic experiences (Weiss, 1993). For example, a gay man I see for psychotherapy was rejected as a child by his father for being a "sissy"; he clearly came to believe that he was weak and unattractive and could never be accepted or loved by another man. Another client witnessed her father emotionally and physically abusing her mother, who never stood up to her husband or said a bad word about him afterwards. This client acquired a strong belief that "One must silently accept any kind of treatment from important others, no matter how terrible." Although such conclusions helped these individuals make sense of their early life experiences and adapt to them, they now get in the way of their pursuing normal developmental goals that would help them achieve happiness. As you can see, this first part of Control-Mastery theory is not that dissimilar from other post-Freudian psychodynamic theories, such as ego psychology, object relations, or self psychology.

Where Weiss's theory is unique is in his assumption that clients seeking psychotherapy are powerfully motivated to "disconfirm" their pathogenic beliefs about themselves and the world in order to become more independent, happy, and achieve more satisfying relationships. Weiss says that when clients seek treatment, they have an unconscious "plan" to seek evidence—through the relationship with the therapist—that their pathogenic beliefs are inaccurate and that it is safe to begin acting as if they were untrue. In Weiss's theory, all clients "test" therapists in several ways to see if they will disprove their pathogenic beliefs.

First, there are what Weiss called *transference tests*, in which the client may see if the therapist accepts and goes along with their pathogenic beliefs, in the same way as early caregivers did. For example, my gay male client was quite confused early in treatment when I asked him why he wasn't trying to date men he found attractive. He said he assumed none of them would ever want to be with him, and he grew notably interested and relieved when I said that I doubted that to be the case. Another kind of test—called *passive-into-active testing*—occurs when clients treat therapists as they themselves were treated as children, to see if the therapists can demonstrate a more effective way of responding. Hence, I was not surprised when the second client I mentioned—who had witnessed her mother silently accepting abuse—one day became unfairly critical and derisive towards me in a session. I had the presence of mind to stand up for myself, and I said explicitly that I did not deserve to be treated that way; at that point the woman calmed down, apologized, and changed the topic. Most importantly, in the following weeks she began to be more assertive with her highly irresponsible boyfriend, who was misusing her terribly, and she started to trust me with more details about their relationship.

One interesting footnote is Weiss's assertion that often, clients reveal their pathogenic beliefs and unconscious plan for change very early in treatment, and more often than not in the first few sessions. Weiss said that sometimes clients will state their unconscious beliefs and plans directly; more often, one must listen "in between the lines" to deduce clients' unconscious agendas.

Control-Mastery Theory and Therapeutic Assessment

As far as I know, no one in the San Francisco Psychotherapy Research Group has yet applied the concepts of Control-Mastery theory to formal psychological assessment. Most likely, this is partly due to the traditional dichotomization of assessment and psychotherapy. Hence, it may only be when one considers Therapeutic Assessment—with its explicit goal of helping clients developing new, more accurate and useful understandings of themselves and the world—that the utility of this theory for psychological assessment becomes evident.

Clients' Unconscious Plans and Their Questions for an Assessment

I have found it useful to consider clients' pathogenic beliefs and unconscious plans in listening to the questions and goals they pose at the beginning of a therapeutic assessment. Sometimes, clients seem to lay out
their worst fears or beliefs about themselves directly, with the overt goal
of using the psychological test results to prove or disprove them. For example, some clients will ask questions like "Are all my problems really
the result of an awful childhood, or am I just using that as an excuse, like
my family tells me?" or "Am I really angry, like my probation officer says,
or just more honest than most people [as I think]?" I never assume before
I see the assessment results exactly how I will end up answering the client's questions by the end of the assessment; but, I generally assume that
the client is testing me to say back directly what he or she has revealed
through the testing. I might end up telling the first client that she has
been severely traumatized, and that her family's expectations for her are
completely unreasonable. Or, her test responses might suggest the opposite, that her background wasn't that dysfunctional and that she over-
plays her background for sympathy because she is terrified of succeeding.
In either case, I believe the client is using the assessment to disconfirm
some worst fear about herself, for example, that she really is a whiny
complainer who simply needs to pull herself up by her bootstraps, or alternatively, that she is so severely damaged that she can never succeed
and deserves pity and sympathy from others. And again, I assume that
clients will tell me which fears to disconfirm through their responses to
the MMPI–2, Rorschach, and so forth.

Like Weiss, I find it rare that clients lay out their pathogenic beliefs for
testing so explicitly; I am more used to situations where depressed and
traumatized clients pose assessment questions like "Why am I so lazy?"
or "Why am I so unreasonably distrustful of everyone?" In such instances, it is usually fairly easy to disprove the pathogenic beliefs embod-
ied in these questions by explaining to clients how the labels they have
for themselves are inaccurate, or lack compassion, even if they have a
grain of truth. I will show the person who thinks he is "lazy" his elevated
Depression scale score on the MMPI–2, and explain to him how chronic
depression can lead to poor work habits, underachievement, and lack of
motivation. I might talk to the woman who views her distrust as a character flaw about her elevated Trauma Content Index on the Rorschach. If

she can acknowledge that awful things were done to her early in life by people who should have been trustworthy, then possibly she can come to see her interpersonal vigilance as an outmoded coping mechanism, and gradually focus on learning when it is smart to be wary and when it is safe to trust.

There is another more striking client presentation I have seen, where the stated goals for the assessment seem unreasonable or clearly contradict information revealed during the assessment. As Weiss (1993) suggested, this can be a clue that the client is unconsciously asking the assessor to refute a pathogenic belief. For example, a colleague and I recently assessed a man who was demoralized after being berated by his wife for years about his "lack of feeling" and "inability to be intimate." One of the questions he posed for his assessment was "How can I come to be satisfied living totally on my own without any intimate relationships?" However, the client's Rorschach was full of color determinants and whole human percepts, and he rated himself on the MMPI–2 as gregarious and highly invested in spending time with others. We told him at the end of the assessment that he wouldn't be happy living the life of a hermit, and that one of his problems was a high degree of emotional sensitivity such that he easily got overwhelmed and sometimes shut down completely. His wife's emotional harangues were the worst possible environment for him to connect to his feelings, but during the safe context of the assessment, he showed that he could be quite tender and emotional. The client seemed visibly relieved at this feedback and agreed to his wife's moving out—something he had been reluctant to consider beforehand.

Similarly, some couples present for conjoint assessment with stated goals that contradict almost everything they reveal during the course of the assessment. Several years ago, I assessed a man and wife who said their main question was "How can we come to forgive each other for past hurts and be happy together again?" They had been vindictively attacking and counterattacking each other for over 20 years. During the individual portions of the assessment, each confessed that she or he no longer loved the other and fantasized constantly about divorce. When I asked, in the assessment intervention session, whether there was simply "too much salt in the soup" for the relationship ever to recover, they both seemed shocked. But when we met a week later to review all the test results, they had already discussed ending the marriage, and reported they had had their best week together in years.

In contrast, another couple I helped assess seemed on the verge of divorce after a number of terrible traumas, including, 2 years earlier, the kidnapping, rape, and murder of their 10-year-old daughter. They had already separated when the assessment began and posed questions like "Is there any hope?" and "What is the best way to tell our families if we divorce?" During the assessment, each shared tender memories of the other, and they both spoke of still being very much in love. I wondered why they were considering divorce, and now think that they had developed a pathogenic belief that they were cursed as a couple. As the assessment progressed, it became clear that they had pulled back from each other after their daughter's death, and had very little support from others to deal with this tragedy. Then, they had projected their guilt and anger on one another, and both secretly feared their spouse blamed them for what had happened. I told them in the final summary/discussion session that I had hope for the marriage if they could get the support they needed to face their collective grief, and that each needed to hear from the other that they were not at fault for their daughter's death. I said I knew talking about all this would take a lot of courage, but that the testing showed that each was a strong person who was up to the challenge. They both began to cry and when I saw them for follow-up a month later, they had moved back in together and were starting to rebuild their marriage.

Behavioral Tests of the Assessor

Sometimes, it seems that clients test assessors behaviorally, much as Weiss said happens during psychotherapy. For example, my colleagues and I rather frequently assess young adults whose high-achieving, successful parents are very concerned about their being underresponsible and failing to individuate. There often are surprised looks all around when—in the first session of such an assessment—I suggest that things will work better if the young man or woman is responsible for getting himself or herself to our sessions. Sometimes, the young adult comes quite reliably—which in itself is interesting—but, in most cases there is at least one missed session. I have come to see these missed sessions as a transference test, and I try to respond according to what I have deduced up to that point about the client's underlying pathogenic beliefs. One young man clearly believed "I am a constant disappointment to others and deserve severe criticism." He seemed shocked when I was fairly nonchalant about the missed appointment and when I casually asked if we should change our meeting time to late afternoons, as I knew that he often stayed up late. He declined my offer and never again missed one of our 10 a.m. meetings. Yet another young woman was clearly overindulged by her parents, who never set limits on her and only brought her for testing at the insistence of her high school counselor. When I recommended to her parents that the girl be asked to pay out of her allowance for her second missed session, she threw a temper tantrum and stormed out of my office. But in a later meeting, she told me that I had earned her respect and she too never missed another appointment. Much later, the young woman confessed that she feared she was incapable of living on her own, but that paying for the missed session had raised her confidence.

Passive-to-Active Tests.   The most common passive-to-active tests I have seen during assessment are those where clients who have been abused in the past turn the tables and try to disparage the assessor or the assessment methods. For example, a young man I helped assess once was seen at the request of his parents because he had virtually cut off all contact with them except for taking their money to pay for college. The young man was very tall, muscular, and emotionally closed off, and the parents were concerned because he had told the mother's therapist that he sometimes thought about "pulling a Colombine." One of the parents' assessment questions was whether they should worry about his killing them. At first this concern seemed outlandish, but as the assessment proceeded, my postdoctoral assistant and I were shocked by how malicious and abusive the boy's parents had been to him as he grew up. For example, when he was 7, his father had insisted that he learn to water ski, and had kept him in the water, sobbing uncontrollably, for over 5 hours until he was finally able to get up on the skis for a brief period of time. The mother sat in the boat with the father the whole time this was happening and did not intervene.

The young man agreed to the assessment but was openly skeptical about whether our psychological tests could tell him anything he didn't know. He was somewhat hostile, but kept this fairly under wraps while I was in the room. Then he had two very significant assessment sessions alone with my postdoctoral assistant. In the first, they talked about his early childhood and he softened considerably as she expressed her horror and sadness about his abuse. At the second session, they did the Rorschach, and afterwards he was so openly disparaging and hostile that he reduced this sturdy young psychologist to tears.

Fortunately, she and I consulted immediately after, and I explained Weiss's idea that the client was hoping that she could demonstrate a way of handling abuse that he had never been able to discover. Apparently, the client's pathogenic belief was that one either had to accept ill treatment, cut off all contact with one's abuser, or become a violent person oneself. At their next meeting, my assistant confronted the client directly about how awfully he had treated her. She did this, of course, without becoming abusive towards him. Later, he also heard me confront his parents when giving assessment feedback about their horrific treatment of him. Like my assistant, I was direct and blunt and forceful, but I never crossed the line to become sadistic or cruel. There were many complicated outcomes to this assessment, but one was that the young man was able to resume contact with his parents, while standing up to them in appropriate ways. By passing his tests, my assistant and I had apparently disconfirmed his pathogenic beliefs and modeled a new way of being.

Failed Assessments

Over the years, I have become quite interested in *failed assessments*, which are defined in Therapeutic Assessment as those assessments that result in clients' feeling diminished or traumatized by the process (Finn & Tonsager, 1997). After reading Weiss and his colleagues, I now hypothesize that certain assessments fail—in the sense of hurting rather than helping clients—because they confirm, in the clients' minds, some key pathogenic belief they hold about themselves. For example, recall the case I discussed in chapter 13, of the woman who experienced her passive, withdrawn husband as abusing her (much as her humiliating and narcissistic father had done). Some of her major questions for the assessment were "Where are my blind spots?" "Where is my 'bad stuff' and what I don't want to see about myself?" and "How am I participating in projective identification in [my marriage]?" I was impressed at the time by the client's psychological sophistication and openness, and I rather naively set myself the task of helping her learn about her part in the dysfunctional marital dance she and her husband were doing. In the summary/discussion session, I talked to the client about her misperceptions of and projections on her husband. I told her I saw no evidence that he was being hostile to her when he shut down emotionally; rather, he simply had no other way of handling his anxiety. I suggested that she had not fully confronted the reality of how sadistic her father had been to her when she was young. Furthermore, her own testing showed a great deal of underlying anger that she was not aware of. I knew these things would be challenging for her to hear, but I was confused and surprised when I learned later that she had been highly traumatized by the feedback session. After learning more about Control-Mastery theory, I have come to see that my feedback must have confirmed—in her mind—some of her deepest held pathogenic beliefs from her childhood: that she was bad, solely responsible for her unhappiness, and did not deserve any sympathy from others.

As mentioned in chapter 13, as a result of my rethinking of this case and other "failed" assessments, I have made a slight, but important modification in the procedures of the first session of a therapeutic assessment. Now, after helping clients to form individualized questions to be addressed by an assessment, I always ask at some point, "What is the worst possible thing I could tell you as a result of our work together?" I have been surprised by how useful clients' answers to this question have been, and I have remembered Weiss's idea that clients are often amazingly insightful in initial sessions about otherwise unconscious pathogenic beliefs. You may want to experiment with asking this question at the beginning of an assessment.

The Role of Theory in Psychological Assessment

This is one of several chapters in this book relating Therapeutic Assessment to various theories of human behavior and psychopathology. Previously I discussed Sullivan's interpersonal theory (chap. 3), humanistic psychology (chap. 4), and family systems theory (chap. 14). In chapter 17, I write about intersubjectivity theory and phenomenology, and elsewhere I have related Therapeutic Assessment—albeit more briefly—to object relations and self psychology (Finn & Tonsager, 1997). Now that I have added another perspective—Control-Mastery theory—to the list, I feel the need to comment on how I use theory in my day-to-day work with clients. This seems important because in the past, after disseminating various papers, I have read some comment later where someone has written "Therapeutic Assessment is based on Sullivanian principles" or "Therapeutic Assessment derives from humanistic psychology" or "Therapeutic Assessment applies family systems theory to psychological assessment." Each of these statements is true, in part, but they all miss the mark in a similar way.

My goal in thinking about a set of test data, or about the process of psychological assessment, in general, is to flexibly consider a variety of theoretical perspectives, and then compare the different insights that result. I find that with one client, object relations theory helps me the most, with another, family systems theory, and with yet another, intersubjectivity theory. But what is most important, I believe, is avoiding the "one size fits all" interpretations I see in so many of the psychological assessment reports I receive from other assessors. Hence I present this exposition of Control-Mastery theory, not because I believe it is the definitive way to understand the complex work we do as assessors, but to provide another lens to aid us in getting in our clients' shoes, helping them find compassion for themselves, and discovering new, more adaptive ways of being in the world.

17

Challenges and Lessons of Intersubjectivity Theory for Psychological Assessment

Intersubjectivity theory is a psychoanalytic perspective developed by Robert Stolorow and his colleagues, George Atwood and Bernard Brandchaft, in a series of seminal books published over the last 20 years (Atwood & Stolorow, 1984, 1996; Stolorow & Atwood, 1992; Stolorow, Atwood, & Brandchaft, 1994; Stolorow, Brandchaft, & Atwood, 1987). Some people have seen intersubjectivity theory as an outgrowth of Kohut's self psychology because both use empathy and introspection as basic guiding principles; however, this is incorrect and there are important differences between the two theories (cf. Trop, 1994). Stolorow (1996) said that intersubjectivity is more closely allied with the personology of Henry Murray, and indeed like Murray's theory, its basic tenets are idiographic, phenomenological, and systemic in nature.

As far as I know, Stolorow and his colleagues have not written much about psychological testing or formal personality assessment, although Stolorow (1994) mentioned learning idiographic personality assessment at Harvard from Irving Alexander, a protégé of Silvan Tomkins. Likewise, with a few notable exceptions (e.g., P. M. Lerner, 1990; Silverstein, 1999; B. L. Smith, 2005), few psychological assessors seem aware of intersubjectivity theory. This may be because at first glance,

---

This chapter is adapted from a paper presented to the Society for Personality Assessment (Finn, 2002a).

intersubjectivity theory and traditional psychological assessment appear highly incompatible.

You see, according to intersubjectivity theory, the "self" is not a separate stable characteristic of an individual—in fact, it cannot be described fully independent of the interpersonal system in which it is observed and/or measured. Objective measures of "self-esteem," "depression," and "borderline personality traits" are quite limited, an intersubjectivist would say, for several reasons. First, behavior always occurs within a certain context, meaning that a client who displays borderline characteristics with one assessor might not display borderline characteristics with a different assessor. Second, there is no such thing as a completely objective measure; assessors can never escape the influence of their own subjective views on their perceptions of clients. My personal history and implicit organizing principles inevitably shape my interpretation that a set of test materials indicates "depression," and this would be true of any other psychologist as well. Third, one can never fully know the extent or nature of one's contribution to an interpersonal context, although one can be open to and curious about such factors. I remember when my friend and colleague, Anna Maria Carlsson, reported at the annual Society for Personality Assessment meeting that different assessors in the large Stockholm Comparative Psychotherapy Study tended to collect different types of Rorschachs (Carlsson & Bihlar, 2000). Some assessors tended to get higher Rs, others more space responses, and yet others lower Lambdas. I remember that many people were troubled by these findings when they were presented, but they are no surprise to an intersubjectivist. In any enterprise that involves human relationships (as psychological assessment certainly does), there is no way to completely remove the influence of the observer and/or assessor. What is unique in the Swedish study is the opportunity to learn about such effects, because usually we don't have the data that permits such comparisons.

To help you grasp these ideas more concretely, let me relate a personal incident that taught me a great deal about intersubjectivity and the importance of perspective. My partner, Jim, and I frequently travel for work. Some years ago, I noticed an interesting correlation between our travel and the state of our queen-sized bed in the morning. When Jim was out of town, I typically woke up to find the sheets and blankets neatly ordered. I could hop out of the bed and make it up in a minute, by simply folding back the corner of the bedclothes where I had slept. In contrast, when Jim was in town, the sheets and blankets were generally in disarray the next morning. (And, I should add, this was not for the reasons you might be thinking.) It might take 3 to 4 minutes to make the bed, requiring one to carefully separate and tuck in each sheet and blanket. After a number of instances of observing this pattern, over some months, I reached a reasonable conclusion: "Jim musses up the bed." I confess I even felt a bit virtuous that my calmer temperament and/or clearer conscience led me to sleep so soundly in contrast to him.

This glowing self-appraisal remained unchallenged until one day when Jim and I were making up an especially disorderly bed together. As we tucked in sheets and blankets on our respective sides, I looked across and asked playfully, "What is that you do to the sheets in the middle of the night, anyway?" "Me?" he replied. "It's you that makes such a mess of them!" "Not me!" I protested. "When you're not here, I simply have to fold back a corner of the sheets in the morning." "But that's what happens to me when you're out of town," Jim retorted. And then we both began to laugh. For we realized, it was neither he nor I who was responsible, but we who mysteriously entangled the bed. In statistical terms we might say that the tendency to mess up sheets resided in the interaction term of the analysis of variance (ANOVA), while each of us had thought it was a main effect. And such mistakes are common, an intersubjectivist would say, because typically we don't have the data we need to see such interactions in two-person systems—each of us has only our personal subjective point of view. Furthermore, we tend to view behaviors or personal characteristics as residing solely in one person or the other because it is so difficult to think systemically and interactionally. If you meditate about it, it really is very complex trying to imagine the exact process through which the sheets on our various beds go awry!

Again, returning to psychological assessment, you can see how difficult it is to apply an intersubjective model to the types of referral questions we traditionally are asked to address. Other professionals ask us, "Is this client borderline?" or "What causes this client to behave so oddly?" or "Will this client be helped by group psychotherapy?" The first two of these questions imply that the source of psychopathology resides in individuals, and that there are people who have borderline characteristics and those who do not. The second question assumes that behavior is linearly determined, and that the purpose of assessment is to discover some "Truth" about people that can then be used to guide treatment. And the third question acts as if some people respond well to group therapy and others do not, without much regard for the type of group, the characteristics of the leader, or the client's attitude towards such a referral. If we adopt an intersubjective perspective, must we be content to answer "It depends," "It's complex," and "I don't know" to such referral questions?

Luckily, another option exists. In 1985, Constance Fischer published a groundbreaking book, called *Individualizing Psychological Assessment*, in which she laid out a coherent view of psychological assessment compatible with intersubjectivity theory, and then derived a set of practical guidelines for psychological assessment. Interestingly, Fischer came to her approach from existential–phenomenological psychology, yet reached a conclusion about psychological inquiry that is remarkably similar to that articulated by Stolorow and his colleagues: Although we can never escape our own subjectivity, we can acknowledge this fact to ourselves and others, and constantly investigate how our internal organizing principles influence our perceptions and conclusions. For reasons I'll explain later, this basic principle led Fischer quite naturally to the practice of collaborative psychological assessment. As described in chapter 1, my colleagues and I later formalized Fischer's methods into the structured approach we call Therapeutic Assessment, emphasizing the fact that such assessments have been shown to be beneficial to clients (Ackerman, Hilsenroth, Baity, & Blagys, 2000; Finn & Tonsager, 1992; Newman & Greenway, 1997).

Next, I want to elucidate for you how intersubjectivity theory fits with the practices of collaborative, phenomenological, therapeutic psychological assessment. I'll organize this section by referencing "lessons" I think intersubjectivity has for psychological assessors.

Lesson #1: Focus on Context

In collaborative assessment, we do not ignore the fact that there are individual influences on behavior; to return to my ANOVA example, we believe in main effects as well as interactions. We even accept that there are potent genetic and biological influences on behavior. However, as Fischer says in her book, we reject conceptions that "trait = fate." We collaborative assessors focus much of our attention on the contextual factors influencing behavior because this is where things get interesting if you're trying to help people overcome problems in living. When a referring professional asks us to determine whether or not a client is "borderline," we might get curious about his or her uncertainty and ask questions like, "Under what circumstances does the client act in a way that makes you think this, and when does he not?" If we can, we assist the referral source in reframing the original question to something like "Sometimes, Bob expresses himself in highly emotional, self-destructive ways and makes sudden decisions in which he doesn't anticipate potential negative consequences. Other times, he is emotionally controlled and thoughtful. How can we understand such behavior patterns?"

Such contextualized referral questions pave the way for what we hope will be the outcome of the assessment—an understanding of the conditions that are necessary and sufficient for a problem behavior to occur, including such things as clients' perceptions or interpretations of events around them. For if we can determine this, we can begin to imagine contexts where the problem behavior might disappear and then, as described in chapter 8, run "experiments" during the assessment where we set up such contexts and see what happens. If these experiments succeed, they lead directly to recommendations of how to alter the client's context outside of the assessment room to minimize the likelihood of a problem behavior occurring.

Lesson #2: Attend to the Frame of the Assessment

Another place where we pay a great deal of attention to context in collaborative and/or therapeutic assessment is in the framing of the assessment itself. We believe it greatly affects our test results how a client views the purposes of the assessment and whether the client and assessor succeed in forming a mutually respectful relationship where they work together to understand "puzzles" the client brings to the assessment. For example, in chapter 6, I've written about my view of "defensive" test protocols, which traditional assessors tend to see as indicative of resistance or lack of cooperation in a client. In Therapeutic Assessment, when we get an MMPI–2 protocol with high L and K and low F, or a Rorschach with a high Lambda and less than 14 responses, we ask ourselves immediately, "Did the client and I adequately discuss her thoughts about the

assessment before beginning testing?" and/or "Do I fully appreciate the
dilemmas facing the client in the evaluation?"

For example, I recently conducted a couples assessment where both
partners produced normal range MMPI–2 profiles, with very high elevations on L, K, and S. This result surprised me at first because (a) the couple was paying a great deal of money for the assessment, (b) the results
would go only to them and their couples therapist, and (c) they genuinely seemed to want help understanding their relational stalemate.
However, as I explored the MMPI–2 findings with them in a session, I
came to understand a piece of the clients' context I had missed. Each very
much wanted to cooperate with the assessment, but also was afraid that
the testing would show that he or she individually was the main cause of
the marital conflicts. So, both of them downplayed their problems and
emphasized their strengths when completing the MMPI–2. Once we all
understood this, we were able to discuss their fears openly, and I shared
my belief that "It takes two to tango." They agreed, and after more discussion vowed that no matter what they learned about each other
through the assessment, they would try not to use it as ammunition. We
agreed it would be helpful if each focused on his or her part in the couple's difficulties. They asked to retake the MMPI–2, I agreed, and both
produced very different unguarded profiles. Also, at our next session,
they reported they'd had their best week together in 5 years!

Lesson #3: Involve Clients in Co-Interpreting Assessment Data

If you are interested in the practice of discussing test data with clients,
you should know that Fischer made it a routine procedure to involve clients in interpreting their own test behaviors. This makes sense to an
intersubjectivist because we recognize that we look through our own
"lens" in understanding any test behavior, test score, or statement of a
client. Thus, we can never really know what a certain piece of assessment
data "means." This does not mean that we give up our own point of view
entirely; it too conveys an important aspect of what is occurring in the
assessment room. However, we do not believe our interpretation reflects
some abstract "reality" and we are curious about others' points of view
(especially that of the client).

For example, several years ago I tested a highly successful and educated businessman, John, who was curious about his tendency to hook up with women who were far less accomplished than him. John explained that these relationships eventually all failed because of a basic incompatibility in interests; however, he still found himself attracted to this type of woman.

John's MMPI–2 was unremarkable, except for a slight elevation on Scale 9, which seemed to reflect his high-driving, busy lifestyle. On the Rorschach, John surprised me by producing eight Morbid responses, and when I asked him to comment on the test right after taking it, he said, "I sure saw a lot of damaged things, didn't I?" I concurred and invited him to speculate on this. He drew a blank. I then suggested that sometimes such responses reflect feelings a person has about himself—that he himself is defective. He considered for a moment and asked, "Could that be from long ago?"

John then revealed that he had spent the first 6 years of his life in a complete body cast because of a congenital spinal rotation. He had never really reflected on the effects this experience had on him, especially as he had completely healed physically and was now an accomplished athlete. As we continued to talk, John remembered feeling different from other kids in the neighborhood and anxious and insecure when he finally was able to attend school. He drew a connection I had not made between such insecurity and the feelings he experienced in the presence of women he considered "highly eligible." Rather quickly, we drew a link to John's selecting women he considered "beneath him" and he left the session highly satisfied. Our joint exploration took us to an understanding of his morbid responses that was based on an integration of our two subjectivities and that neither of us could have reached alone.

Lesson #4: Consider Other Points of View

In Fischer's book, she comes up with numerous pragmatic ways of dealing with the subjectivity problem in psychological assessment. One of my favorites is this: After you have looked at a set of test scores and developed a tentative understanding, force yourself to look at the data again, while trying on different theoretical "hats." Ask yourself, "How would a cognitive behaviorist understand this data, or a family systems therapist, or a social learning theorist?" Obviously, it helps to be widely read and to have training in different personality theories. Even attending roundtables and symposia at professional meetings can assist with this exercise because they help us personify the different points of view. Even if the next Monday morning you can't remember the intricacies of the different presenters' papers, you might ask yourself as you look at some test data, "What would presenter A, presenter B, and presenter C say about this particular person?" Or if you work in a setting with other psychologists, you can share cases and challenge each other to look at assessment results from different perspectives. One of the best reasons I can think to be part of an assessment consultation group is to become more aware of the biases and organizing principles with which we all perceive the world and our clients.

Lesson #5: Acknowledge Your Influence on the Assessment When Reporting Results

Next, I'd like to say a word about collaborative, intersubjective assessment reports. If you have not seen any, Fischer has numerous examples in her book or you can read those examples I've included in chapter 7 and chapter 10. One of the first things you notice if you were trained to write traditional reports is our liberal use of first person to refer to the assessor. You see if we can't escape our own influence on the field of the assessment, why not acknowledge it, document it, and put it out there so other readers can take it into account?

The following is an excerpt from a report Fischer wrote about her assessment of a boy with academic difficulties:

> When I asked Robbie to copy some geometric designs freehand (the Bender-Gestalt), he started right away and then had to erase part of the first design. Similarly, he scattered the designs on his paper without regard for the total number that would have to go on the page. Midway I interrupted to identify this continuing pattern. Robbie agreed that *starting without planning* is what leads to the messy papers that are so dissatisfying to his teachers. We explored the possibility that he could *stop and think before beginning*. For example, he could have counted the dots beforehand instead of midway as he had done. I suggested that he also could have made each figure smaller. Then he enthusiastically volunteered to start over. This time he numbered the figures, arranged then sequentially, corrected an error from the origi-

nal sheet, and pronounced that the second sheet was much better (as it indeed was, although both were adequate for a 10-year-old. (Fischer, 1985/1994, p. 32)

Do you see how there's no attempt on Fischer's part to pretend she was a detached, objective "examiner"? In fact, as one reads through the complete report, one gets a sense of what Fischer herself is like and how her way of being influences and in turn responds to this young boy. Other readers, such as Robbie's teachers, could read this report and begin to imagine their own contribution to the "interaction effect" with Robbie, which resulted in their being frustrated with him and his hating school.

The Challenge of Thinking Intersubjectively

In closing, I wish to acknowledge how challenging it is to think intersubjectively and to practice collaborative psychological assessment. Part of this difficulty lies in the fact that we live in a world that is dominated by logical positivism and what intersubjectivists call the "Myth of the Isolated Mind" (Stolorow & Atwood, 1992)—the view that each of us is independent from the world and people around us and that our perceptions represent objective views of reality. Additionally, although this philosophy is increasingly rejected in physics and botany, it continues to dominate most psychology and psychiatry training programs in the United States. We need only pick up a copy of the *Diagnostic and Statistical Manual of Mental Disorders* (4th ed. [*DSM–IV*]; American Psychiatric Association, 1994) to see why traditional, logical–positivist psychological assessment continues to direct our profession.

Second, you will notice that an intersubjective or phenomenologic point of view is difficult to maintain psychologically, as it leads to a sense of being more vulnerable, less in control, and less sure of oneself. We become aware of what Stolorow and Atwood (1992) call *the unbearable embeddedness of being,* and sometimes this awareness seems too much to handle. If I really remember the lesson of the bed-sheet incident with my partner Jim, I must constantly realize that there is an impossible-to-quantify interaction term in all of my experiences of self, friends, and clients. I feel less sure of where I stop and another person begins. The Rorschach I recorded yesterday might say important things about me, as well as about the client. That MMPI–2 profile I scored this morning has no fixed, invariant interpretation. The client I'm struggling to treat in psychotherapy might do better with my colleague down the hall. To the extent that my security depends on seeing my world and me as separate, defined, and unchanging, such thoughts can generate a great deal of anxiety.

So what are the benefits of thinking intersubjectively? I believe that it helps us cultivate a realistic humility that benefits our work. You see, although many of us are learned and wise, and our psychological instruments are wonderful, our tests don't reveal some fundamental "Truth" about our clients. What we have to offer through assessment is a unique and rare perspective, a new "story" if you will, about how to understand a particular person. And if we use our tests for what they are—as empathy "magnifiers" to better understand a client's subjectivity—the story we jointly construct with that person through the assessment will lead to increased compassion, envisioning new possibilities, and an increased sense of connection.

On my good days, I find the intersubjective perspective fascinating and invigorating. What an amazing and wonderful puzzle it is to try to understand how my perceptions of and reactions to clients intersect with their perceptions of and reactions to me to create a set of events that are reflected in test scores and other events during an assessment! And as I work with more and more clients, I think I'm learning about some of my "main effects." (Another time I may write about the types of Rorschachs I tend to collect.) Of course, this too is constantly shifting, as I change and am influenced by my clients.

For this is one last implication of intersubjectivity theory: Assessments have the potential to change not only clients, but also assessors. If we are open to clients' ideas and impressions of us and to their differing interpretations of test scores, us, and themselves, we will be affected—no doubt about it. (This idea is explored further in chap. 18.) To me, the main benefit of collaborative, intersubjective assessment is that it helps us grow as psychologists and as human beings. Really, not bad wages at all when you think about it!

18

How Psychological Assessment Taught Me Compassion and Firmness

I began practicing psychological assessment in 1979 as a 23-year-old graduate student. When I look back on myself at that time, I see a bright, energetic, and rather insecure young man who was concerned about people and who covered up his self-doubts and anxieties with an air of self-importance and accomplishment. Many things have happened in the intervening 28 years that have helped me become who I am today—a wiser and somewhat more secure middle-aged man who sometimes covers up his anxieties with an air of self-importance and accomplishment. Among the things that have shaped me the most, I count my work as a practitioner, teacher, and researcher of psychological assessment. My goal in this chapter is to illuminate several ways that I think practicing assessment has affected me and to reflect on how this happened.

My title focuses on learning compassion and firmness because these are two of the most important ways assessment has changed me. I want to start with a story about learning compassion that happened in 1982 when I was a psychology intern at Hennepin County Medical Center in Minneapolis. As part of my usual duties, I was assigned to do a personality assessment with a male client about my same age who had been admitted recently to the inpatient psychiatry ward following a suicide at-

---

This paper was previously published in the *Journal of Personality Assessment* (Finn, 2005b).

tempt. This client, whom I'll call John, was memorable in that in just a few days, he had managed to alienate a good deal of the highly experienced nursing staff—not to mention the rest of the people being treated on the ward—with his condescending and disdainful demeanor. In the treatment groups, John called the other patients "idiots" and offered penetrating but harsh comments on why they had the problems they did. One day he reduced a well-liked occupational therapist to tears with his biting remarks about her suggested craft project. And John and I got off to a bad start in our first meeting when he made it clear how impossible it was that a psychology trainee like myself could teach him anything about himself that he did not already know. I left that session with a major dose of negative countertransference, and my supervisor, Dr. Ken Hampton, patiently listened to me rant about why I should even "waste my time" on someone who obviously did not want to be helped when there were so many other deserving people needing assessments. I think Dr. Hampton knew this could be an important assessment for me, and he calmly and firmly instructed me to do the best I could with John, explaining that if we could understand John's off-putting behavior better, it would be of considerable help to the other staff.

John's Minnesota Multiphasic Personality Inventory (MMPI; Hathaway & McKinley, 1943) profile was extremely guarded and had no significant elevations on any of the clinical scales. In my mind at the time, this just confirmed the futility of my doing any further testing with John. Again, Dr. Hampton insisted that I persevere, and I gave John a Rorschach (Exner, 1993). This was quite a different experience. John produced five reflection responses in his average length protocol, confirming my impressions of his narcissism. He also gave a series of extremely depressive percepts, including a number of morbid images such as people with "empty" insides and a poignant final response about a person who had fallen apart into pieces.

Furthermore, John seemed quite undone by the process of the Rorschach, and for the first time, I felt some sympathy for him. When I inquired gently about how he was doing, he turned on me viciously, saying I might truly be the biggest fool he had ever met in all his contacts with the mental health system and that I needn't bother talking to him about the results of the assessment. He then stormed out of the testing room, got a nurse to let him back in the locked ward, and then refused to talk to me when I followed a few minutes later. To my embarrassment, the nurses and other staff observed all this and couldn't hide their knowing grins.

As a 26-year-old psychology intern, I took this all quite personally, and I stormed off myself to my supervisor's office, where I too had a temper tantrum, although it was slightly more intellectualized than John's. Again, Dr. Hampton listened patiently and asked me to show him the MMPI and read him the Rorschach. I've since come to understand a great deal about the types of MMPI–Rorschach discrepancies represented in John's testing (see chap. 7), but at the time, I needed help resolving the apparent contradictions.

Could I see, asked Dr. Hampton, how John's offensive interpersonal tactics and defensiveness on the MMPI were so strong because of the extreme inner pain and emptiness he was trying to protect? I thought I could, but why wouldn't John just admit to this pain and let us help him when it obviously troubled him enough to make a serious suicide attempt? Dr. Hampton nodded slowly, looked me in the eye, and asked if I could find no empathy for a person who would rather hide his pain and insecurity with an air of competence and self-sufficiency rather than face the shame of admitting that he needed help. I nodded slowly, starting to "get it." Dr. Hampton watched me closely and then explained projective identification to me in simple language. In fact, he said, what I was now experiencing—in terms of rage and embarrassment and the desire to retaliate—was a version of the feelings John struggled with daily. And for this to have happened, it must mean that I was vulnerable to some of the same dynamics as John.

That interpretation was quite a challenge for me at that point in my personal development, and I needed quite a bit of support in supervision and my own therapy to "metabolize" it over time. Dr. Hampton's timing was perfect in that I was able, fairly quickly, to shift my view of John to that of a fellow human being rather than someone who was totally different from me. Also, as I completed the assessment with my supervisor's help, writing the report, and eventually giving feedback to John and the staff working with him, I found more compassion, not only for John, but also for the part of myself that was so like him.

Over the years, I've come to see this experience as representative of one of the most challenging and exciting parts of being an assessor. To really be empathic to the clients we assess—and I'm using the word "empathy" in the Kohutian sense, as the ability to "put ourselves in our clients' shoes"—we are challenged repeatedly to find in ourselves a personal version of the conflicts, dynamics, and feelings troubling the people we assess. And although it's certainly possible to conduct psychological assessments without engaging in such personal exploration, I believe that if you do so, your reports will be wooden, your clients will not really feel moved and understood when you talk about their test results, referring professionals won't feel enlightened, and after a while, you'll feel bored with psychological assessment.

Of course, psychotherapists face a similar challenge to identify on some level with their clients. If you do a lot of assessment, it's even more challenging for a number of reasons. First, we assessors get asked to comprehend and explain the clients that no one else can understand, often because those clients exhibit qualities that even experienced mental health professionals prefer to deny in themselves. Over my years of doing assessments, I've stretched myself to empathize with how one might commit murder, perpetrate sexual abuse, repeatedly set oneself up to be victimized, engage in all kinds of compulsions, really truly wish to die, and use every known character defense and mind-altering chemical to ward off inner pain. Recently, I was really struggling with an assessment I was doing, so I sought consultation with Dr. Paul Lerner, who helped me see that I didn't really understand my own or other's capacity for sadistically holding other people hostage by being a martyr (see chap. 14).

There is another way that doing personality testing challenges us differently than doing nonassessment-based psychotherapy. Our tests are powerful tools that give us access to clients' inner worlds in ways we don't have otherwise (except perhaps through clients' dreams). I have written elsewhere about my view of psychological tests as "empathy magnifiers" (Finn & Tonsager, 1997, 2002). Well, sometimes we see things clearly through magnifying glasses that we might not otherwise choose to see. For example, to go back to my assessment with John, after talking about his Rorschach with Dr. Hampton, I found myself quite haunted by some of the images John reported. This was heightened after my psychotherapist at the time pointed out the similarities to some of my own Rorschach responses, from a protocol administered 2 years earlier just before my first Rorschach course. Open-response tests are not the only tests that can have these types of effects. I think we can have similar strong emotional reactions just by reading slowly and thoughtfully through the MMPI–2 (Butcher et al., 1989) critical items endorsed by a highly distressed or disturbed client.

Now, I implied in my title that assessment has taught me firmness as well as compassion, and I want to relate one more, briefer personal story that illustrates this second point. Early in my clinical practice, I became aware of a particular "blind spot" I had by doing an exercise that Alex Caldwell (2003) talked about during his Klopfer award acceptance speech to the Society for Personality Assessment. I used to challenge myself after interviewing clients I was assessing to sketch my best guess of their MMPI profiles before the answer sheets were scored. Over time, I saw a glaring pattern: I consistently failed to predict elevations on Scale 4 or both Scale 4 and Scale 9. And although the hypothesis Dick Rogers (2003) mentioned in his Master Lecture is intriguing—that we will tend not to see people as psychopathic unless they surpass our own level of psychopathy—in fact, I'm pretty sure the opposite was true in my case. At that time in my life I had so clamped down on my own "inner psychopath" that I simply kept expecting other people to be as nice as I thought myself to be.

I knew something was off about this and was grateful to have the MMPI to "watch my back." Still, fairly quickly, another problem became glaringly apparent. Even when I knew from my assessment materials that clients tended to act out in antisocial ways, I tended to be rather ineffective with them during assessments. I would talk with them about their impulsivity, excitement seeking, and ability to be coldhearted, but I remember feeling at the end of such assessments that I had missed something and that the clients were vaguely disappointed. Similarly, when I saw such clients in therapy, they would tend to leave after four or five sessions. At first, I consoled myself with the maxim that antisocial clients don't respond well in general to mental health interventions. The only problem was, the clients I was seeing weren't hard-core psychopaths at all but simply people who tended to act out as a coping mechanism. Also I was acutely aware that some of my colleagues had much better track records than I did with this type of client.

In this case, it was a client and an assessment workshop that helped me make the personal shift required. I was assessing a young woman named Mary who had gotten into some legal trouble for threatening a man at a party with a knife because he refused to have sex with her when the bash was done. At one point, I was talking with Mary about her MMPI (a 4–9–2–7 profile for those of you who are interested) and she looked at me and said, "I wish you wouldn't be so damn nice all the time!" When I looked confused she said, "You always try not to hurt people's feelings. But sometimes it's not good. It would work better if you'd just call a spade a spade!" This impressed me, in part because I had just attended an MMPI workshop with Alex Caldwell where he had discussed his hypothesis about Scale-4 elevations being related to a combination of overly harsh and overly permissive parenting in childhood. I suddenly realized that I was repeating history by acting like an overprotective parent and failing to provide what self psychologists call an "adversarial transference" experience (Wolf, 1998) for these individuals where they could bump up against a firm, savvy, and yet benevolent authority figure. Years later, Carl Gacono explained to me that antisocial clients can't idealize us if they feel that they can outsmart us and get away with things in the therapy and/or assessment relationship.

True to form, Mary appeared for our assessment feedback session with a beer in her hand and a glint in her eye that seemed to say, "So what are you going to do about this?" I calmly pointed at the small kitchen off the waiting room and said firmly, "You can put that in the refrigerator and pick it up when we're done." We then went over the assessment results together, which I had worked hard to put into no-nonsense, direct, blunt language. Mary listened respectfully, asked a few questions, and said at the end, "You really got me!" I remember feeling that tremendous excitement of having risen to an occasion and knowing that I would never be quite the same afterwards.

As it turned out, I ended up working in psychotherapy with Mary after the assessment, and years later, she told me how relieved she had been when I made her put up her beer, because in her words, "Mom always let me play in the middle of the highway." The lesson I learned from Mary helped me not only in that assessment but in almost every assessment I've done since then. For I've come to see that our job is not only to find compassion for our clients and to understand the psychological dilemmas underlying their problems in living but also to talk with clients about these issues in clear, forceful language. For many clients, an assessment may be the first time that someone respected them enough to bring up such topics, and our doing so conveys a certain faith in the part of them that wants to grow and change. We do no one any good by constructing excessively sympathetic apologias for clients' psychological "shortcuts." As Mary said, most times it's best just to "call a spade a spade." Our reluctance to do this is, I believe, is in fact due to a common empathic error: We project our own shame on clients and assume they will be devastated if we speak frankly about the less savory aspects of their personalities. In fact, some part of them is longing to get such things out in the open and to better understand why they behave in self-destructive or cruel ways and how to begin to make changes.

In conclusion, I believe that the work of an assessor is not for the faint of heart. To do our jobs well, we must continuously confront our inner shadows and courageously say things to people that no one has said before. This work takes energy, lots of support from others, and an ability to appreciate and even be amused by life's individualized, "remedial classroom"—by which I mean our tendency to create and encounter the same life lessons over and over until we master them sufficiently to move on to the next. Perhaps because—rather than in spite of—these very challenges, I count myself lucky to be a psychological assessor.

19

Conclusion: Practicing Therapeutic Assessment

By this point in this book, I hope to have inspired you, convinced you about the potential of psychological assessment as a life-changing experience, and have interested you in Therapeutic Assessment in particular. Thus, in this final chapter, I address certain practical matters regarding the practice of Therapeutic Assessment: When is this approach not appropriate? Who pays for an assessment conducted in this manner? How does one get referrals? What kind of support is needed to learn and practice Therapeutic Assessment?

Possible Contraindications for Therapeutic Assessment

Are there times when Therapeutic Assessment is not the best approach and it may be better to use a traditional, noncollaborative format? Quite possibly, there may be situations when this is true. Here are four instances that come to mind:

An Assessment is Being Done for Selection and/or Classification Purposes Only

Occasionally, at our clinic, we receive requests for psychological testing that are solely for the purpose of qualifying an individual for some psychological or educational service. A common example would be a parent who requests that a child be given an IQ test to see if the child qualifies for a school program for "gifted and talented" children. Often, the only assessment question is whether the child has a documented IQ score of 135 or greater. I typically talk with these parents to make sure there are no other issues that should be explored through an assessment. If there are not, I arrange for the IQ test and for a brief summary/discussion session where I talk with the parents about their child's intellectual functioning. Occasionally, something arises in the IQ testing that warrants further discussion, and I may suggest to the parents that it could be helpful to expand the focus of the assessment. Typically, however, a full Therapeutic Assessment would be "overkill" for this kind of referral question and others like it.

A Client Is in Acute Crisis or Severe Emotional Distress but an Assessment Is Still Needed

When clients are in severe acute distress, most types of psychological testing are inadvisable, and some clients with whom I have worked have expressed resentment about being tested under such circumstances in the past. Imagine being asked to participate in a WAIS–III when you were severely suicidal, or being told while acutely psychotic that you could only have visitors to the inpatient ward after you completed an MMPI–2! These are events clients told me that actually happened to them. Psychological assessment may still be appropriate at such times, and may involve observing and interviewing the client, talking to family members and collateral professionals, and reviewing records from past evaluations. But the client may have diminished capacity to engage in full collaboration, and if so, attempts to engage the client as a participant observer may miss the mark. Some acutely distressed clients may not even be able to give true informed consent. Under such circumstances, I would still try to collaborate with family members of the client and other members of the treatment team, and I would treat the client as respectfully as possible, for example, explaining everything I was doing and offering to answer any questions. However, I would freely deviate from the Therapeutic Assessment flow chart (see chap. 1), and hope that I might involve the client more fully at a later point in time.

Involuntary Assessments

When clients are referred against their will for a psychological assessment, collaborative assessment techniques may be somewhat useful in gaining the clients' cooperation. For example, Purves (1997, 2002) wrote moving accounts of collaborative assessments of incarcerated adolescents and of mothers referred for possible termination of their parental rights. Again, I would do everything I could in such instances to treat the client respectfully, give informed consent, share my thoughts about the test findings, and listen to the client's explanations, modifications, and corrections. But clearly, in those instances where client confidentiality is limited and much is at stake, it may not be in clients' best interests to generate questions about themselves, share reactions to assessment feedback, and so forth. My goal in such situations is to incorporate enough of the spirit of Therapeutic Assessment that the clients do not feel abused by the assessment process; but rarely is it possible to adhere to the complete collaborative model.

You may remember from chapter 14 that I have a particular way of handling the assessment of adolescents who are brought for assessment against their will by their parents. I ask parents to put their questions concerning those adolescents "on the table" for their children to know, and to allow the adolescents to have their own private assessment questions, to which they will receive answers before their parents get feedback at the end of the assessment. If the adolescent is still uncomfortable and unwilling to be assessed, I am likely to suggest to the parents that we wait and do the assessment at some point in the future. (I may or may not continue working with the adolescent during this interval to build more of a relationship.) I realize that even when parents do agree to my proposal, legally they have the right to full access to my records. But in all my years of assessing adolescents, I have never yet had parents renege on their promise of privacy for their child regarding an assessment.

An Assessment Is Likely to Be Used to Harm the Client

Rarely, at the beginning of an assessment, I have sensed that one part of a client's interpersonal system is likely to use assessment results to try to humiliate or punish the client. For example, I wrote in chapter 9 about a referring therapist who wanted an assessment of his client to "prove"

EXHIBIT 19–1
Sample Bill for a Therapeutic Assessment

Bill For Professional Services

August 9, 20XX

Client: Barbara Jones
100 Main Street
Smalltown, TX 78XXX

D.O.B.: 7–1–56

DSM-IV: 300.40

Date	Activity	Time	CPT Code[a]	Fee
7–5–06	Diagnostic Interview	1 hour	90801	$180
7–12–06	Psychological Testing	1.5 hours	96101	$270
7–19–06	Psychological Testing	3 hours	96101	$540
7–26–06	Psychotherapy	1.5 hours	90808	$270
8–1–06	Psychological Testing	2 hours	96101	$360
8–2–06	Psychotherapy	1.5 hours	90808	$270
8–4–06	Psychological Testing	4 hours	96101	$720

Total Charges **$2610**

Stephen E. Finn

Stephen E. Finn, PhD
Licensed Psychologist
(TX license 12345)
Tax ID: XX-XXXXXXX

[a]These CPT codes are those that are current at the time of this book's publication.

that an interpretation the therapist made was "actually correct." In another instance, two parents were intent on using assessment results concerning their child as ammunition in an escalating marital battle, and I could see no way to protect the child's best interests. Clearly, in such situations, an assessor can first try to confront the parties whose agendas would be harmful to the client. If this tactic were unsuccessful, I myself would decline to conduct the assessment. But if I did not have that kind of freedom, I would either inform the client of my suspicions (if I could do so without putting the client in a bad spot), or conduct a routine traditional assessment that did not ask the client to be a vulnerable collaborator.

Billing for a Therapeutic Assessment

Two questions I am asked frequently are: "How do you bill for a Therapeutic Assessment?" and "Do insurance companies pay for this type of assessment?" There are no fixed answers to these questions, but I gladly share my experience. Also, a colleague and I addressed these two questions in a chapter published elsewhere (Finn & Martin, 1997). In general, however, I caution you that questions of billing and appropriate charges vary to some extent by state, third-party payor, and the particular client. Therefore, it is always good to check with your own licensing board, professional society, attorney, or contract provider if you are unsure of whether your billing practices are appropriate.

Because Therapeutic Assessment is a mixture of psychological testing and psychotherapy, when I am asked to provide an itemized bill for an insurance provider, I often bill some of the sessions as diagnostic interview, some as psychological testing, and some as psychotherapy.[1] I am as transparent about this practice as possible, and have sometimes sent an accompanying letter explaining this breakdown. Exhibit 19–1 gives an example of a bill from a recent assessment of a 50-year-old woman, Barbara Jones. At the first session, Mrs. Jones and I met for 60 min to develop questions for the assessment and discuss background information, and I billed for 1 hour of diagnostic interview. At the next session, Mrs. Jones spent 1.5 hours completing the MMPI–2 (for which I did not charge) but then we spent 1 hour discussing her experience of taking the test, and I spent 30 min scoring and interpreting the test, so I billed for 1.5 hours of psychological testing. The following week, Mrs. Jones and I completed and discussed her experience of the Rorschach together (2 hours), and I spent an hour scoring and interpreting it, so I billed for 3 hours of psychological testing. Our next session was a 90-min assessment intervention session, which I billed as psychotherapy. I then spent

---

[1]Again, some third-party payors may object to this kind of breakdown, and may ask you to bill all the sessions as psychological testing. I suggest you clarify this with companies with which you have service contracts.

2 hours interpreting and integrating the testing and writing a detailed script for the summary/discussion session (billed as psychological testing). Mrs. Jones and I then met for 1.5 hours for a summary/discussion session (billed as psychotherapy), and subsequently I spent 4 hours writing a report about the assessment that Mrs. Jones needed for her work, which I billed as psychological testing. I was not under contract with Mrs. Jones's insurance provider, so in this instance she paid me and then submitted the bill on her own for reimbursement. Therefore, I am unaware of how her company processed the bill and how much was paid.[2]

You will notice from Exhibit 19–1 that I bill at the same rate for psychological assessment as I do for psychotherapy. As I have spoken about (Finn, 2003a), I believe the common practice of charging less for psychological assessment than psychotherapy fails to recognize the many professional and personal demands of psychological assessment. If anything (and this is not to put down the challenges of being a psychotherapist), psychological assessment often requires more knowledge, training, and overhead costs than does psychotherapy, and this is especially true if one is practicing Therapeutic Assessment. Also, as this book explains, I do not see psychotherapy and psychological assessment as wholly distinct enterprises. I recognize that not all insurance carriers operate according to this logic, but we as professionals will not begin to change such attitudes unless we ourselves value the work that we do. I also believe that if psychologists are not appropriately reimbursed for their time doing psychological assessment, many will simply find it easier to practice psychotherapy and will give up doing psychological assessments completely. In my mind, this would be a loss of something distinctive and valuable about being a psychologist.

Negotiating Contracts With Third-Party Payors

This brings up the question of how one negotiates service provider contracts that honor the value of psychological assessment with third-party payors. As I have written about elsewhere (Finn & Martin, 1997), I found the key to success in this area involved: (a) developing relation-

---

[2]I find that even middle-class clients will pay these kinds of fees for a psychological assessment and feel that they got their money's worth! Currently, I also do a portion of my assessments gratis or on a sliding-fee scale for clients whose finances are limited.

ships with gatekeepers and other "powers that be" in such organizations, (b) educating them about the validity and potential therapeutic value of psychological assessment, (c) demonstrating to them that the assessments I conducted were useful in ways that previous psychological assessments they encountered were not, and (d) supplying them with research data and client satisfaction data that supported the points I was making. With these tactics employed, in several instances, insurance providers who were previously quite resistant to paying for psychological assessments started referring difficult and complex clients for comprehensive evaluations.

Marketing Therapeutic Assessment

So how does one successfully develop referral sources for Therapeutic Assessment? First, hone your assessment and psychotherapy skills so that you do really excellent work, for as the old saying goes, "Quality is the best advertisement." (I write more to come about how to become trained in Therapeutic Assessment.) Next, you have to get the word out to referring professionals and the community at large about what you do. When I started the Center for Therapeutic Assessment in 1993, I asked each of three highly successful clinicians in Austin to lunch. I told them about Therapeutic Assessment and offered a free assessment of their "hardest client." All three of them took me up on my offer, and as I expected, they found the assessments extremely helpful to them and their clients. Before long, I had more referrals than I could handle, and had to hire more staff. I am pleased to say that each of those three therapists still refers many clients for assessments today.

There were other ways I spread the word about my work:

(1) I gave talks about Therapeutic Assessment to various professional organizations, especially those for nonpsychologists. I found many masters-level psychotherapists and psychiatrists who were eager for input and support on their difficult clients, and psychological assessment provided a graceful venue for them to get this.

(2) I took part in supervisor-led or peer-organized psychotherapy consultation groups. I not only welcomed the support and assistance with my own cases, when another therapist presented a cli-

ent whom I thought might benefit from psychological assessment, I spoke up and said so. In many instances, the therapist had never even considered this option.

(3) I accepted invitations to talk in graduate school courses for psychologists, social workers, and so forth about Therapeutic Assessment. Many of these students went on to get their degrees and practice in the Austin area, and some remembered my presentation and made referrals.

(4) I visited and spoke with ministers and pastors about therapeutic couples assessments. Many were working with extremely challenging couples and jumped at the chance to get help from a psychologist. (Some of these churches even funded the couples assessments they referred.)

Some of my best referral sources have been satisfied clients. At this point, approximately 20% to 30% of my requests for Therapeutic Assessment do not come through another mental health professional, but directly from people who have heard about our assessments from their family, friends, and neighbors. I have never done any direct advertising to the public, but I know of a colleague practicing collaborative assessment who once ran an ad in her local newspaper reading something like: "Facing a major life decision or at a personal turning point? Get input from a psychologist through the process of psychological testing..." She got a number of calls from people interested in brief assessments.

In sum, I have a firm belief that if you do excellent psychological assessments and let others know about what you are doing, then the word will spread and soon you too can have a thriving practice in Therapeutic Assessment.

Learning Therapeutic Assessment

I am currently thinking a great deal about how to develop training materials and training opportunities for the increasing number of psychologists who want to learn to do Therapeutic Assessment. This book is one step in that direction, and I also give training workshops around the world, so contact me if you would like to receive announcements about those or schedule a workshop in your area. I also hope to be developing future training materials that include DVDs of exemplar interactions with clients, such as those videos I show in my workshops.

In the meantime, if you want to become expert at Therapeutic Assessment, I urge you to:

(1) Read everything you can about Therapeutic Assessment and collaborative assessment. The references at the end of this book contain many important articles that can teach you a lot.

(2) Begin experimenting with some of the collaborative assessment techniques written about in this book. Feel free to start small, perhaps by asking clients for assessment questions or by stopping after a test administration to inquire what clients noticed or experienced. You're unlikely to do any harm with such efforts, and gradually you will find yourself becoming more confident.

(3) Become as skilled as you can at using and interpreting a number of psychological tests. Because Therapeutic Assessment is about "getting in clients' shoes," you need not only your empathy, but as much knowledge as you can about what various test scores might mean. If you listen to the great "MMPI–ers" and "Rorschachers" of our time, you'll notice that they excel at knowing how a particular score or response translates into clients' subjective experience and how to put this experience into words.

(4) Become as knowledgeable about and as skilled as you can with different types of psychotherapy. This will not only help you envision what treatment options different clients might need, you can also draw from different techniques and ways of conceptualizing problems when conducting Therapeutic Assessments.

(5) Finally, expand your self and your compassion and wisdom through reading novels, traveling, psychotherapy, mindfulness or spiritual practices, or dedication to a sport, music, art, and so forth. As I covered in chapter 18, one of the challenges of practicing Therapeutic Assessment is that often we are asked to "feel our way into" clients' subjective experiences that we may find terrifying, disgusting, confusing, or initially incomprehensible. The more "inner blocks" you can remove and the more self-

awareness you have before you see a client, the more likely you will be able to understand and ultimately help that person.

Getting Support

As I have said at various points throughout this book, collaborative and/or Therapeutic Assessment is a challenging line of work, and I believe it is best practiced in the context of a supportive community of like-minded professionals. If none exists in your area, what should you do? You might consider inviting other colleagues to start a reading group on collaborative and Therapeutic Assessment. If there is enough interest, you could eventually discuss your assessment cases with each other, or puzzle together about such questions as, "What might be an appropriate assessment intervention for this type of client?" Sometimes, it can be invaluable just to read a difficult set of TAT stories, or a Rorschach protocol, and have others help you "hold it."

I also urge you to attend regional and national meetings where we collaborative assessment people hang out, such as the Society for Personality Assessment. You can join this organization online at www.personality.org and get the *Journal of Personality Assessment* (where many articles on Therapeutic Assessment have been published) with your membership fee.

Finally I welcome you to write or e-mail me about your questions and experiences with Therapeutic Assessment. I know that as this model develops, many of you will introduce innovations that I have never even considered. I look eagerly forward to that day.

References

Abidin, R. R. (1995). *Parenting Stress Index, 3rd ed.: Professional manual*. Odessa, FL: Psychological Assessment Resources.

Achenbach, T. M. (1991). *Manual for the Child Behavior Checklist/4–18 and 1991 profile*. Burlington, VT: University of Vermont Department of Psychiatry.

Ackerman, S. J., Hilsenroth, M. J., Baity, M. R., & Blagys, M. D. (2000). Interaction of therapeutic process and alliance during psychological assessment. *Journal of Personality Assessment, 75*, 82–109.

Agazarian, Y. M. (1997). *Systems-centered therapy for groups*. New York: Guilford.

Allen, J. G. (1981.) The clinical psychologist as diagnostic consultant. *Bulletin of the Menninger Clinic, 45*, 247–258.

American Psychiatric Association. (1994). *Diagnostic and statistical manual of mental disorders* (4th ed.). Washington, DC: Author.

American Psychological Association. (1992). Ethical principles of psychologists and code of conduct. *American Psychologist, 47*, 1597–1611.

Aranow, E., Reznikoff, M., & Moreland, K. (1994). *The Rorschach technique: Perceptual basics, content interpretation, and applications*. Boston: Allyn & Bacon.

Arbisi, P. A., & Ben-Porath, Y. S. (1996). An MMPI–2 infrequent response scale for use with psychopathological populations: The Infrequency Psychopathology Scale, F(p). *Psychological Assessment, 7*, 424–431.

Archer, R. P., & Krishnamurthy, R. (1993a). Combining the Rorschach and the MMPI in the assessment of adolescents. *Journal of Personality Assessment, 60*, 132–140.

Archer, R. P., & Krishnamurthy, R. (1993b). A review of MMPI and Rorschach interrelationships in adult samples. *Journal of Personality Assessment, 61*, 277–293.

Armstrong, J. G., & Lowenstein, R. J. (1990). Characteristics of persons with multiple personality and dissociative disorders on psychological testing. *Journal of Nervous and Mental Disease, 178*, 448–454.

Atwood, G. E., & Stolorow, R. D. (1984). *Structures of subjectivity: Explorations in psychoanalytic phenomenology*. Hillsdale, NJ: Analytic Press.

Atwood, G. E., & Stolorow, R. D. (1996). *Faces in a cloud: Intersubjectivity in personality theory*. London: Jason Aronson.

Barton, A. (1994). Humanistic contributions to the field of psychotherapy: Appreciating the human and liberating the therapist. In F. Wertz (Ed.), *The humanistic movement: Recovering the person in psychology* (pp. 215–232). Lake Worth, FL: Gardner Press.

Becker, E., Gohara, Y. Y., Marizilda, F. D., & Santiago, M. D. E. (2002). Interventive assessment with children and their parents in group meetings:

Professional training and storybook feedback. *The Humanistic Psychologist, 30*, 114–124.

Bender L. A. (1938). *Visual Motor Gestalt Test and its clinical use: Research monograph number 3*. New York: American Orthopsychiatric Association.

Ben-Porath, Y., Graham, J. R., Nagayama Hall, G. C., & Hirschman, R. (1995). *Forensic applications of the MMPI–2*. Thousand Oaks, CA: Sage.

Berg, M. (1986). Toward a diagnostic alliance between psychiatrist and psychologist. *American Psychologist, 41*, 52–59.

Berg, M. (1988). Diagnostic benefits of analyzing the group dynamics of the assessment team. *Bulletin of the Menninger Clinic, 52*, 126–133.

Bernstein, E. M., & Putnam, F. W. (1986). Development, reliability, and validity of a dissociation scale. *Journal of Nervous and Mental Disease, 174*, 727–735.

Blanchard, W. (1959). The group process in gang rape. *Journal of Social Psychology, 49*, 259–266.

Blanchard, W. (1968). The Consensus Rorschach: Background and development. *Journal of Projective Techniques and Personality Assessment, 32*, 327–330.

Bruhn, A. R. (1992). The Early Memories Procedure: A projective test of autobiographical memory (Part I). *Journal of Personality Assessment, 58*, 1–15.

Bugental, J. F. T., & Sapienza, B. G. (1994). The three R's for humanistic psychology: Remembering, reconciling, and reuniting. In F. Wertz (Ed.), *The humanistic movement: Recovering the person in psychology* (pp. 159–169). Lake Worth, FL: Gardner Press.

Butcher, J. N. (1990). *The MMPI–2 in psychological treatment*. New York: Oxford University Press.

Butcher, J. N., Dahlstrom, W. G., Graham, J. R., Tellegen, A., & Kaemmer, B. (1989). *MMPI–2: Minnesota Multiphasic Personality Inventory–2: Manual for administration and scoring*. Minneapolis: University of Minnesota Press.

Caldwell, A. M. (2001). What do the MMPI–2 scales fundamentally measure? Some hypotheses. *Journal of Personality Assessment, 76*, 1–17.

Caldwell, A. M. (2003, March). *A love affair with an instrument*. Paper presented at the annual meeting of the Society for Personality Assessment, San Francisco.

Carlsson, A. M., & Bihlar, B. (2000, March). *Rorschach assessment before or during psychotherapy: Does it make a difference?* Paper presented at the annual meeting of the Society for Personality Assessment, Albuquerque, NM.

Cohen, L. J. (1980). The unstated problem in a psychological testing referral. *American Journal of Psychiatry, 137*, 1173–1176.

Craddick, R. A. (1972). Humanistic assessment: A reply to Brown. *Psychotherapy: Theory, Research, and Practice, 9*, 107–110.

Craddick, R. A. (1975). Sharing oneself in the assessment procedure. *Professional Psychology, 6*, 279–282.

Dana, R. H. (1982). Communication of assessment findings. In R. H. Dana (Ed.), *A human science model for personality assessment with projective techniques* (pp. 217–251). Springfield, IL: Charles C. Thomas.

Dana, R. H. (1984a). Personality assessment: Practice and teaching for the next decade. *Journal of Personality Assessment, 48*, 46–57.

Dana, R. H. (1984b). A service-delivery paradigm for personality assessment. *Journal of Personality Assessment, 49*, 598–604.

Dana, R. H., & Graham, E. D. (1976). Feedback of client-relevant information and clinical practice. *Journal of Personality Assessment, 40*, 464–469.

Dana, R. H., & Leech, S. (1974). Existential assessment. *Journal of Personality Assessment, 38*, 428–435.

Dorr, D. (1981). Conjoint psychological testing in marriage therapy: New wine in old skins. *Professional Psychology, 12*, 549–555.

Driggs, J. H., & Finn, S. E. (1990). *Intimacy between men: How to find and keep gay love relationships*. New York: E. P. Dutton.

Evans III, F. B. (1996). *Harry Stack Sullivan: Interpersonal theory and psychotherapy*. London: Routledge.

Evans III, F. B. (2000, March). The relevance of Sullivan's interpersonal theory and psychiatric interview to psychological assessment. In F. B. Evans III (Chair), *Harry Stack Sullivan and psychological assessment*. Symposium conducted at the annual meeting of the Society for Personality Assessment, Albuquerque, NM.

Exner, J. E., Jr. (1993). *The Rorschach: A comprehensive system: Vol. 1. Basic foundations (3rd. ed.)*. New York: Wiley.

Exner, J. E., Jr. (1995). *A Rorschach workbook for the comprehensive system* (4th ed.). Asheville, NC: Rorschach Workshops.

Exner, J. E., Jr. (1996, March). Toward an understanding of Rorschach and MMPI relationships. In G. J. Meyer & R. Krishnamurthy (Chairs), *The Rorschach and MMPI disagree: Implications for research and practice*. Symposium conducted at the annual meeting of the Society for Personality Assessment, Denver, CO.

Exner, J. E., Jr., Armbruster, G., & Mittman, B. (1978). The Rorschach response process. *Journal of Personality Assessment, 42*, 27–38.

Finn, S. E. (1993, March). *Using "softer" tests to demonstrate MMPI–2 findings to clients in treatment planning*. Paper presented at the 28th Annual Symposium on Recent Developments in the Use of the MMPI, MMPI–2, and MMPI–A, Saint Petersburg Beach, FL.

Finn, S. E. (1994, April). *Testing one's own clients mid-therapy with the Rorschach*. Paper presented at the annual meeting of the Society for Personality Assessment, Chicago, IL.

Finn, S. E. (1996a). Assessment feedback integrating MMPI–2 and Rorschach findings. *Journal of Personality Assessment, 67*, 543–557.

Finn, S. E. (1996b). *Manual for using the MMPI–2 as a therapeutic intervention*. Minneapolis, MN: University of Minnesota Press.

Finn, S. E. (1996c, March.). Using the Consensus Rorschach technique as brief marital therapy. In S. E. Finn (Chair), *Collaborative assessment of couples*. Symposium conducted at the annual meeting of the Society for Personality Assessment, Denver, CO.

Finn, S. E. (1997a, March). Collaborative child assessment as a family systems intervention. In S. E. Finn (Chair), *Collaborative assessment of children and families*. Symposium conducted at the annual meeting of the Society for Personality Assessment, San Diego, CA.

Finn, S. E. (1997b, March). One-up, one-down, and in-between: A systemic model of assessment collaboration. In S. E. Finn (Chair), *Collaborative consultation between assessor and therapist*. Symposium conducted at the annual meeting of the Society for Personality Assessment, San Diego, CA.

Finn, S. E. (1998). Teaching therapeutic assessment in a required graduate course. In H. Handler & M. J. Hilsenroth (Eds.), *Teaching and learning personality assessment* (pp. 359–373). Mahwah, NJ: Lawrence Erlbaum Associates.

Finn, S. E. (1999, March). Giving clients feedback about "defensive" test protocols: Guidelines from therapeutic assessment. In R. J. Genellen (Chair), *Defining, detecting, and dealing with defensive responding*. Symposium conducted at the annual meeting of the Society for Personality Assessment, New Orleans, LA.

Finn, S. E. (2000, March). Therapeutic Assessment: Would Harry approve? In F. B. Evans III (Chair), *Harry Stack Sullivan and psychological assessment*. Symposium conducted at the annual meeting of the Society for Personality Assessment, Albuquerque, NM.

Finn, S. E. (2002a, March). Challenges and lessons of intersubjectivity theory for psychological assessment. In M. L. Silverstein (Chair), *Concepts of the self: Implications for assessment*. Symposium conducted at the annual meeting of the Society for Personality Assessment, San Antonio, TX.

Finn, S. E. (2002b, March). *The power and potential of psychological assessment*. Presidential address presented at the annual meeting of the Society for Personality Assessment, San Antonio, TX.

Finn, S. E. (2003a, March). *Obstacles to practicing psychological assessment*. Presidential address to the annual meeting of the Society for Personality Assessment, San Francisco, CA.

Finn, S. E. (2003b). Therapeutic Assessment of a man with "ADD." *Journal of Personality Assessment, 80*, 115–129.

Finn, S. E. (2004, March). "But I was only trying to help!": Therapeutic Assessment and Karpman's triangle. In S. E. Finn (Chair), *What can we learn from failed assessments*. Symposium conducted at the annual meeting of the Society for Personality Assessment, Miami, FL.

Finn, S. E. (2005a, July). Collaborative sequence analysis of the Rorschach. In S. E. Finn (Chair), *Collaborative/therapeutic uses of the Rorschach*. Symposium conducted at the XVIII International Congress on the Rorschach and Projective Methods, Barcelona, Spain.

Finn, S. E. (2005b). How psychological assessment taught me compassion and firmness. *Journal of Personality Assessment, 84*, 27–30.

Finn, S. E. (2005c, March). Please tell me that I'm not who I fear I am: Control-Mastery theory and therapeutic assessment. In C. T. Fischer (Chair), *Conceptual innovations in personality assessment*. Symposium conducted at the annual meeting of the Society for Personality Assessment, Chicago, IL.

Finn, S. E. (2006, March). *Therapeutic assessment: Definitions, distinctions, and current developments*. Master lecture presented at the annual meeting of the Society for Personality Assessment, San Diego, CA.

Finn, S. E. (in press). Therapeutic assessment: Definitions, distinctions, and current developments. *Journal of Personality Assessment*.

Finn, S. E., & Kamphuis, J. H. (2006). Therapeutic Assessment with the MMPI–2. In J. N. Butcher (Ed.), *MMPI–2: A practitioners guide* (pp. 165–191). Washington, DC: APA Books.

Finn, S. E., & Martin, H. (1997). Therapeutic assessment with the MMPI–2 in managed health care. In J. N. Butcher (Ed.), *Objective personality assessment in managed health care: A practitioner's guide* (pp. 131–152). New York: Oxford University Press.

Finn, S. E., Schroeder, D. G., & Tonsager, M. E. (1994). *The Assessment Questionnaire–2 (AQ–2): A measure of client's experiences with psychological assessment.* Unpublished manuscript available from the first author.

Finn, S. E., & Tonsager, M. E. (1992). The therapeutic effects of providing MMPI–2 test feedback to college students awaiting psychotherapy. *Psychological Assessment, 4*, 278–287.

Finn, S. E., & Tonsager, M. E. (1997). Information-gathering and therapeutic models of assessment: Complementary paradigms. *Psychological Assessment, 9*, 374–385.

Finn, S. E., & Tonsager, M. E. (2002). How *Therapeutic Assessment* became humanistic. *The Humanistic Psychologist, 30*, 10–22.

Fischer, C. T. (1970). The testee as co-evaluator. *Journal of Counseling Psychology, 17*, 70–76.

Fischer, C. T. (1972). Paradigm changes which allow sharing of results. *Professional Psychology, 3*, 364–369.

Fischer, C. T. (1978). Collaborative psychological assessment. In C. T. Fischer & S. L. Brodsky (Eds.), *Client participation in human services* (pp. 41–61). New Brunswick, NJ: Transaction Books.

Fischer, C. T. (1979). Individualized assessment and phenomenological psychology. *Journal of Personality Assessment, 43*, 115–122.

Fischer, C. T. (1982). Intimacy in assessment. In M. Fisher & G. Stricker (Eds.), *Intimacy* (pp. 443–460). New York Plenum.

Fischer, C. T. (1994). *Individualizing psychological assessment.* Mahwah, NJ: Lawrence Erlbaum Asociates. (Original work published 1985)

Fischer, C. T. (2001). Collaborative exploration as an approach to personality assessment. In K. J. Schneider, J. F. T. Bugenthal, & J. F. Pierson (Eds.), *The handbook of humanistic psychology: Leading edges in theory research and practice* (pp. 525–538). Thousand Oaks, CA: Sage.

Forness, S. R., Kavale, K. A., King, B. H., & Kasari, C. (1994). Simple versus complex conduct disorders: Identification and phenomenology. Differential diagnosis in ADD. *Behavioral Disorders, 19*, 306–312.

Fromm-Reichmann, F. (1950). *Principles of intensive psychotherapy.* Chicago: University of Chicago Press.

Fulmer, R. H., Cohen, S., & Monaco, G. (1985). Using psychological assessment in structural family therapy. *Journal of Learning Disabilities, 18*, 145–150.

Ganellen, R. J., Wasyliw, O. E., Haywood, T. W., & Grossman, L. S. (1996). Can psychosis be malingered on the Rorschach? An empirical study. *Journal of Personality Assessment, 66*, 65–80.

Handler, L. (1995). The clinical use of figure drawings. In C. Newmark (Ed.), *Major psychological assessment instruments* (pp. 206–293). Boston: Allyn & Bacon.

Handler, L. (1997). He says, she says, they say: The Consensus Rorschach. In J. R. Meloy, M. W. Acklin, C. B. Gacono, J. F. Murray, & C. A. Peterson (Eds.), *Contemporary Rorschach interpretation* (pp. 499–533). Mahwah, NJ: Lawrence Erlbaum Associates.

Handler, L. (2000, March). How Harry Stack Sullivan taught me therapeutic assessment. In F. B. Evans III (Chair), *Harry Stack Sullivan and Psychological Assessment*. Symposium conducted at the annual meeting of the Society for Personality Assessment, Albuquerque, NM.

Handler, L. (2006). Therapeutic assessment with children and adolescents. In S. Smith & L. Handler, (Eds.), *Clinical assessment of children and adolescents: A practitioner's guide* (pp. 53–72). Mahwah, NJ: Lawrence Erlbaum Associates.

Handler, L., & Hilsenroth, M. J. (Eds.). (1998). *Teaching and learning personality assessment*. Mahwah, NJ: Lawrence Erlbaum Associates.

Hanson, W. E., Claiborn, C. D., & Kerr, B. (1997). Differential effects of two test-interpretation styles in counseling: A field study. *Journal of Counseling Psychology, 44*, 400–405.

Harrower, M. (1956). Projective counseling—A psychotherapeutic technique. *American Journal of Psychotherapy, 10*, 74–86.

Hathaway, S. R., & McKinley, J. C. (1943). *The Minnesota Multiphasic Personality Inventory*. Minneapolis: University of Minnesota Press.

Jourard, S. M. (1968). *Disclosing man to himself*. Princeton, NJ: Van Nostrand.

Kamphuis, J. H., Kugeares, S. L., & Finn, S. E. (2000). Rorschach correlates of sexual abuse: Trauma content and aggression indices. *Journal of Personality Assessment, 75*, 212–224.

Karpman, S. B. (1968). Fairy tales and script drama analysis. *Transactional Analysis Bulletin, 7*, 39–43.

Klopfer, W. (1969). Consensus Rorschach in the primary classroom. *Journal of Projective Techniques and Personality Assessment, 33*, 549–552.

Kohut, H. (1977). *The restoration of the self*. New York: International University Press.

Kohut, H. (1984). *How does analysis cure?* Chicago: University of Chicago Press.

Lance, B. R., & Krishnamurthy, R. (2003, March). *A comparison of three modes of MMPI–2 test feedback*. Paper presented at the annual meeting of the Society for Personality Assessment, San Francisco, CA.

Lerner, H. G. (1985). *The dance of anger*. New York: Harper & Row.

Lerner, P. M. (1990). Rorschach assessment of primitive defenses: A review. *Journal of Personality Assessment, 54*, 30–46.

Lerner, P. M. (2005a). On developing a clinical sense of self. *Journal of Personality Assessment, 84*, 21–24.

Lerner, P. M. (2005b). Red beavers and building bridges between assessment and treatment. *Journal of Personality Assessment, 85*, 271–279.

Lewak, R. W., Marks, P. A., & Nelson, G. E. (1990). *Therapist guide to the MMPI & MMPI–2*. Muncie, IN: Accelerated Development.

Loveland, N. (1967). The relation Rorschach: A technique for studying interaction. *The Journal of Nervous and Mental Disease, 145*, 93–105.

Lovitt, R. (1993). A strategy for integrating a normal MMPI–2 and dysfunctional Rorschach in a severely compromised patient. *Journal of Personality Assessment, 60*, 141–147.

Meyer, G. J. (1997). On the integration of personality assessment methods: The Rorschach and MMPI. *Journal of Personality Assessment, 68*, 297–330.

Meyer, G., Finn, S. E., Eyde, L. D., Kay, G. G., Kubiszyn, T. W., Moreland, K. L., Eisman, E. J., & Dies, R. R. (1998). *Benefits and costs of psychological assessment in healthcare delivery: Report of the Board of Professional Affairs Psychological*

Assessment Work Group, Part I. Washington, DC: American Psychological Association.

Meyer, G .J., Finn, S. E., Eyde, L. D., Kay, G. G., Moreland, K. L., Dies, R. R., Eisman, E. J., Kubiszyn, T. W., & Reed, G. M. (2001). Psychological testing and psychological assessment: A review of evidence and issues. *American Psychologist, 56,* 128–65.

Middelberg, C. V. (2001). Projective identification in common couple dances. *Journal of Marital and Family Therapy, 27,* 341–352.

Murray, H. A. (1943). *Thematic Apperception Test manual.* Cambridge, MA: Harvard University Press.

Papp, P. (1983). *The process of change.* New York: Guilford.

Nakamura, S., & Nakamura, N. (1987). Family Rorschach technique. *Rorschachiana, 16,* 136–141.

Newman, M. L., & Greenway, P. (1997). Therapeutic effects of providing MMPI–2 test feedback to clients at a university counseling service. *Psychological Assessment, 9,* 122–131.

Noy-Sharav, D. (2006). The Rorschach and TAT as relational instruments: Evaluating young couples with Consensus Rorschach and TAT. *Rorschachiana, 27,* 139–163.

Perry, H. S. (1982). *Psychiatrist of America: The life of Harry Stack Sullivan.* New York: W. W. Norton & Co.

Psychological Corporation. (2002). *The Wechsler Individual Achievement Test, 2nd ed. (WIAT–II).* San Antonio, TX: Author.

Purves, C. (1997, March). Therapeutic assessment in juvenile hall: Can it be done? In S. F. Finn (Chair), *Collaborative assessment of children and families.* Symposium conducted at the annual meeting of the Society for Personality Assessment, San Diego, CA.

Purves, C. (2002). Collaborative assessment with involuntary populations: Foster children and their mothers. *The Humanistic Psychologist, 30,* 164–174.

Rapaport, D., Gill, M., & Shafer, R. (1968). *Psychological diagnostic testing* (Rev. ed.). New York: International Universities Press.

Rogers, C. R. (1951). *Client-centered therapy.* Boston: Houghton Mifflin.

Rogers, D. (2003, March). *Standardizing DSM–IV diagnoses: The clinical applications of structured interviews.* Master lecture presented at the annual meeting of the Society for Personality Assessment, San Francisco, CA.

Roman, M., & Bauman, G. (1960). Interaction testing: A technique for the psychological evaluation of small groups. In M. Harrower, P. Vorhaus, M. Roman, & G. Bauman (Eds.), *Creative variations in the projective techniques* (pp. 93–138). Springfield, IL: Charles Thomas.

Schore A. N. (1994). *Affect regulation and the origin of the self: The neurobiology of emotional development.* Mahwah, NJ: Lawrence Erlbaum Associates.

Schroeder, D. G., Hahn, E. D., Finn, S. E., & Swann, W. B., Jr. (1993, June). *Personality feedback has more impact when mildly discrepant from self-views.* Paper presented at the fifth annual convention of the American Psychological Society, Chicago, IL.

Shafer, R. (1954). *Psychoanalytic interpretation in Rorschach testing: Theory and application.* New York: Grune & Stratton.

Siegel, D. J. (1999). *The developing mind: Toward a neurobiology of interpersonal experience.* New York: Guilford.

Silverstein, M. L. (1999). *Self psychology and diagnostic assessment: Identifying self-object functions through psychological testing*. Mahwah, NJ: Lawrence Erlbaum Associates.

Singer, H. K., & Brabender, V. (1993). The use of the Rorschach to differentiate unipolar and bipolar disorders. *Journal of Personality Assessment, 60,* 333–345.

Singer, M., & Wynne, L. (1963). Thought disorders and family relations of schizophrenics, III. Methodology using projective techniques. *Archives of General Psychiatry, 12,* 187–200.

Smith, B. L. (2005). The observer observed: Discussion of articles by Evans, Finn, Handler, and Lerner. *Journal of Personality Assessment, 84,* 33–36.

Smith, T. P. (2002, September). Therapeutic Assessment with a client who couldn't reveal her questions. In S. E. Finn (Chair), *Recent advances in therapeutic assessment*. Symposium presented at the XVII International Congress on the Rorschach and Projective Methods, Rome, Italy.

Steere, D. (1985). *Where words come from*. London: Quaker Home Service. (Original work published 1955)

Stolorow, R. D. (1994). Subjectivity and self psychology. In R. Stolorow, G. Atwood, & B. Brandchaft, B. (Eds.), *The intersubjective perspective* (pp. 31–39). London: Jason Aronson.

Stolorow, R. D. (1996, February). Comments made during an address to the Austin Society for Psychoanalytic Psychotherapy, Austin, TX.

Stolorow, R. D., & Atwood, G. E. (1992). *Contexts of being: The intersubjective foundations of psychological life*. Hillsdale, NJ: Analytic Press.

Stolorow, R. D., Atwood, G., & Brandchaft, B. (Eds.). (1994). *The intersubjective perspective*. London: Jason Aronson.

Stolorow, R. D., Brandchaft, B., & Atwood, G. E. (1987.) *Psychoanalytic treatment: An intersubjective approach*. Hillsdale, NJ: Analytic Press.

Sullivan, H. S. (1953). *Conceptions of modern psychiatry, 2nd ed*. New York: W. W. Norton & Co. (Original work published 1940)

Sullivan, H. S. (1953). *The interpersonal theory of psychiatry*. New York: W. W. Norton & Co.

Sullivan, H. S. (1954). *The psychiatric interview*. New York: W. W. Norton & Co.

Sullivan, H. S. (1962). *Schizophrenia as a human process*. New York: W. W. Norton & Co.

Sullivan, H. S. (1964). *The fusion of psychiatry and social science*. New York: W. W. Norton & Co.

Swann, W. B., Jr. (1996). *Self-traps: The elusive quest for higher self-esteem*. New York: Freeman.

Swann, W. B., Jr. (1997). The trouble with change: Self-verification and allegiance to the self. *Psychological Science, 8,* 177–180.

Swann, W. B., Jr., Stein-Seroussi, A., & Giesler, B. (1992). Why people self-verify. *Journal of Personality and Social Psychology, 62,* 392–401.

Swann, W. B., Jr., Wenzlaff, R. M., Krull, D. S., & Pelham, B. W. (1992). The allure of negative feedback: Self-verification strivings among depressed persons. *Journal of Abnormal Psychology, 101,* 293–306.

Tharinger, D. J., Finn, S. E., Wilkinson, A. D., & Schaber, P. M. (in press). Therapeutic Assessment with a child as a family intervention: Clinical protocol and a research case study. *Psychology in the Schools*.

Triolo, S. J., & Murphy, K. R. (1996). *Attention Deficit Scales for Adults (ADSA): Manual for scoring and interpretation.* New York: Brunner/Mazel.

Trop, J. L. (1994). Self psychology and intersubjectivity theory. In R. Stolorow, G. Atwood, & B. Brandchaft (Eds.), *The intersubjective perspective,* (pp. 77–91). London: Jason Aronson.

Wechsler, D. (1997). *WAIS–III manual: Wechsler Adult Intelligence Scale* (3rd ed.). San Antonio, TX: Psychological Corporation.

Weiner, I. (1993). Clinical considerations in the conjoint use of the Rorschach and the MMPI. *Journal of Personality Assessment, 60,* 148–152.

Weiss, J. (1993). *How psychotherapy works.* New York: Guilford.

Wolf, E. (1998). *Treating the self: Elements of clinical self psychology.* New York: Guilford.

Zamorsky, J. (2002). Deviating from the TA model: Choosing not to do an assessment intervention. In S. E. Finn (Chair), *Recent advances in therapeutic assessment.* Symposium conducted at the XVII International Congress on the Rorschach and Projective Methods, Rome, Italy.

Ziffer, R. L. (1985). The utilization of psychological testing in the context of family therapy. In R. L. Ziffer (Ed.), *Adjunctive techniques in family therapy* (pp. 33–66). New York: Grune & Stratton.

Author Index

Subject Index